C000214780

Published 2017 by
**The National Crime Syndicate**

**Copyright ©National Crime Syndicate**

Mr Bert Rossi
Mr Teddy Adams
Mr Jimmy Andrews
Mr Frankie Rossi

**Foreword:** Jimmy "The Whirlwind" White (MBE)

**Internal Photos**: Bert Rossi

All rights reserved. No part of this publication may be reproduced, distributed, or transmitted in any form or by any means, including photocopying, recording or other electronic or mechanical methods, without the prior written permission of the publisher.

**ISBN:** 978-0-9956548-0-8

# SPECIAL ACKNOWLEDGEMENTS

All the Rossi Family ( London and Nationwide )

All the Andrews Family ( London / Liverpool )

The Adams Family ( Clerkenwell - N. London)

The Mancini Family ( London and Manchester )

The Boffa Family ( Clerkenwell, N. London )

The Sabini Family ( E. London )

The Fury Family, Peter - Hughie - Tyson - John ( Manchester )

Bobby and Albert Reading ( E. London )

Steve and Davy Hunt ( E. London )

Jimmy "The Whirlwind" White, MBE ( Epsom, Surrey )

Barry Hearn ( Essex )

Eddie Hearn ( Essex )

Francis "Rocket-Pocket" ampofo ( Norwich )

Terry Adams ( London )

Garry Delaney ( E. London )

Darcy Delaney ( E. London )

Jimmy Andrews ( London / Liverpool )

Kathy Andrews ( Liverpool )

Terry Haley ( W. London )

Andy Jones ( Gloucester )

Robbie Butler ( Liverpool )

Joey and Franny Bennet ( Liverpool )

Johnny Burton ( Liverpool )

Frank and Robert Warren ( N. London )

Harry and Billy Hayward ( S. London )

Dennis and Memhet Arif ( S. London )

Kenny Bloom (London/Southampton)

Eddie Richardson ( S. London )

Steven Berkoff ( E. London )

Michelle Richardson ( S. London )

Danni Lou ( S. London )

James Morton ( Barnet, N. London )

Shirley Hine ( S. London )

Joey Pyle Jr ( S. London)

Mitch Pyle ( S. London )

Eddie and Billy Blundell ( Essex )

Johnny Eames ( E. London )

Liam and Yvonne Galvin ( Northampton )

John Conteh ( Liverpool )

Gary Jacobs ( Glasgow )

Terry Downes ( W. London )

Charlie Magri ( E. London )

John H Stracey ( E. London )

Jamie Mclean ( London )

Kelly Mclean ( London )

Gary Shaw ( Essex / Lincolnshire )

Anna and Greg Steene ( S. London )

Chris and Jamie Saniger ( Bristol )

Lee Haskins (Bristol)

Charlie and Jackie Rumble ( S. London/Kent )

Charlie Jr and Billy Rumble ( S. London/Kent )

Freddy Rumbol ( S. London )

Tommy and Franna Lamb ( Liverpool )

Darryl and Miguel Wickham ( Liverpool )

"Little" Darryl Wickham ( London / Liverpool )

Dessie Bayliss ( Liverpool )

Charlie Seiga ( Liverpool )

Jimmy Malloy ( Liverpool )

Jimmy Tibbs ( E. London )

Mark Tibbs ( E. London )

Alan Levene ( Liverpool )

Jimmy and Joey Swords ( Manchester )

Arthur and Jimmy Donnelly ( Manchester )

Vinny and Louis Scarfo ( Manchester )

Micky Francis ( Manchester )

Ray Winstone ( E. London / Essex )

# SPECIAL ACKNOWLEDGEMENTS

Glen Murphy MBE ( E. London )

Terry Marsh ( Essex )

Craig Fairbrass ( Kent )

Garry Booth Sr ( Manchester )

Bobby Rimmer ( Manchester )

Ricky Hatton ( Manchester )

Guy Ritchie ( London / Los Angeles )

Mark Murrell ( E. London )

Chrissy Murrell ( Essex )

John Mcvicar ( London )

Alison Sharpe ( Portsmouth )

"Big" Alan Williams ( North West )

"Big" David Renolds ( Ireland )

"Big" Matt Legg ( Milton Keynes )

"Big" Stevie Sinclair ( Blackpool )

"Big" Spencer Brown ( Blackpool )

"Big" Joe Egan ( Birmingham )

Jock and Sammy Gordon ( Birmingham / Redditch )

Adam Mcracken ( Birmingham )

Tommy Powell ( Birmingham )

Monty Powell ( Birmingham )

"Big" Al Stephens ( Birmingham )

Jon Pegg ( Birmingham )

"Big" Dale Brendan Hyde ( Wakefield )

"Big" Anthony Thomas ( Wales )

Brendon Driscoll ( Wales )

Bernard Driscoll ( Wales )

Julian Davies / Juggs ( Wales )

Lee Wortley ( Yorkshire )

"Big Daddy" Bunce ( London )

Cassius and Helder ( IFL - Tv London )

Glyn Rhodes MBE ( Sheffield )

Errol Graham ( Sheffield )

Steve Ellis ( Manchester )

Peter Walsh ( Kirkham )

Craig and Steph Timmins ( Midlands )

# SPECIAL ACKNOWLEDGEMENTS

All the Timmins Family inc Gordon Timmins (R.I.P) ( Midlands )

Frankie Rossi and Chelsea ( N. London )

Jules Annan ( Gloucestershire )

Charles Defelde ( Cambridge )

Simon Twilley Plus sons Ben and Joe ( W. London )

Brian Twilley ( W. London )

Sammy and Sara ( Bournemouth )

Tom Pettifor - The Mirror

Mike Sullivan - The Sun

Bill Ackerman RIP - Son Stephen Ackerman ( Bournemouth )

and a very special thank you to Duncan Campbell and his
beautiful wife Julie Christie

Not to forget the friends over the pond who
all made this book possible,

"Big" John C. Berkery ( Philadelphia )

Meyer Lanksi II ( New York )

Joe Gambino Jr ( New York )

Giovanni Gambino ( New York )

Teresa Gambino ( New York )

Phil Genovese ( New Jersey )

Nino Belduono  ( New Jersey )

Plus the rest of Mr Rossi's Mafioso associates.

Anyone named in the acknowledgements above please do not hesitate to make
contact with The National Crime Syndicate to receive a complementary signed
copy of Mr Rossi's book.

Mr Rossi will be donating 10% of each sale towards
The Macmillan Nurses Trust.

# FURTHER ACKNOWLEDGEMENTS

# FURTHER ACKNOWLEDGEMENTS

Mo Hussain ( E. London )

Adrian Elliot ( E. London )

Tony Sims ( Essex )

Peter Sims ( Essex )

Frank Buglioni ( Enfield )

Georgie Schofield ( Liverpool )

Shea Neary ( Liverpool )

Paul Lomas ( Manchester )

Derry Mathews ( Liverpool )

Alan Rukin ( Liverpool )

"Big" Albert Chapman ( Birmingham )

"Big" Norman Buckland ( Northampton )

"Big" Alfie Buckland ( Northamption )

Norman Simpson ( London )

Tommy Winstanley ( Wales )

"Big" Richard Towers ( Sheffield )

Ian John Lewis ( London )

Teddy and Gary Dennis ( W. London )

Kirsty Connors ( Shrewsbury )

Gary Jacobs ( Glasgow )

Steve Wraith ( Newcastle )

Del Lovell ( Southampton )

Kim Peat ( London )

Neil Jackson ( Newcastle )

Wayne Lear ( South East )

Gareth Goves ( South East )

Freddie Foreman and godson Christian ( London )

Wilf and Ross Pine ( Christchurch )

Paul Ferris ( Glasgow )

John Petra ( Glasgow )

Gary Stretch ( St Helens / Los Angeles )

Colin "Sweet C" Macmillan ( Essex )

Nathan Cleverly ( Wales )

# JIMMY WHITE MBE: FOREWORD

I first met Bert Rossi — Mr Rossi to me in those days—
back in 1980 when I'd just won the world amateur
championship. Sometimes I used to practice in the
Mazurka Club in Denman Street and he'd often come in
there. We both liked snooker and we both liked boxing.

In those days Soho was a trap for young people but I could
always go to Bert. He wouldn't stand no nonsense . And
it wasn't just in Soho. He had friends all over London and
a call from him would sort things out. And if he did you a
favour he didn't want anything in return.

**He was both a Godfather and a Goodfellow
in the best sense of the words.**

# ROSSI BIBLIO

If you want to read more about what I've written then the place to start to look for a lot of stuff is in the National Archives at Kew. Many of the files are closed for 50, 70 a hundred years but some are open. Ernie Isaacs murder for a start and there some bits of the Gold murder you can look at. The judgment in Errol Heibner's appeal's also on the web. There's the Croydon Airport robbery (MEPO 3/1387) and also the Clerkenwell Bullion robbery (MEPO 3/898) the one which Harry Bryan got bird for. There's the Babe Mancini case, not only the trial but there's also a file on the efforts made to save him from the gallows. (CRIM 1/1314; HO 45/25560) There's a file on the Spot slashing (MEPO 2/9837) and to show you how big it was at the time there's also a file about who got tickets for the public gallery. There's a few files on Darby and Alf White and the racecourse wars. There's literally hundreds of files about the Kray Twins there.

As for America there's almost hundred if not thousands about the various mobs. My friend John Berkery has written K&A Kid : The Young Manhood of Johnny Burke which is about his relationship with the Philadelphia Mafia. There's quite a bit on John's friend Major Coxson in S.P. Griffin Philadelphia's Black Mafia: A Social and Political History.

If you want to know about the early days of the racecourse gangs there's Carl Chinn's Better Betting With A Decent Fellow. Carl's family was Birmingham bookies and he knows all about it. There's more about bookies and the Sabinis in William Bebbington's Rogues Go Racing. There's also a bit about the Colombo fight at Wandsworth in it. There's quite a bit about the Sabinis in Raphael Samuels' East End Underworld and there a good bit in James Morton's East End Gangland and Gangland Soho. Brian Macdonald wrote about his family who feuded with Darby and his family in The Elephant Boys. He also wrote The Gangs of London.

Of course there's plenty of books about fights and fighters but the bit about Albert and the Pender fight is in the boxing writer Frank Butler's The Good, the Bad and the Ugly. James Morton wrote a lot about Freddie Mills in Fighters.

Billy Hill wrote Boss of Britain's Underworld but that gives all sorts of pseudonyms so the Whites become the Blacks and Teddy Hughes is Teddy Odd Legs and so on. His son updated it a couple of years back. Hank Janson wrote Man of a Thousand Cuts which is Jack Spot's version of what happened. Michael Connor wrote The Soho Don a biography of his father Bill Howard.

There are dozens of books about the Twins and the best has got to be John Pearson's The Profession of Violence. Those should be a start.

# 1 : SAFFRON HILL

A reporter from a television company once said he thought I'd killed as many as eleven people both here and in the States.... Bastard.

What the police could never do was make up their minds what part they thought I played in the murder of Biddy Gold. Whether I was the planner, the middle man, the look-out, the actual gunman while a blagger Erroll Heibner acted as lookout, or just to have been the go-between who gave Heibner the gun used. This is what one of the coppers DCI Reginald Dixon said to me when I was being questioned a month or so after she was killed:

> In my estimation, Mr Rossi, you are the vile and treacherous person who planned this murder for your own ends or for someone else.

Well, he was entitled to think whatever he wanted and that's what I told him. Doesn't necessarily mean he was right though.

That woman Biddy Gold was killed in her office of the clothing factory she ran in Clerkenwell with her husband, Eric. September 1975 it was. Him and his secretary had gone out to buy some wine and food for the goldfish and while they were gone, in comes a gunman and shoots poor Biddy. No one could make out why. There'd been a big bullion robbery down the road in Bowling Green Lane the previous few months earlier and a lot of gold went missing. No one was ever done for the robbery but one fellow Ronnie Stafford did something like eight years for receiving. The speedway rider Split Waterman did some bird over it as well. He was going to smelt some of it down. Was it to do with that? Then there was a story that she'd been killed because she was a Zionist. She certainly went to gay parties when it wasn't really the thing to do. There were stories she'd written a couple of porn novels which had never been published and it seems like some well known people were described in it. Was it a contract? And if so who paid for it? Or was it a robbery gone wrong? What I do know for a fact is I got pulled in by the police at the end of October and they did me for her murder. And it all come about because I rented a few rooms in Hatton Garden from a couple of fences, George Meisl and Matty Constantinou and the fellow Errol Heibner — people called him John — was a friend of my son.

••••

There's a saying that the best criminal is the one you've never heard of and in a way that fits me. My name does crop up in books like Duncan Campbell's Underworld, Billy Howard and Frankie Fraser's books and some by Ron and Reggie, but to all extent I've been a ghost.

How have I kept under the radar? By not doing stupid things. For example, in the old days whenever a crime went to court the coppers all went down to see who was in the public gallery watching his case. And the men didn't have the intelligence to wait for another case after his and then trickle out one by one. No, they streamed out after their mate had been dealt with and the coppers clocked who they were associating with. I just never went down to watch. I'd get the result soon enough. And I never bought a racehorse or wanted to mix with film stars or write my story. Jack Spot, whose real name was Comer and who I cut to ribbons in 1955 , always reckoned his downfall was because of getting too much publicity. If you do and you're thought to be active that's a good reason for the coppers to lean on you. Moreover I never went and shot a man in a pub in front of straight people like Ronnie Kray did.

So why am I writing a story after all this time? I can answer that saying why haven't I? And that's because while people have been still alive, I've not been prepared to name names. I wouldn't have done it at 50 but now I'm 94 and all my friends are dead it's not going to hurt them, so I think it's time to set the record straight about what happened over the years. Who was really the Guv'nor at any one time? Who really did what? The people I knew, from Darby Sabini through the Messina brothers who ran all the girls in the West End, Billy Hill and Jack Spot, the Upton Park Mob, the Philadelphia Mafia, the Krays and the Richardsons, right up to today. The clubs in Soho and who ran them and the brasses, the bent coppers. It's social history really.

I'm the last one left who can write about people who were legends in their time and, without undue modesty, that includes me. People write a lot about the East End but I can tell what it was like growing up an 'Eyetie' in the slums of Clerkenwell —there was actually a well there in Farringdon Lane which is how the area got its name —and getting out so that I was mixing with top American criminals. People will ask what have I been doing for the last forty years since the Gold murder case? Well, I suppose the best answer to that is keeping my head down again, running a few spielers, a bit of buying and selling and a quite a bit of consultancy work. That's what Godfathers do best.

They were immigrants my parents. My brothers, Bernie, Peter, Louie and sister Enrichetta, who we called Rita, and me were born here but my father Michele came from Piacenza in northern Italy, the same region as the Sabini family who lived in Bowling Green Lane, and my mother Rosa was from Parma.

Over the centuries Clerkenwell was known for being a big brothel area and then it became fashionable and a bit after, like so many areas, it went down. Charles Dickens set Oliver Twist in Field Lane off Saffron Hill. You wouldn't believe it now but Saffron Hill got its name because people grew saffron there.

Then because it was poor and no one else wanted to live there Italians started arriving in the 1850s. My parents must have arrived about the end of the 1890s. My father used to call me Dillinger after the American gangster because as a boy I was wild. I used just to call him 'Papa'. My mother called me Umberto or Berto after the King of Italy.

When I say my father called me Dillinger he was my stepfather. We lived in a slum, 22 Eyre Street Hill, and we shared it with three other families one of which was the Guiliottis. Mrs Guiliotti couldn't stand the pressure, had a breakdown and went off to the mad house leaving behind all her children. My mother took to looking after them, cooking for them and then she took up with Mr Guiliotti. My real father found out and he upped and offed so Mr Guiliotti became my step-father.

When you come from the slums if you didn't get out and grab it you suffered; struggled to pay the rent, struggled to put food on the table. Thieving's better than jumping on a bus every morning, struggling to pay for a holiday once a year. Do what your brains tell you. The first thing I ever stole was a turkey one Christmas.

We was on the breadline then. My father did his ice cream sales in the summer and worked as a mosaic layer in the winter and my mother took in extra laundry. My poor mother was a slave, poor woman, a slave. Every time I went home for lunch there'd she'd be up to her elbows in soap suds doing the washing she had to take in. Then in the summer of an evening she'd make the ice cream for my father to put in his barrow and push it up the hill from Eyre Street, over Holborn, down Chancery Lane into Fleet Street and then push it up to St Clement Danes which is where he sold it

The flat had no electricity — there were gas mantels which were very fragile and were always breaking and I'd be sent to the local shop to get some more. They gave off a white light. We all washed outside in the yard under a cold tap. It was no different for anyone. There was nothing to keep us indoors. No television of course; for a lot of the time there was no wireless. We played football or cricket in the street until the light went. The ball was old newspapers wetted down and tied with string. The wicket was a lamp post. We made the bats out of bits of wood. Same as all the kids from slums up and down the country did. There were some families such as the

Terronis who had shops — there's still a Terronis in the Clerkenwell Road — but they were the exception. That family had been here much longer than us and were much more settled in.

Do you know that at the time in the 20s there were 20,000 families in the area and over 4000 of them lived in one room and another 7000 lived in two rooms? Only 4 per cent had private baths.

People say that before the war Clerkenwell was all Italian but that's not true. There were plenty of Irish and plenty of English and we all rubbed along together. True the Italians had their own clubs like the Central and the Fratellanza but we all rubbed along together because we were all poor.

It wasn't all bad. It was a real community. At one time there was even an Italian cinema in Roseberry Avenue, The Avenue Picture Palace, but it closed before I was born and we used to go to The Globe in Skinner Street if we could find sixpence for the Saturday matinees. They were silent at first and then talkies with a cartoon, an educational film like a travelogue, a serial which always ended with the hero in a bad spot, like being knocked out and unconscious in a burning building so you had to come back next week and see what happened, and then a western with Tom Mix or someone like that. We'd all cheer and stamp our feet so you'd think the building was shaking. At the end we all had to stand up while there was 'God Save the King'. That sort of thing continued well into the 1960s. You didn't dare walk out while it was playing. Sometimes people even sang it. I don't know why. What did royalty care about people?

In the summer at weekends people played the barrel organ and there was dancing in the streets of an evening. Sometimes Darby Sabini would sing. He'd got a really good tenor voice. My mother would point him out to me, 'That's Darby Sabini' and there he was with a shirt with no collar, just a stud in it. He wore a dark brown suit with a high buttoned waistcoat, a black silk stock and a light-checked flat cap. People said he'd chosen this outfit when he was twenty and wore it for the rest of his life — indoors, outdoors and, so it is said but not in front of him sometimes in bed. It was also said he kept a gun under his pillow. Of course it didn't mean anything to me when I was five or six except that he was a man who had to be respected.

There were other big families who were respected also like the Cortesis and the Fuscos, and some of them were often best avoided but, of course, the best known of them was the Sabinis.

What do I know about Darby and the rest of the family? Well they was at their heyday when I was just a baby really so everything is what I've been told, stories which became legends.

I don't know how many Sabini brothers there were because they all used each other's names. Darby wasn't the oldest but he was the leader. His real name was Ullano but from time to time when it suited him, he was known as Fred or Charles, the names of two of his older brothers. Their father was Italian and long dead before I was born and their mother Scottish.

Fred was the eldest and he traded as a bookmaker, Bob Wilson, at the Harringay Greyhound Stadium. Then came Charles, who was two years younger and he was a list supplier working for the bookmaker Joe Levy. He owned shares in West Ham Stadium and the coppers thought he was 'slightly mentally deranged'. I know that by just before the war he'd spent some time in a mental hospital. If something like that happened in a family, even if they'd moved out of the Hill, everyone knew. Just like with my step-father's first wife. Then came Joseph, who on paper was both the hero and the villain of the family. He had been in the First World War in the Royal Welsh Fusiliers and then the Cheshire Regiment and had been wounded in France. He'd been injured and he got a few shillings a week pension.

Darby left school at the age of 13 and boxed professionally from 1909. He first won a novice competition in the February and at one time it was thought he could, in the words of Marlon Brando, 'have been a contender'. It is said that while still in his teens he had knocked out the fancied middleweight, Fred Sutton, in the first round. There was nothing in his record about it. Maybe it was a set to in a gym; maybe the fight was at a fairground booth. In those days it was common for licensed boxers to take on all comers at booths. A lot of them, like Freddie Mills who went on to be the light heavyweight world champion, got their basic training there.

Then booth fighting was banned by the British Boxing Board of Control sometime in the 1970s.

A lot of good boys didn't like training, hours running on the streets and some trainers were pretty brutal in those days. If you needed to take weight off they'd make their boys run with a mattress wrapped round them. From what people said Darby didn't like training but that can't be right because he boxed right up to 1917 when he lost over sixteen rounds at the National Sporting Club. He'd have been in his late twenties by then. After that he became a helper for the promotions of another Anglo-Italian Dai Sullivan's at the Hoxton Baths, keeping the locals from attacking the fighters. All Italian boxers had to have English names if they were going to get anywhere.

How did Darby become the Godfather of Little Italy then, the person we all touched our caps to? The story is that just after the war, that's World War One, Thomas Benneyworth, who they called Monkey' and was a leader of the Elephant Gang, deliberately tore the dress of an Italian girl serving behind the bar of The Griffin pub in Saffron Hill. Darby intervened and knocked Benneyworth out and showed him up as the bully he was who picked on women. When his broken jaw had mended Bennyworth returned with members of the Elephant Gang but this time they were driven out of Little Italy by Darby with the help of young Italians who had got behind him. As for Monkey he became a Jack Spot man and he was there when Billy Goller's throat was cut in the Nut House off Piccadilly after the war. I heard he'd died in the 1950s.

Of course I was a baby really in Darby's heyday. Everything I heard was from stories around the Hill and later from Bert Marsh whose real name was Pasqualino Papa. He wouldn't have any prostitution in the area and there was the story of how he went into Soho to see one of the Frenchmen who'd got hold of an Italian girl. The French were running prostitution in those days; white birding it was called. The girls would think they were being part of a dance troupe but really they were going to brothels in Buenos Aires and places like that. They weren't drugged and kidnapped. Just silly girls who never thought about things. Darby went round and explained things to the Frenchman and the girl came home with him.

His brother Harry, who was much younger, was from a different cut of cloth. Always known as Harryboy, and much more smartly dressed than Darby, he went to St Peter's Roman Catholic School in Clerkenwell same as me and my brothers but a bit earlier. Later, when I knew him better, he told me when he left school he went to work for an optician and during the First World War he worked in a munitions factory. After that he became a bookmaker's clerk, working first for Gus Hall and later for Walter Beresford who helped sort out the racecourse wars in the 1920s.

It was after the end of the First World War that Darby and the others began to take an interest in the racecourses and they made a lot of money from that. So much so that Darby could always be relied on to help out with the rent if people got behind; and no question of any interest either.

# 2 : THE TWENTIES

To understand how I came to cut Jack Spot to ribbons in 1955 you have to go back to before I was born and see just who ruled Soho and Clerkenwell and the racecourse pitches and who wanted control of them. It's the story of men I knew and worked with and so it's really a history of the London underworld from the 1920s to the 1960s, and the end result of it al was the Krays.

Of course much of it happened when I was a kid and, as I say, I picked up the stories from my parents and my elder brothers as well as from the other boys in the area and things I read in books. I was also told a lot by Harryboy Sabini when I did some driving for him after the Second World War . And of course I heard a lot from Darby's right hand man who boxed as Bert Marsh . His real name was Pasqualino Papa and he was always talking about the good, or bad, old days.

Racecourses have always been a place for the likes of us to make money. One way of stopping a bookmaker attracting any business was to surround his stand so the punters could not get to it to place their bets. It was like what happened at Walthamstow dogs when there was a big coup in the 1950s. People in it just blocked the Tote windows so they could rig the price of the race. Then there was the bucket drop. If a bookmaker wished to avoid trouble he'd drop a tosheroon (25p) in a bucket containing water and a sponge which was carried between races up and down the line of bookies by a bucket boy. The sponge was used to wipe out the odds next to the printed sheet of runners on the board. If he didn't pay, then the bucket boy would wipe the odds out just when he needed them most. He always had a man standing by him in case the bookie cut up rough. You could allocate pitches, and bookmakers had to give you a share of the day's takings; you also sold them the tissues, which were the sheets with the names of horses on them, before it all went electronic.

There were other tricks such as starting fights near a bookmaker's pitch, claiming a non-existent winning bet, and having other pitches put so close to the non-paying bookmaker than he physically just could not operate. Quite apart from that there was the straightforward demand for a non-repayable loan of £5 or £10. All this may seem small today but, added up, it came to what was big money then. When a team went to a course like Brighton they could clear as much as £4,000 or even £5,000. At Epsom on Derby Day, it was said it could be as much as £15,000 or £20,000.

Then there were crooked games like Find the Lady and Crown and Anchor which were played on trains to and back from the races and on waste ground outside the courses theirselves to separate the mugs from their money. I can't have seen a Crown and Anchor board in fifty years. As for Find the Lady that was old as the hills. You had to tell which of three cards which were being shuffled face down was the Queen. The mug punter could never win. If anyone seemed to it was because he was acting as a shill for the team which could be four or five strong. If by any chance the punter got it right then some of the others in the team would say it was their bet and there'd be a rerun or someone would call 'Bill' which meant the police were coming. Then the board would be folded and the team would scarper. If they were unlucky ou'd see the Three Card men, as they were called, coming up in court first thing the next day. They'd always be fined and paid cash. But then the coppers started putting a conspiracy to cheat charge on them which meant bird, and over the years they've died out.

Before the First World War the Birmingham gangs had established a hold on racecourse protection in the north and now they tried to expand. You've seen Peaky Blinders on television and that's based on their leaders Billy Kimber and Andrew Townie. They became known as the Brummagem Boys despite the fact that most of the members came from the Elephant and

Castle south of the river. For a time Kimber's mob took control of southern racecourses such as Newbury, Epsom, Earls Park and Kempton. But then Darby saw that small time Jewish bookmakers on these tracks needed to be protected from Kimber and his mob.

Billy Kimber was big. He was not a layer but instead he controlled the best pitches on the courses. He'd lease them out for the day on a half profit but no loss sharing basis. Some people said he was well liked and it wasn't him who terrorised the Jewish bookmakers in the cheaper rings at the southern courses but it was sort of loose elements who were attached to him. The Jews accepted their lot fairly philosophically but it was something Darby and Harryboy intended to sort out.

It seems that it all came on top one day when the Kimber mob forced bookmakers at Salisbury at gunpoint to make them pay for their pitches, so they formed the Bookmakers Protection Association and that was run by Darby. There were fights all over the country and that year or the next, one of Darby's men Alf White got charged with the attempted murder of Fred Gilbert when he shot him in a fight outside the Yorkshire Gray in Holborn. That day Alf was with Joe Sabini and a lot of Sabini men; just because they had English names it didn't mean they weren't Italian. Most of them got not guilties but Joe got three years and Alf had his conviction overturned on appeal. Then Alf thought Joe was having a hard time in Maidstone prison and tried to give a screw money to get letters into him. The screw doubled him and Alf got 18 months.

Alf had been a member of the Titanics which later became known as the Hoxton Mob. The Titanics had been around for years. At their peak there were about 50 of them. Pickpockets really and they worked railways stations, football matches and music halls. The police said they'd been broken up in the early 1920s and maybe that's how Alf White came to join up with Darby but I know there were bits of the Titanics still around in Hoxton during the Second World War.

It was after Fred Gilbert got shot that the bookmaker Walter Beresford stepped in and got Kimber and Darby together to put a stop to all this violence. It wasn't doing any good; people were staying away from the tracks. After a meeting they did agree to divide the racecourses between them and the racecourse wars died down. Darby got the tracks in the south and Kimber and his friends the rest.

There were so many stories about Darby and horse racing. I remember being told the one about Jack Leach the jockey who was a friend of Fred Astaire. He come out badly in a race at Longchamp in France and the crowd was about to set on him when he left the weighing room to go back to his hotel. A load of men circled him and got him through. When he asked why they'd helped him one of them told him, 'Darby said we was to protect you'. Then Darby would make sure young jockeys didn't fall into bad company. They used to travel to the races by train and Harry Carr, who later became the Queen's jockey, and another apprentice got in a carriage full of Three Card tricksters and they did their money. Darby came into the carriage, asked how much Carr and his friend had lost and they said a fiver which was a lot in those days. He made the men give it back and then another big white fiver each for the trouble. But Carr didn't escape scot-free. He said he got a lecture from Darby about how he was never to mix with villains. There was another story about how a racing Lord got his bins stolen and appealed to Darby who had them returned in five minutes. I forget who his Lordship was.

But with Kimber settled Darby started having internal troubles. Some of the troops wanted more of the takings. The four Cortesi brothers (Augustus, George, Paul and Enrico, who were known as the Frenchies, decided they'd act as sort of shop stewards to put the case to him. Almost immediately afterwards some of the Jewish element in the gang also formed a breakaway group known as the Yiddishers. Darby negotiated as he always did. The Cortesis would be given a greater percentage. The Yiddishers got permission to lean on one, but only one, of the bookmakers under protection.

However, peace did not last long. More and more the Yiddishers began to side with the Cortesis and by the autumn of 1922 the new team had effectively nicked the Sabini money from the bookmakers at Kempton

Park. It couldn't be allowed to go unnoticed and as a result Harryboy was convicted at Marylebone Magistrates' Court of an assault on George Cortesi.

The next bit of the story — the Fratellanza Club shooting — is like one of those fairy stories your mother tells you before bedtime with a heroine who saves the hero's life. But this wasn't a fairy story; it was real. You can read it for yourselves in the old papers.

The club in Bath Street was a place mainly for Italians and in November 1922 Darby and Harryboy went down there for a drink when they were ambushed by Enrico Cortesi and his brother Augustus who lived just five doors down from the club.

Darby was given a beating and was hit with some bottles and Harryboy was shot. Louisa Dorelli, who was the daughter of the club's secretary and who was said to have been a bit sweet on Harryboy, tried to get in the way. She'd already knocked Augustus's hand when he tried to shoot Darby and the bullet went through a window. Then when Enrico tried to shoot Harryboy she got in front of him but Enrico pushed her out of the way and Harryboy took a bullet in the stomach. It all ended up at the Bailey when that judge who had had the Steinie Morrison trial give the jury a lecture on how the Sabinis were descended from ancient Romans, though what that had to do with things no one in the Hill never understood. Augustus and Enrico got three years each. The judge also said he could have had them deported which is what the jury had wanted, but he didn't. What he did say was that if there was any more trouble in the colony then out they would go along with their wives and children. He couldn't have said that today; not with their Human Rights. My mother used to say that what Darby minded most about the whole thing was that his false teeth got broken.

Next up was the 1924 killing of Buck Emden, who was known as Barney Blitz, in the Eden Club off the Hampstead Road. Darby wasn't directly involved in that, only in trying to sort things out. It was Alfie Solomons who killed him. There was no doubt about that. It was just the circumstances.

What had happened was Buck Emden thought an Edward Emmanuel

— some people said he was the brains behind Darby — had grassed him over an earlier case for which he'd been put away. He got after Emmanuel with a broken glass and when Solomons saw what was happening he stabbed him to save his friend. At least that was how the story came out. Buck wasn't what people might call an angel himself. He'd done a copper with a bayonet a bit earlier.

What Darby did was to go and see the great brief Sir Edward Marshall Hall at his home in Welbeck Street and try to give him a bunch of old white fivers — when they were new they actually crackled — to defend Solomons. That wasn't the way to go about things. People like us didn't go to the homes of top barristers but it shows what nerve Darby had when he wanted something. Marshall Hall told him to go and see his clerk the next day and he took the case and defended Solomons.

By all accounts Marshall Hall was wonderful and got a manslaughter which since Solomons had stabbed Buck in the back of the neck was going some. One of the troubles for the prosecution was that although there was about forty people in the club they could only get half a dozen to give evidence. One man who was there but said he was drunk and couldn't remember anything was Jack Solomons, the boxing promoter. I don't think he was any relation to Alfie.

What Darby did was have good briefs even if they were crooked. There was a solicitor Sharman from West Ham and that man George Edjali who did a spell for maiming horses but got released after the writer Conan Doyle set up a campaign for him. There was always a story that Sharman was more than a brief and that he fenced stuff and there was even talk that he was another of Darby's backers. He certainly went down for seven years not long after I was born — receiving stuff stolen from mailbags on trains — but there again, his story was one of the more or less legends in the Hill even though he come from West Ham.

Darby did keep a tight ship and if you defaulted, well there was a price to pay. Lambi's in Back Street was where Shonk Mazzarda — his real name was Silvio— got his nose cut and he got his name as a result. Lambi's was a great restaurant, the smell of the cooking was wonderful. We kids used to hang around outside because Darby and the others might give us tuppence or even sixpence if they'd had a good day at the races. I'd say, 'Can I look after your car, Mr Sabini?' and he'd give me some coppers. Of course, it didn't need looking after. No one would have dared to touch it even if it had stayed in the street for a year. Well, maybe they'd have given it a wash. Anyway, one night they come back from Epsom and Darby says where's the money to Shonk who's meant to be holding it and Shonk says, 'Well it went on a horse in the 4.30' or whatever, and with that Darby whips out a knife and just slashes his nose. Straight down the nose, it split it. Blood all over the place and Shonk has to hold it back with one of the white serviettes they had. A group of us were hanging about outside the restaurant and I seem to remember seeing Shonk running out with his face covered but at my age memory can play tricks and I may just have been told about it. But that was the end of the punishment. Shonk didn't get expelled or anything like that and he knew he was in the wrong.

Things was quiet for a bit but then in 1927 there was what the papers called the Battle of Ham Yard off Piccadilly over who should be running clubs in Soho. Darby's hangout there was the Admiral Duncan in Old Compton Street. The fight was between Wal McDonald and his Elephant Boys and Harryboy who got cut across the cheek. After that things died down again for a time. From what I've been told it was because another Elephant Boy, Wal's brother, Bert went to America along with Billy Kimber.

Things flared up again at the beginning of 1930 when another old villain Jack 'Dodger' Mullins who had had a long history of rivalry with Darby, along with half a dozen others, went looking for Sabini men in Soho and found Angelo Costognetti in the Argus Club in Greek Street. Angelo was given a real beating and thrown on the fire while a woman Edith Milburn, who tried to protect him, was also given a seeing to. At the beginning of May Mullins and the Steadman brothers, Charles and George, were acquitted. A few years earlier in July 1926 Dodger had picked up four years and his friend Timmy Hayes nine at the Bailey after they was found guilty of blackmail and assault. Mullins said he could prove the case had been got up by the Sabinis and 'some of the Yiddisher people' in order to get him and Hayes out of the way. It didn't do him any good.

I was told the fight in February 1930 in the Admiral Duncan came about when Sid Baxter, who was a Sabini man, wanted £10 from another Elephant Boy, Jim McDonald at Sandown Park. McDonald knocked him down and as a result was on offer. Baxter and the father of the well-known actor ex-boxer George Sewell, who was a great friend of Darby and who liked to be known as the 'Cobblestone Kid', sorted him out. In turn Billy Kimber asked the Phillips brothers, John and Arthur, to help McDonald. The brothers and four other men attacked George and Sid cutting their faces with a piece of broken glass. John got five years and Arthur three. That was the one of last of the big Soho fights. After that George went down to Brighton for a time to be with Darby who'd more or less left things to Harry by then.

But there was still the biggest racecourse fight of them all to come. And that, of course, was the Battle of Lewes Racecourse in 1936.

# 3 : THE THIRTIES

It's funny how once someone is involved in a murder they often get involved a second time. I don't mean they commit a murder but somehow they're on the fringes of one. But Eddie Fleischer, who was a Russian and called himself Fletcher, was more than on the fringes. He was part of the Whitechapel Mob which wanted a share of Soho. In January 1931 him and Harry White, Alf's son, got involved in a fight outside the Phoenix Club in Little Denmark Street. They did the manager who wrestled as Carl Reginski — they cut his throat— and Fred Roche, who'd been one of Darby's men, as they left the club and were done for malicious wounding. But when the case came up for committal it had all been squared up. Roche said he had made a mistake while still suffering from the effects of the attack. Now he was sure that, whoever hit him, it wasn't neither White nor Fleischer. There was one independent witness but he also said he's made a mistake earlier. Ten years later it was Fleischer who caused the row in Wardour Street in which the ponce Hubby Distleman got killed and thirty years after that it was in his club in Mayfair where Jack Buggy got done. I used to play cards there but I'll come to that story later.

From what Bert Marsh and Harryboy said the Battle of Lewes Racecourse sorted things out once and for all. Well at least until the war. Before that it had become clear Alf White and his boys wanted more of the pot and some people said he was the one who was behind that fight. Other people said it was revenge for a member of the Whites having his throat cut at Liverpool Street station. Anyway a whole coach load including Porky Gilder and Jimmy Spinks from West Ham go down to Lewes racecourse which was just outside the town and they're all tooled up. While they're there they attack a Sabini bookmaker Arthur Solomons and his clerk Mark Frater and they lay into them with hatchets. Now someone has warned the coppers that it's all on top and they are there in force as well. There's really only one result and the end is that Alf White's man, Jimmy Spinks gets a five and Porky gets a three. Fourteen others went down as well including Thomas Mack, who was once one of Darby's men, and he got a three as well. Of course Alf was nowhere to be seen but it was after that there was an agreement Alf White could have Kings Cross and Darby and Harryboy would keep Clerkenwell.

Of course, it wasn't all racecourse fights and looking after clubs in Soho. People from the Hill were involved in blags and one of the best of the pre-war robberies has to have been the one at Croydon Airport. No violence, nothing recovered, just three boxes of gold bars, sovereigns and dollars spirited away early one morning. In March 1936 it was. Of course I wasn't there. I'd have been 13 at the time but it was the talk of the Hill for years and one of the men who set it up was a fellow I got to know when I grew up, Silvio Mazzardo who, as I've said was known as Shonk . But the coppers said he used the English name John Silvester.

The gold came in on what was then an Imperial Airways flight and you won't believe it but in those days there was only one man in charge of the airport overnight. He had to do everything. And around 4.15 that morning he had to guide in a German airliner which had landed. Of course, someone had taken an impression of the keys which locked the safe room and while he was out on the tarmac away went the boxes.

What the police said was that a cab had been hired from King's Cross and the boxes were brought back to Harringay. A fellow who worked for the gas thought something was suspicious when the cab was being loaded and he took the number. The cab driver, a fellow called Manson, said that he'd been frightened into taking the boxes but what he was was an accomplice. He was lucky not to have been nicked but they needed him as a prosecution witness. Shonk and two other fellows John O'Brien and Cecil

Swanland were nicked. There wasn't a lot of evidence except the cab driver against Shonk and John but wrappers and seals were found in Cecil's room in Harringay.

His defence according to the papers was that the boxes were empty when they arrived at his room. There was a bit of ID evidence and the usual rubbish from a grass in the same cell rand Shonk and John got not guilties. In fact the judge threw out the case early on against John. The ID of Shonk was by Manson, a man who'd known him for 20 years, and the judge was a bit severe with the police saying they shouldn't have had an ID parade — who else was he going to ID? —and the only reason they had was to try to trap Shonk into saying something incriminating. Poor old Cecil got seven years. It was funny because what he really was was a forger and he's done a five, a six and a seven already back in 1909 and after. His wife had the European Café in Dean Street and when she went to the prison to give him some money the Governor got hold of the police and told them. They said they couldn't prove the money come from Croydon and let it go but it shows how spiteful people could be. Shonk later set himself up as a rails bookmaker trading as Nick Gold which didn't amuse the coppers and that's when I got to know him

You can see how much interest there was in Shonk after the Croydon case. Next year The Times reported how he'd been done for speeding and been fined the maximum of £50 and disqualified. After that he got a driver.

That year the police had another try at finding who'd supplied the keys and they came up with the name of a loader, fellow called Peters. They went to see him and got hold of his bank account which showed he'd had about £1500 at the time of the robbery. He said it was his savings from when he was at sea and he's bought a pub in Hertfordshire with it. They leaned on him a bit but he stuck it out and in the end they just gave up.

People always hinted that Bert Marsh was the brains behind Croydon but I don't know. If he was he didn't tell me. If he was the organiser of that it was a busy year and overall really a lucky one for him.

Dog racing was just starting to be popular and one of the men who ran the betting at the Wandsworth track was Jim Wicks, who later was big in boxing and the manager of Henry Cooper. He handed the bookmakers' pitches out – in return for a fee of course.

The stadium was a big place which could hold over 20,000 people. The trouble Bert got into was all about the pitches in the half crown ring. For some reason Jim Wicks wouldn't give one to the Colombo brothers, who lived down the street from us, but Bert Marsh and his friend Bert Wilkins, who lived in Sekforde Street down near Smithfield Market, they had one. Years earlier Bert Marsh bashed a couple of bookmakers at Wye races, which used to be a small jumping track near Maidstone, and got a month for it along with Antonio Mancini — now there was an unlucky man — and Tommy Mack. He lived at Cavendish Mansions in the Clerkenwell Road.

Bert Marsh was only a small man but the Colombos were big. There were three of them at the track that night — Lemelli, Camillo and Massimino — and the Berts knew it was off. Bert Marsh had to stand up to them. The Colombos hadn't gone to the track that night tooled up in the sense they had knives but Bert Marsh had.

I wasn't there that night, of course, I was only 13, but reading the accounts of the trial and hearing what people told me it seems that the row started when Massimino tried to hit Bert Marsh with a stool or threw one at him. And from then it was all on top.

When Massimino was stabbed he knew he had had it and he was calling out to Camillo, 'Scappare, scappare', 'Escape'. I'm dying'. After the fight the Berts had a drink at the track and then they went to see a doctor giving a couple of false names but there was no doubt Bert Marsh had taken a beating himself; been hit with a life preserver. Then they went and handed themselves in to the police which was about the most sensible thing they could do.

When the news got back to Clerkenwell, Carlo, the eldest brother, wanted to go out and look for Bert Marsh to shoot him straight away. He was raving about what he was going to do. I can remember my mother and father in our front room pleading with him to give them the gun, 'Don't throw your life away. You have a wife and family and they'll hang you'. Carlo was crying and my mother was weeping. Eventually he did listen to them and he did hand over the gun. Years later the other brother Camillo showed me how he'd been cut from his right shoulder down to his hip.

Massimino's funeral was massive. He'd lain in state for three days in an undertakers in Chadwell Street and thousands of us went to pay tribute. Four tall white candles and a massive crucifix. Of course my parents and me went as a matter of respect and even though the funeral was on a Thursday and therefore a workday, I should think everyone from the Hill went that day also. There were forty cars and the Daily Express said there was £500 worth of flowers at the cemetery in Kensal Green. People came from as far away as Manchester. Poor Massimino, he was only 27. The sad thing about it was that until a bit before the fight they'd all been good friends.

Bert Marsh must have had quite a bit of money put by because he had the top barrister Norman Birkett as his brief. Along with Marshall Hall, Birkett must have been about the best there was in the country at the time and for many years after. He'd just defended Mrs Hearn, the woman accused of poisoning her friend's wife in Cornwall, and he'd got her a not guilty.

It was put about that the money for Bert's defence had been raised by his wife pawning her jewels and drawing out her savings, as well as a subscription from what were called racing men. There was no question of a door to door collection or people being tapped. Far too many liked the Colombos for that. It was also said Bert had eight children but that was rubbish. He only ever had one daughter, Virgilia. That bit sounded like a bit of clever embroidery by Darby.

The two Berts went down for manslaughter only and this was where Bert Marsh had done a clever thing. While he was in Brixton on remand he'd paid a fellow to attack a screw and he and the other Bert had pulled him off. The fellow got the Cat but it counted a lot in sentencing and the Berts got less than two years. It was something Billy Hill did later with one of the Rosa brothers when he was in the nick.

I was never that close to Bert Marsh. For a start he was twenty years older than me. He was never a thief, he was a leader. In fact he was a lot like Billy Hill. As dangerous as any one of them. He gave the impression he didn't have any compassion for anyone. If you were a cripple or a dummy he wouldn't give you the time of day. It was only if he thought you could be of use to him he'd entertain you. Same with Billy Hill once he'd made it.

It was one day in December when I was 12 or 13 the subject of Christmas and a turkey came up and my father said we couldn't afford one; we'd have to get a chicken and that wouldn't go far between five of us. There was two turkeys hanging in a butcher's shop window in Bath Streetand I knew the people who owned it had plenty of money so one evening I put a brick through the window and took one of them. I told my mother I'd got it from my school pal Mario Terroni whose family had a delicatessen. I told her he'd won it in a school raffle and his family already had one. The shop owner gave me a pull about it but I said it wasn't me. It could have been any one of a number of people because a lot of us was in the same boat so it all came out all right. And that's how I started. Not a lot of boys from the St Peters when into crime; a couple like me and a couple more became big businessmen but that was about it.

I left school a couple of years later and my mother asked the man who lived on the top floor of our house if he could help get me a job. He worked at the Savoy hotel. Could he get me one there? So he asked the manager of the section where he worked and I got an interview. A place like that always had a high turnover of staff and I was a good-looking, polite, well-mannered boy so when I went for the interview I got a position as a commis waiter; 4 p.m. to 1 a.m. The man had done me a big favour because if I'd just turned up on my own there was no way I'd have got a job. My mother made me a white waistcoat and collar. Now I don't know if it's changed but in those days the waiter took the order and brought it behind a curtain where us commis waiters stood and then we had to take it to the kitchen and when we got a call the food was ready, bring it back to the waiter who took it to the table. It seemed to me to be an awful lot of standing around doing nothing. What I didn't like was seeing all these rich people in evening dress waste all this expensive food. I used to take things which hadn't been eaten back on the tram to my mates. But I watched how these people used their knives and forks and learned from it. What I did like was watching the floor come up with the band on it for the dancing. I suppose it must have been that famous bandleader Carroll Gibbons.

I stuck it four weeks and then I couldn't stand it no more. I'd been a boy of the streets and this wasn't for me. Is that what I was going to be for the rest of my life? The manager didn't want me to go; he thought I was shaping up well and my mother certainly wasn't pleased. But I went my own way. First, I did shops and then offices and that's when I came to the notice of the two best thieves I ever knew —Jock Wyatt and Harry Bryant — and they both came from Clerkenwell.

No, that's not right. Billy Hill must have been the best from the early 1950s on after he pulled off the Eastcastle Street robbery which brought in over a quarter of a million in those days, and then the Lincoln's Inn gold snatch a few years later. He was exceptional. But he was more like a magician who starts off producing doves from his sleeves and ends up as an illusionist making the Eiffel Tower disappear. He started out as nothing more than a thief and cardsharp from Seven Dials. His sister was one of the all women gang the Forty Thieves that lasted for years. The only men who worked for them were drivers and decoys. I remember one of the girls telling me that one of the store detectives at Selfridge's used to greet her in a morning thinking she was a great customer but she'd never bought a thing there in her life. Frankie Fraser's sister was one of the Forty and there was a long waiting list to join. One of the downsides of Billy Hill was he had a nasty temper and he pulled people into things. Maybe that's two downsides.

There again, people might say Jock and Harry can't have been that good thieves because both of them did a lot of prison but they had some good touches and they ended up having a film made about them which is more than you can say for most of us. Jock had once worked with the White family and he was always a Billy Hill man. Him and little Eddie Raimo who looked like George Raft — he always wore a black shirt and a white tie — had been chucked at London Sessions a couple of years earlier. They'd been done for cutting Michael Macausland, who was a White man, outside his home in Kings Cross in March 1938 along with a John Phillips who'd gone to protect him. The pros offered no evidence but when Macausland died four months later his family would never believe it hadn't been as a result of that cutting and beating and not from a kidney disease which is what the doctors said.

When I met Jock and Harry it would have been the end of the '30s just before the war. I knew who Jock was, of course, but I was a young man and I couldn't go cap in hand and say,''Please Mr Wyatt can I work with you?' No, the approach came from him and Billy Hill one day when a car pulled up on Bath Street and Jock beckoned me over. That was when he asked me to have a cup of tea with them in the Lyons Corner House at the Angel, opposite where the tube station is. It was quite casual. 'There's a friend I'd like you to meet. Come and have a cup of tea tomorrow about three thirty'. Jock knew I was a likely lad and reliable so to speak. You get a reputation and I was known as a good climber and that was what they wanted. I must have done every factory in Old Street one year. What do you need to be a good climber? Strong arms for a start. You don't want to be too heavy although Peter Scott, who was one of the best in the business, was a big man. You need to be agile, able to jump and to run. And of course you've got to have nerve and in those days I had all those things.

What they had in mind was a load of jewellery in a room at the Savoy hotel. They took me down to have a look at a drainpipe which led to the room and we went back again that night. They waited in a car down in the gardens between the hotel and the river — there were no parking problems then. I climbed up it all right but when I was outside the room I could see the window had little wires down it. It was belled up. I came down, told them and they gave me a few quid for my trouble. What you must be sure is that a job is right. It would have been plain stupid to have tried anything. That was the first time I worked with them but there were plenty of others.

It was Harry though who had pulled off the Clerkenwell Bullion Robbery in 1936 and again it was the talk of the town so to speak. And like all robberies it was simple and in fact it was the second Bullion Robbery within three years. In the days before the railways got nationalised there was a London North Eastern line and one of their vans carrying a packing case with gold and ingots, stuff like that, was taking the stuff from King's Cross station to the Sheffield Smelting Company in Clerkenwell.

It had to go through Aylesbury Street off the Farringdon Road. Now Aylesbury Street like so many streets around Farringdon was narrow. You couldn't overtake anything in it and that morning it was blocked by a barrow. The van driver doesn't realise he's been followed so out gets the van boy to move the barrow and both he and the driver are threatened with iron bars and a box is lifted from the van. Then the car which was behind him goes up on the pavement, the barrow's pushed back in the middle of the road and they're away. Headlines in the evening papers that people had to jump for their lives. Jimmy Francis, who'd been at it since the turn of the century, was caught and so was Harry where they were grassed up.

What was so surprising about the whole thing was that there had been an identical raid four years earlier. Both Harry and Jock's names were in the frame for that one as well but no one had been nicked. The railways had done nothing to change things and they got a bollocking from the judge saying it wasn't fair on the insurers making it so simple for thieves.

# 4 : THE WAR

When I say Italians were popular pedalling round on their bikes selling ice cream, we were. That is until Italy declared war on 10 June 1940 when Count Ciano said Mussolini was backing Hitler and from then on it was 'fucking Eyeties' and our houses and shops were fair game. That night the police raided the Italian Club on the Charing Cross Road and took away the waiters. There was a women's march on Old Compton Street and windows were smashed before an Italian woman, Rose Blau, stepped in and pleaded with them saying that Soho's Italians were mostly British born. Shopkeepers had to put up signs such as 'We are Swiss' and overnight the Spaghetti House which had been running for years became the British Food Shop. There were plans that all Italians between sixteen and sixty who had been here for over twenty years should be interned. It didn't matter that the men were in the British forces. A lot of other boys from the Hill went in the army but their fathers were still interned. Both my brothers were in the army and Peter died at Dunkirk. He'd been in the Black Watch. One of Darby Sabini's boys went down in the war as well. That didn't count. We were the enemy. We was all dangerous, so far as the authorities were concerned that is; speaking a foreign language and ready to start an uprising, just waiting for the nod from Mussolini.

There was something like 35, 000 Italians in Britain and between ten and fifteen thousand were children born here. There was 700 rounded up in the first swoop and over time there was something like four thousand Italians locked up and a lot of Anglo-Italians as well. People were just rounded up and no one knew where they'd been taken. Innocent people like a fellow who played the violin at Quaglinos which was a fancy restaurant in Mayfair and the Manetti brothers who'd been clowns at Bertram Mills circus for something like fifteen years. Pepe Leoni who'd struggled to establish Leoni's Quo Vadis in Dean Street was another. Just scooped up. People were just rounded up and we didn't know where they were being taken. Eventually, off they went with Darby who'd been picked up in Brighton and Harryboy Sabini and Bert Marsh to places like Ascot racecourse where there was a detention camp. I suppose my father was lucky that he wasn't sent to it with them but there was still other things. I came home one day and I couldn't see the radio. I said, 'Dad, where's the radio?' and he said, 'I'm not allowed to have one. The police came and took it'.

In a way Bert Marsh kept order among the people in the camp. The Anglo-Italians weren't that keen on the Mosleyites and they were having a bit of trouble. Bert went over to a man Arthur Swan who was a Blackshirt and told him if he could get a bottle of Chianti or two from the other side of the wire there'd be no more trouble. He did and there wasn't.

So far as Darby and Harryboy were concerned they were on a special list of people who the authorities thought would lead an Italian uprising against the British government. The fact that half of them couldn't speak Italian didn't count. There was a list of the ten most dangerous people in the event of an uprising and it was put together by that crooked copper Ted Greeno. There was a fair number of English on it who couldn't be detained, more's the pity the authorities thought. A friend of mine got hold of the list and copied it out for me. Top was Alfred Vince whose real name was Raffaele Spampinato. I never heard of him. Then came Augustus Cortesi. The coppers said he could often be found in the Coach and Horses in Soho. Third was Darby and fourth Harryboy. Fifth was Bert Marsh, but the sixth was a bit of of a surprise. It was Shonk who the coppers said used the name John Silvester and was managing the Imperial Club in Leicester Square. Then came their English associates, Alf White, James and Harry Ford who weren't related, Bert Marsh's friend Bert Wilkins and Edward Smith known as Edward Emmanuel who was said to be the financial backer of Darby and

Harryboy. And finally, last on the list there was Jock Wyatt.

Of course Darby and Harryboy should never have been detained and eventually they got out but it took Harryboy nine months to do so. Unfortunately he'd also denied he ever used the name Handley and he got an extra nine months for that. We were all convinced it wa just to break up that Raddies as Darby and the others were known and there was still bad feeling over that gold from Croydon.

Meanwhile a tragedy struck the whole community. On 2 July 1940 the Arandora Star taking to Canada a whole load of straight Italian people, barbers, shopkeepers, people like that who'd been interned, was sunk by a German U boat. There was around 750 of them , around five hundred Germans who'd been interned, a bit under a hundred German prisoners of war. And guards and crew made up nearly another 400.

There had been a swastika flying to show she was carrying German prisoners of war but she was still torpedoed. She hadn't been given an escort and when the torpedo hit the ship on the starboard side many of our people who had been on the lower decks were afraid to leave it. Over 800 people died and among them were nearly 450 Italians. For the next month or more bodies kept being washed up in Ireland. Anthony Eden give it all a whitewash saying that all of those on board had been either Nazis or Fascists. So good riddance.

There's a plaque in St Peter's Church which commemorates the dead but they didn't even leave us with that church in the war. It was handed over to Irish Pallotines and we didn't get it back until 1953.

Things could have been even worse. In 1940, I think it was, a bomb hit the top of the Temple Press building on the corner of Mount Pleasant and Wardner Street where 600 of us Italians were sheltering. Fortunately it didn't go off. Tommy Falco and Phil Nataro were there playing cards and the story is they never even looked up.

Meanwhile boys I'd been at school with, played football on the street with, were going round smashing windows of Italian people down the Hill. I wasn't having that and I hurt one or two of them, and I mean hurt. It wasn't just a slap. Anyway I'd hurt someone who had a brother or a cousin who said he was going to shoot me. I'm in this pub in Hoxton and the fellow I'm with says, 'That the man who'd looking for you.' I could see him coming down the stairs and I could see he'd got a gun with him. I went up to him — I was tooled up don't worry about that — and I said, 'I understand you're looking for me. Do you really want to pull that?' I was right up against him and he got the message. He just shook his head.

Before the Second World War protection had been pretty low level. A fight was started in a club and a certain amount of damage was done. Maybe a foot went through the skin of the drum, tables were overturned, a few glasses were broken, nothing much really, just a calling card you could say. The next day came a visit from a sympathetic representative of Darby or the others who would point out things like this were frightening off punters and how they could be avoided by payment of a small weekly sum. By 1941 however the rules of the game had changed. Now smash it up properly. If the club closed for good so much the better. There was one less competitor.

On 20 April 1941, 'Fair Hair' Eddie Fletcher, who'd up that wrestler and Joseph Franks were involved in a fight with Bert Connelly, the doorman of Palm Beach Bottles Parties, a club in the basement of 37 Wardour Street. There was also the Cosmo on the ground floor, the West End Bridge and Billiards Club on the first and also in the building there was a load of prostitutes run by the Messina brothers. In fact that was where the girl Martha Watts who ran the girls for him first met Eugenio Messina. Now Fletcher was given a beating and banned from the club by the manager Joe Leon, whose real name was Niccolo Cariello. You see how all had to become English.

Ten days later Fletcher is back and Sammy Lederman, a Soho face for something like thirty years —he was a friend of Jack Spot and later gave evidence against the Twins — went into the Palm Beach to tell Antonio Mancini, who we all call Babe who was the club's catering manager and on the door for the night, that 'They're smashing up the [Bridge and Billiards] Club'.

What had happened was that Fletcher and other members of the Yiddisher Gang including Moishe Cohen had been playing pool and cards in the club when in walked Albert Dimes, who was on the trot from the Royal Air Force along with Joseph Collette and Harry Capocci. Fighting had broke out and the witnesses said Albert started it. The police and the papers thought that it was us Eyeties breaking up a Jewish club. Fletcher copped another beating and was taken to Charing Cross Hospital, which then was just a few minutes away. Patched up he went back to Wardour Street to pick up his coat, at least that's what he said.

At first Babe seems to have wanted to stay out of trouble but Joe Leon then asked him to go to the door of the Palm Beach and let no one in. He changed out of his evening clothes and went upstairs to see the damage.

As he was on the stairs he heard someone say, 'There's Babe, let's knife him'. He thought it was Fletcher. He sensed someone was behind him and went into the club followed by Fletcher Harry 'Little Hubby' or 'Scarface' Distleman and another man.

Then it all went off again, with Albert being held back by his elder brother, Victor. Distleman was stabbed. Babe had then chased after Fletcher and had almost severed his arm. Only a few of the forty people in the club would talk to the coppers but most of them who did agreed it was Babe who stabbed him. In fact Distleman had said when it happened, ' I am terribly hurt. Babe's done it'. Now that might not be as strong in evidence as what was called a formal dying declaration when the fellow believes he's about to snuff it but it certainly didn't help Babe. The coppers may have had it right that trouble had been deliberately caused because just at the end of the fight who should arrive but that other Sabini man Thomas Mack.

When he was interviewed he told Detective Inspector Arthur Thorp, 'I admit I stabbed Fletcher with a long dagger which I found on the floor of the club, but I don't admit doing Distleman. Why should I do him? They threatened me as I came up the stairs and I got panicky.' The next day, however, when he was questioned a bit more he said he had the dagger wrapped in a rag with him when he went up the stairs. Like the Berts had known the Colombo brothers Babe had known Little Hubby Distleman for something in the region of fifteen years.

Babe was unlucky at his trial. The brief to the prosecution which is now in the National Archives suggests that if he offered a plea to manslaughter, 'Counsel will no doubt consider it, as the witnesses of the assault on Distleman are vague and shaky'. That was because there was such confusion about what went on they couldn't guarantee what their witnesses were going to say at all. Anyway Babe wouldn't have it. He said he was not guilty. In any event the Judge had said he wouldn't allow it either because of the length of the blade on the knife but if the pros had insisted he'd have had to agree. Anyway Babe was adamant and it cost him his life.

What didn't help was that Babe had asked a fellow in Brixton James Boyle to give evidence matching a statement he gave him and offered him £50. Boyle straightaway asked to see the copper Thorpe.

Babe's brief argued that if the jury wouldn't wear self-defence, a death in a gang fight in such circumstances should only be manslaughter and indeed the judge eventually more or less agreed. But the jury didn't stay out long and convicted Babe of murder in less than an hour. So it was the black cap. Babe appealed, of course, and the Court of Appeal heard it twice but it went against him. The judge had, if anything, been too favourable in his summing-up, said the Lord Chief Justice. There was another appeal to the House of Lords but that also failed and Babe became what the papers called the 'first London gangster', to be hanged for nearly twenty-five years,. That was a fellow Joseph Jones in the First World War.

Following Babe's trial Albert , Callette and Capocci were again brought up , this time before the Recorder of London, Sir Gerald Dodson. One by one the witnesses for the prosecution failed to identify them and the case collapsed. Capocci was acquitted but Albert and Collette were bound over in the sum of £5 to come up for judgment in the next three years. 'You were probably expecting prison,' said Dodson, 'and no doubt you deserve it'. Albert was returned to the RAF but he didn't stay for very long.

Poor old Babe went to the condemned cell. The papers made a

whole lot of the killing of Hubby Distleman as part of a gang war protecting nightclubs and saying Distleman was part of the Whitechapel Boys and Babe was the Italian Mob.

Babe's solicitor and barrister did a lot to try and save him, writing to the Home Secretary and going to see him but it wasn't any good. Poor Babe was in the condemned cell for something like three and a half months as as his appeals were heard. His lawyers said that was too long and cruel to him keeping him on tenterhooks so to speak but that didn't work; they also said that it was a heat of the moment thing and not a planned murder. Nor did it count that he'd only got a bit of form for violence. What Babe was was a pickpocket. Then there was the fact that the prosecution had said they'd take a plea to manslaughter. His parents had been here since the 1870s and his brother had fought in the First World War. He'd wanted to join the army and he'd been turned down because he was Italian so he'd joined the Ambulance Service. None of that counted either.

With the papers yelling, 'Gang Warfare' and us Italians not being too popular the Home Secretary wasn't having anything. It was a black day for the Italian community when he was hanged. Saffron Hill couldn't believe it.

Funnily enough Babe wasn't the longest in the condemned cell. A couple of years later a Canadian serviceman machine-gunned his married girlfriend when she said she wouldn't go out with him as she was going out with another man. Her old man was already a prisoner of war in Germany. It was down in Sussex and the fellow was in the death cell for even longer.

As for me I did a bit of work on bomb sites in the city and there was a photo of me working away, but I was only looking to see if there was anything worth having. I could see the safes but when I got into them the money was just burned to a crisp. That's when I was congratulated for my work by the King and Queen and I think there was actually a photo of me with them in the evening papers. Not bad for a boy from my background but if they'd known what I was really doing I bet they wouldn't have been see near me.

It was June 1941 I got married. My wife Irene came from a nice, good family; above board, comfortable. They had a piano. I met her when I was about 17 so we were just kids. She became my girl and then one day she told me she was going to have a baby. I loved her in a way and her to go back to her parents Mr and Mrs Kiddy and tell them would have been a terrible thing. In those days it was not uncommon for girls who weren't married to get slung on the streets by their families. I had no money at the time but I said I'd marry her. I went and met the family. I'm sure her father would have preferred his daughter to have married an English fellow but they accepted me. It's still like it today; you'd want your daughter to marry an English face. Years later I realised it was a marriage of convenience.

Just at the beginning of the war I'd picked up five months at Clerkenwell. Charlie Dear and Ted Collins who were with me got six months apiece ay North London. We'd got hold of a lorry load of sugar and things like that in Dalston Lane and driven it off. We were nicked while we were unloading it. It was one of those cases when the judge likes to sound off. 'I could not imagine a worse case' is what he was reported as saying in the papers, calling the stuff we stole 'goods of national importance'. I was lucky. I'd been nicked again this time stealing some wine from a place in the Farringdon Road with Henry Buglione and Billy Dunks and I was lucky because I got a month less than Charlie and Ted at Clerkenwell.

It was around then that I got shot at the first time. I was out screwing a pub with a friend Georgie. We waited for the landlord to go to bed but we must have made a noise because we could hear him getting up. We were straight on our toes. We got out of the place and are running down the street when we hear a bang and he's shot at us. He wasn't that far behind us either. If he'd hit me it would have been the end. He could have been an ex-serviceman. Who knows?

So here I was, married with a baby on the way and if I'd been straight I'd have earned about 80 pence a week and have to give 50 pence to Mr Kiddy. Don't tell me about the fucking conditions today. I knew I wasn't wanted.. The beginning was really the start of the end of the marriage and I can't say I really blame her or them.

Anyway I have one or two nice bits of work and I bought clothes for Irene and of course she needed a pram. She saw one she liked and I was flush so I bought it. It must have been the best pram in the whole of Clerkenwell. And so her father thinks, 'He may be Italian but he's a good boy'. But my photo don't go on the piano like one of his other daughter's husbands. 'He's in the navy.' Not one of me and when it's pointed out they have to say, 'He's on his toes'. If you mix with straight people they don't want a deserter in the family.

I had another bit of luck after that as well. A couple of years later Bobby Reed and me were found behind a bedroom door on the Holly Lodge Estate, Highgate. Now Highgate and Hampstead were the places to go for a screwing in those days. It was the house of a Squadron Leader and we haven't been in the place two minutes when he comes home. I was about to make a run for it when the Squadron Leader pulls out a gun and tells me to stand where I was. I still make a run at some French windows but they're locked. I'm fucked. I told him my wife was in hospital which she was. The decent thing was the Squadron Leader come to court and says I was a game boy, the sort who would do well in the service. They needed boys like me.

I was given a three week lay down for reports – we both were in fact – but Bobby didn't have the sense to go along with the probation officer and he ended up with three months. I was given probation. The report said that I seemed to want to go straight and 'appeared unfortunate in his associates'. That was me showing a bit of intelligence. If you're nicked bang to rights, then it should be 'Yes, sir', 'No sir', 'I did it for my poor mother, sir'. That's the way to the shortest sentence and quickest release.

Then I'm called up and overall I didn't have what people call a 'good' war. I was drafted into the Royal Army Service Corps and it would have been all right if I was just killing Germans but it was the discipline I couldn't stand it. Think about it. At the start, my father was in his sixties and my mother was getting on for that. One brother Peter died at Dunkirk and the other was serving. There was only the four of us in the house including my sister Rita . I was the only one with any fire who could stop people breaking things up. In my mind I knew what was going on and it was my job to protect my family. The army was not for me.

Now if I'd had a good war, thrown a grenade into a Jerry dugout and got the DSO and things like that for bravery, it would have been all right. I'd have been welcomed back, had my photo on the piano with my brother in law in naval uniform, and there'd probably have been a street party for me.

But the army wasn't for me whatever the Squadron Leader said even though I thought I'll give it a week. Then if I'm going on the run I can at least say I tried. When it come to us I only stood it one day. There was this fellow shouting' Left right, left right, about turn' at us instead of talking and when we had tea I was sat with straight boys. They weren't my kind of boys. I wasn't going to get on with them and so I became one of the Trotters as we were called. I think I absconded five times in all. Nothing like as much as Porky Bennett from Millwall who was known as the 'King of the Trotters' from the times he was off.

People will tell you that escaping is easy enough, it's the staying out that's difficult and they're right. Of course you can't go home. That's the first place they look for you. That's why the Krays were such idiots. First thing they do is go straight back to Vallance Road and breakfast time the next day where did the coppers go straight to? Found them in bed. Top class gangsters they were. People don't learn. What is it? November last year a fellow gets out of Pentonville. Brilliant escape, seems like he's used a diamond cutter which come in over the walls by drone. You wouldn't believe it possible would you? Never had things like that in my day, but then three days later maximum he's found more or less with his family, same old haunts. I'd have been out of the country before they knew I was missing.

Now I've walked off couldn't go home. Irene had four sisters and all their husbands was doing well in the Services. As I say they were straight people. So I went into Soho. I'd spend four or five nights a week in the Turkish Baths in Jermyn Street; they're long gone now. Then you could always find a brass to stay with for a bit if you didn't mind her coming and going. I was never short of money; I did a few jobs. I mixed with good and bad in dives, gambling clubs. Villainy. That's how you exist. You don't get real wages for being straight. When you're on the run you've got to earn as well. I was living a life of survival and it was inevitable I was captured.

It was in April 1943 I was pulled over some forged coupons. This time it was again five months. Day before I'm coming out I'm taken to see the Governor and he tells me I'm to be handed over to the army.

Next day two Redcaps come for me, a sergeant and a private. I'm in civvies and I'm handcuffed to the buck to go to Worley Barracks on the train. Once we're in the compartment there's no one with us and I say to the sergeant can I have the cuffs off? He lets the buck uncuff himself but I've still got the handcuff on my wrist. When we come to Brentwood station I'm still unlocked. I've behaved myself and I think this is the one chance I've got, so on the platform I give the buck a dig. It's sheeting down with rain and he slips over and I'm off. Now its uphill to the barracks and the sergeant is chasing after me. There's some workmen sitting having tea and one of them has left his bike propped up against a wall so I hopped on it and I pedalled all the way to London where I got a mate to file off the handcuff.

Next thing I did was go and find my wife to let her know I'm all right. There she is in Clerkenwell walking the baby Peter in the pram and talking to a girlfriend. I wait till they've finished and I go up to her and her reaction is one of disappointment and concern. 'Don't let my dad see you', she says. I thought, 'That's a fucking reaction.' Nothing like 'How are you? Have you eaten? Do you want some money? No, it's don't let my Dad se you" I walked away knowing her concern was not for me but for her family. I still saw her, and after the war we had a daughter but by then I'd met Mary. She was another local girl and she's been an angel. We've been together now nearly sixty-five years.

Another time I was on the trot I was in The Standard when I was picked up and I broke out of Grays Inn Road nick. This time I got detention and I was handcuffed properly and it started all over again.

After that I was escorted everywhere while I was waiting for a court martial. I was there three or four days when a new army screw comes in. He doesn't know me and he unlocks me and says, 'Football', There was a PT instructor and he made us put big benches up against the wall. I thought, 'You won't get a better chance' and I made sure I was the goalkeeper. After about ten minutes I got the ball gave it a big kick up field and while people was watching the ball I ran to the benches and was up over the wall. I think I was out four, five weeks that time and after that it was back to Brentwood barracks.

With all my escapes I ended in the mental hospital at Banstead. I wanted out of there as well and so when after a bit I was put on the ward there were some drapes across the windows because it was blackout. I picked up a chair and bang, I did the window. It was locked but not barred. I got through it and I was across the fields but I never got far that tiem

I think I was there at Banstead a bit under three months. I remember it was a couple of weeks before Christmas when who comes in but Porky Gilder who got three years over the affray at Lewes Racecourse when one of the Sabini bookmakers got badly cut. And who was with him but Jimmy Spinks who'd had a five over the same thing. A week or two later Porky gets his discharge out of the army. Just like that and I've been there getting on for three months. I couldn't stand it. I thought to myself, 'How is it all these people are coming in and going out with their tickets (discharge papers) and I'm not?' One morning I got myself an interview with the officer in charge of the ward – a Major Blair he was.

He sits down at the desk — I'm standing of course — and he asks, 'What's bothering you Rossi?' 'People coming in and being discharged. What do you intend to do with me?' Then a woman nurse came in with a tray and put a cup of coffee on his desk. He takes a sip and then says, 'Rossi. I've examined you. I've got your record and I'm about to send it off now. Yes, Rossi, I've found nothing wrong with you physically or mentally. I'm recommended RTU'. 'What's that, sir?'. ' Returned to Unit, Rossi'. I was so angry I banged on the table and upset his coffee. My mind had gone with all the fucking aggro.

I thought now is this ever going to end? Was I ever going to get out? I thought the only way was to show I was unfit for the army and so I decided to cut my wrists and take my chance. When you shaved you were given a razor blade, thin and double sided, nothing like they have nowadays. I thought if I talked to the fellow who handed it out he might not notice I'd not given it back and that's how it worked. Once he'd gone and I was in my cell on my own I thought, 'Now I'll do it'. I knew I had to do it bad enough for me to go to hospital proper. And I did my left wrist. You can still see the scars. Blood pumping out all over me and the cell. Some of it actually spurted up and hit me on the nose. And then I thought, 'I've got to be found'. There was no way anyone was going to answer the bell if I rang it and so I started to smash up the cell; made as much noise as I could so someone would come. And eventually they did coming running in. By then I'd nearly passed out.

And that was it. There was some sort of rule coming in that the army didn't have to waste their time on people like me and we were just thrown out. And that's what happened. Blair had me in again and told me that he was keeping me for a bit longer until this came into force and when it did I was out.

After that for a time Jock Wyatt and I did well in the war with the black market. There was a farm we knew where we could get eggs and they were at a premium. Me and Jock would go down to a farm and pick up a crate of eggs and there was always a butcher you could go to. A lot of housewives would give it away to them to get a cut of meat or extra eggs for the family.

Then there were places like Bobby's Club in Rupert Court where you could sell anything but the real open air informal black market was outside the Rainbow Club on the corner of Shaftesbury Avenue. That was a club for American servicemen which had opened in November 1942 and from then on watches, cameras, silk stockings and pens were all on offer in Berwick Street market. There was a big supply of condoms in the club — the US army didn't want their men picking the pox up frm our girls — and the GIs would sell these on as well.

Of course being in the black market was a dangerous game, not just because of the law but because of each other. One man I knew well was Russian Robert whose real name was Reuben Martirosoff. He wasn't Russian at all. He was one of three or four Poles who used to hang out together. He was into just about everything he could be — forged notes, changing stolen money, buying and selling diamonds, running a few girls and, what I didn't know, he was a grass.

His life was like something out of a spy novel. He moved from Warsaw to Constantinople and then to Paris where he did a couple of years for fraud. Then he went to Berlin and did a bit of time there before he came to England . He used to be a big card player in a club called the Bagatelle where at one time Albert's brother Victor had a share. I think it was in an alleyway at the back of the Phoenix Theatre but over the years there were so many Bagatelle clubs in and around Soho. Of a day if you wanted to find Robert you had to go to Warren Street at the top end of Tottenham Court Road. Later on he also had a tobacco kiosk on the Embankment which he ran with his wife. He was a charmer. Good looking and he'd splash money about. He could pull women like picking fruit off a tree, but he also had them on the game if they weren't careful.

What Robert was also was an expert pickpocket. Racecourses were just opening up again after the bombing and he'd take me with him sometimes. I wasn't acting as a stall for him or anything. I was just out for the day but on the way home he's show me what he'd picked up. And one day he shows me a wallet he's got and who do you thinks name is in it? John Capstick, the copper who liked to be known as Johnny Artful. I told Robert he'd better stay off the courses a bit.

I've never had too much to do with brasses; I've never liked that sort of work but back during the war and just after if you were in Soho for more than half an hour you got to know a lot of them. And dangerous work it was for them. There was a fellow Gordon Cummins who killed a whole load, in 1942 I think it was. There was a lot of brasses got killed during the war and many more we don't know about. As I say you got to know them. Now with him killing the girls he was a serious danger to anyone on his toes from the forces. The law was out en masse. People said it was another Jack the Ripper but the law decided he was just a thief who cut up the women afterwards to make it look like a sex fiend. He'd used an old- fashioned tin opener on one of them. He got caught because he left his gasmask behind in one attack. He called another girl as an alibi but in those days anyway juries didn't take notice of what brasses said. A lot of people said the evidence had been mixed up and some of it put on him but he was topped in the June.

In a way it was best if the girls worked for the Messina brothers. They looked after their girls even if they weren't allowed more than ten minutes a client and they got a whipping with wire if they caused trouble. At least the brothers provided some protection from the punters. What there was in the war was a whole lot of half brasses who worked around Leicester Square and were known as the Piccadilly Commandos. Now, they could be trouble. Often the punter didn't even get to a bed; it was up against the railings in an alley and have your pocket picked while you were doing it. That or a bang over the head from behind.

I was always getting stopped by the coppers. It was inevitable really. If you were in your early twenties coppers looked at you. They'd come in pubs and say 'Everyone stay where you are' and they'd check your papers and ask why you weren't in the army. I was nicked a few times but you could often buy your way out. I'd like to have the money I've given to the law over the years. Not having papers would cost around a pony.

It was always a help if you knew faces in the place where you got a pull. That was true peacetime as well as wartime. So I knew the people from the old Titanic Mob in Hoxton. They'd been a great gang of shoplifters and pickpockets even before the First World War and although the police said they'd been broken up, they hadn't. They'd merely splintered a bit.

One day I'd been with some of the them, Jimmy Spinks, Victor Chandler and the others in their boozer to do a bit of business and when I walk out to look for a cab when two plain clothes coppers give me a pull and said they want to see my ID. 'I must have left it in my old suit'. 'Why aren't you in the army?' 'I'm exempt.' So the older one asks me my occupation. 'I'm an asphalter,' I say. 'Let's see yourhands then,' says the sergeant. I show him knuckles up. 'And the other side'. The moment I turn them over he can see they're not the hands of a working man and I'm nicked. You can always try it on and on the way to the station I asked, ' Can I talk to you?' This was standard. He wanted to know what I was doing down his way and I told him I'd been with Spinskie and the others from the Hoxton Mob. He said 'All right' and let me go. When I went back to the pub Victor said I must give him a pony to give to the copper. That was about the tariff. If I'd been nicked for a screwing then it could have been up to a monkey.

By the end of the war Billy Hill had things going for him. There was said to be over 20,000 criminals or trotters on the run. He could have papers printed up that would fool the coppers. Take the beginning of December 1945 there was a raid checking clubs, dance halls and cafes in Soho for deserters. Bridges were sealed off but what did they find? Out of over 15,000 people who were questioned the coppers only found 32 deserters.

There were three bits of business in those war years which got me my name as someone to be reckoned with. The first actually started when I was a kid. I was on my way with some friends to the Merlin Street Baths and we had to pass a café where Joey Fusco was sitting. I'd have been about eleven I suppose because the Baths hadn't been open that long. It had 90 cubicles and a washing tough for clothes and mangles. People thought it was wonderful.

Joey was from one of the big families along with the Cortesis, the Montes, the Sabinis and they all were hard men. The Fuscos were just as dangerous. You would have a row with them and they could hurt you. I had my towel under my arm and Fusco snatched it and wouldn't give it back. My mother was leaning out of the window at the time and she yelled at him in Italian to give it back to me. He just started mimicking her. I hated him for it but there was nothing I could do.

Years later when I was about 18 I started going on a Sunday morning with people from the Angel to play dice on the roof of a dilapidated building. Who's there one Sunday but Joey Fusco. I was betting 'In and Out' which means if you bet 'In' you want the player to get the number he first threw before he rolls a seven. Or the other way around if you bet 'Out'. I won and went to pick up my winnings but Fusco snatched them and said, 'You bet ''Out''. I made up my mind to do him. If I didn't he'd lean on me forever. They all carried razors and I went over to a fellow Tony Nappi and asked if I could have a loan of his but he said, 'No'. He didn't want trouble. So I picked up a window sash which was laying around and I went for Fusco. I just smashed it over his head and shoulder and I kept on until I was pulled off. It was Albert Dimeo who pulled me off and held my arm and that's both what stopped me killing Fusco and how Albert and me became the closest of friends. It lasted the rest of his life.

Then there was the second bit. It took place in the Duke of York in Hoxton where some Canadian soldiers were drinking when me and Jimmy Spinks and Porky Gilder went in. They were at one end of the bar and near us was Bert Marsh's adopted son Peter who was a straight boy with his girlfriend. One of the Canadians come over and started stroking the girl's arm. Peter wasn't a fighting boy and I thought this was a liberty. I said, 'Do you mind' and the soldier said, 'What's the problem, Dimples?' I just went bosh. From then on it was mayhem. Now, we want to get away and get Peter and his girl out of the place but one of the Canadians is outside waiting for us with the others chasing us out. Someone had dug a great big hole six or eight feet deep and one of the Canadians goes down it. There was a boulder nearby and I picked it up and dropped it on him. I just left him there screaming. I don't know if it broke his fucking back. Serves him right if it did. It was all over that soldier taking liberties with people who can't defend themselves. That's something I can't stand.

Even late in the war when the Italians had come over to the British side the working Italian boys from around the Angel still had troubles. There was a gang led by Patsy Reagan, nothing but hooligans, beating us up. Not a week went by without someone being cut or café windows being smashed and the Italian boys weren't what you called 'racing people'; they were straight men. Frankie Ciano was cut and so was Kenny Fields. Reagan and the others would just go into a pub or a café and say, 'We're here' and 'Fucking Raddies' and then the smashing would start. Then Nestle the youngest of the Montecolombo family was cut. It was going on and on. I'd never met Reagan but I knew the name. I heard about things in the Central that Reagan and his team had stormed into a pub and left five Italian boys on the floor. Who was he to do this?

Late one evening I'm sitting having a chat with one of the Terronis at the café the Malagonis owned when in comes Reagan; he's with about five others and he comes straight over to me and says, 'You're Bert Rossi. I hear you've been asking about me.' Straight away I knew I'm at a serious disadvantage. He and the others are going to be tooled up and I'm not. I said, 'If you want a straightener, just you and me, let's have it outside'. Now a straightener is with no weapons but I know he's carrying. He nods and he and the others walk outside. I dash behind the counter and start looking for some knife, but there just isn't one there. You'd think there'd be something useful in a café for cutting vegetables but there's nothing except one which bent when you touched it. There's nothing I can do. I know I'm going to get cut but I can't back down and so I take the knife and wrap a tea towel around it so that there's only a bit of the blade showing. At least this holds it firm. He looks back in the café, 'When you coming?' And the moment I'm through the door he cuts me behind the left ear.

When you've a tool in your hand you want to lay them out as quick as possible — the neck, the eye. It's like two gladiators, one of them will be sanded. It's a very dangerous situation. You've got no option. You're going to hurt him or he's going to hurt you. You don't think. When you're roused to that extent you throw caution to the wind and you do just what you got to do.

And that's what happened. I got in close and cut him back and forth with this little one inch blade and I drove him from Malagoni's into Hatton Garden. He was like so many people. He could dish it out but he couldn't take it. And then it was, 'All right, Bert, all right. No more tools. I'll give you a straightener'. I knew I had him. 'I said, 'Now you've got less chance'. I hit him and I hit him again and again until he drops his hands. He deserved it. He took liberties. He and the others were nothing but wannabee gangsters. Of course we both had to go to hospital and this is where I was clever. I said to him, 'Look we've got to say we was attacked as we came out of the café and we didn't see who it was, it was so quick'. And he went along with it.

I never saw him nor any of his mob around the Angel or Hatton Garden again.

There was one thing came out of the fight with Reagan, apart from the scar on my neck which is still there, what is it seventy or more years later. It was a message out of the blue from Billy Howard, who was then the boss of South London. Would I meet him and Jimmy Emmett who was a big name in Soho clubs. I didn't know Emmett but I knew of Billy Howard. Emmett was a man with what you would call a reputation. 'Yes,' I said, 'I'd be pleased, where?' And it was agreed we'd meet on Blackfriars Bridge. I walked down the Clerkenwell Road —I'd still got my bandages on —and there they were half way across the bridge. They'd heard about my fight and Billy asks, 'Is there going to be any trouble?' Meaning was there going to be reprisals. 'No, I don't think so. I haven't heard of him in the area again'. Now what I didn't want was for them to think I couldn't manage Clerkenwell and they could move in. I wanted them to think Clerkenwell could take care of itself. 'That's all right,' says Billy. 'It's just that if there is we want you to know we're with you'. And off they went.

I saw Billy over the years and we became good friends but Jimmy Emmett and I fell out and I'm not even sure whose fault it was but he blamed me for his getting a long stretch of bird. It was a misunderstanding really that wasn't cleared up until it was too late.

Now Jimmy Emmett was a handful. During the war or just after for some reason or other he'd done old Dodger Mullins and Archie Hill and Billy Hill, who was his brother, decided that's enough, so when he hears Jimmy's in the Paramount Dance Hall in Tottenham Court Road he goes along with Teddy Hughes and a couple of others and Jimmy gets a few stripes. The Paramount was a funny place. It catered a lot for black American servicemen and the papers were always full of pictures and how jitterbugging was corrupting young white girls.

My trouble with Emmett was over an old boy named Chill Quotramino who I saw in Clerkenwell one day with a black eye. He was a small man five three, five four, who in the war and just after made his money selling whisky, which no one could get, to American servicemen at Rainbow Corner. I asked him how he got his black eye and he said Emmett had given him a slap and he thought he might get another. I said I'd go and see Jimmy in Soho, have a talk with him. I'd no intention of offering Jimmy out. All I was going to say was, 'Look Jim, Chill's getting to be an old man, drop it out'. I went up and asked around in one or two clubs I knew he was connected with. 'Tell him Bert Rossi called'. I never heard from him and neither did Chill.

It was only later when I was in Pentonville where I was doing 15 months over a jewellers in Edgware, I met up with Jim. He was serving ten years after being found with a gun outside the Café de Paris where Princess Margaret used to go. He was down in Dartmoor but you could save up your visits and be transferred to your home town for a short while so your family could come and see you. In those days people didn't have the money to go to Dartmoor and stay a few days so they could get to see their folk. It was lunch time and Jim came past with his tray. I said, 'Hello Jim, what was all that about with the gun?' He just looked at me and said, ' All through you'. I'd expected him to sit down but he was standing up and people were looking at him. 'I got that gun because I knew you were looking for me,' he says. 'You were looking for me and that gun was for you'. I said, 'Jim, I think you're a friend, you think I'm an enemy'. He just turned and walked away and never spoke to me again. I think he must have believed it until the day he died. If I'd run into him he'd have shot me, simple as that.

# 5 : AFTER THE WAR

One man who didn't last long after the war was Russian Robert. Someone shot him in his car near where he lived in Chepstow Place, North Kensington in November 1945 and it wasn't difficult for the law to work out who it was. It was a couple of Poles who were trotters and who'd been staying with him. A couple of days later one of them, Marian Grondkowski, was found down the East India Dock Road with Robert's watch and wallet and his cigarette lighter. What he then did was grass his mate Henryk Malinowski. But they'd been mad. One of them had bought a second hand Polish officer's uniform with Robert's money. When it come to the trial each of them said it was the other who had shot Robert and forced him to go along with it. I'll tell you who defended one of them and that was Melford Stevenson who was Ruth Ellis's brief and who was the judge at the Kray trial. But the law had them nailed down tighter than a coffin lid. Both of them were hanged. Robert had been a bit flash with his cash and they'd taken about £150 off him after they shot him.

As I've said once Albert Dimes pulled me off Joey Fusco him and me became really close. He was a funny fellow though. He was what you might call a man about Soho. Someone would always know where he was. He may have been like a brother to me but he was one who could be difficult. I think the Dimeos or Dimes were only half Italian like the Sabinis. Their father had a wooden leg. Albert had had this row with his brother Victor, who was known as Italian Jock and was two years older than Albert and he wouldn't talk to his brother for months, even years at a time. I never found out what that was about. Albert ought to have been grateful to him because

Victor stopped him getting stuck into the Distlemans and Eddie Fletcher in the Palm Beach Club when Babe Mancini got done. Victor was a thick set fellow, opened a club here and there, ran a few brasses. If Albert and I went to one of his clubs it was 'Hello Bert' and he'd ignore Albert.

It was one Sunday morning the October after the war ended that I'm home and Albert Dimes comes round to say his sister's rung and told him Victor's been shot and is in hospital. Although Albert's not talking to his brother, I say we ought to go and see him. There's Victor with a gun shot wound in his arm and another in his leg. He's still not talking to Albert and so I ask, 'Who's done this?' And Victor says. 'That bastard over there.' And who was that bastard over there? More or less in the bed opposite is the fellow who's shot him and he's in a far worse state on a drip. It's Elliman Bah. the son of a Gambian chief. I'd run into Bah before; an enormous man, 6'4" at least and built with it. He'd come over here before the war to study so he said but he'd soon started to run a few clubs and a few greyhounds. He had one dog which was a real winner, Bob's Choice. In the war he was the favourite of the Colonial Office because they sort of sponsored a club he owned, the Fullado Club in New Compton Street for black servicemen. Big place for jazz it was; opened three in the afternoon until midnight. He was a big gambler and you'd often see him in the clubs; some he owned some he just played in.

I was in one of Bert Marsh's club's around midday one day playing a bit of solitaire. There's only me and the barman when in comes Bah wearing an overcoat. I waited for him to sit down for a game. He puts his coat on a chair and calls the tea boy, tells him to look after it. So the boy puts it in the kitchen. We're halfway through our game when in comes the law, tells Bah he's wanted and they walk off with him. He never mentions he has a coat. I ask the boy to go out and get me a cigar and while he's gone I dive into the kitchen and in the coat pocket there's Bah's gun.

What had happened this time was him and Victor had had an interest together in the Cromwell Club in Nottingham Place and there's been a row and Victor wouldn't let him in. Bah shot Victor and then Victor managed to get the gun off of him and accidentally shot him. Of course the law's involved straightaway.

When it got to the Bailey they've sorted things out as best they can. Bah's charged with attempted suicide and attempted murder. Attempted suicide must have been the only offence where you couldn't be charged with the completed act. His story was that he wanted to get £1500 which was what he'd put into the club and Victor wouldn't let him in and he'd threatened him with a knife. So Bah shoots him and then somehow shoots himself in the stomach. Bah says he's then trying to empty the gun and it goes off. In the end Bah got a not guilty on the attempteds and 18 months for wounding Victor. His counsel said he wanted to go back to Gambia as soon as possible and the judge more or less said it was a pity he ever left.

Back after the war we all had guns. It wasn't a bit thing. If you were in that environment it was only common sense even to this day. It didn't mean you carried it wherever you went but it was a precaution. They were cheap to pick up. Once the war ended the price plummeted. You could pick up a gun for under a couple of quid.

I was about 23 so it would be at the end of the war or just after I was down in Clerkenwell when two or three law come down and got hold of me. My pals were ready to have a punch up and get them off me but I knew I'd done nothing and I told them, 'No'. All right, they'd have got me away but it would have meant a kicking when I was found and I couldn't stay away forever over some silly little thing.

The guv'nor of Clerkenwell comes to see me in my cell and I'm wondering what he's got for me. It's a simple message. He wants me to be a grass and, if I am, I'll have a bit of licence in the manor. 'Work with me or work against me'. He wants information and I want out so I give him a promise for the future. A couple of weeks later I'm nicked and again he comes to my cell though this time it's, 'I told you didn't I? If you'd done what you promised you wouldn't be here.' And then he kicks me out. It would have been easy for him to make a suspected person charge stand so I stayed out of the way for a bit. The ordinary public wouldn't know how corrupt they were then.

The first time I ever went to the races was in 1945 and it was the start of a lifetime obsession. Not that I hadn't been into cards and dice but racing was something else. Over the months at the end of the war I had a touch or two and so I went up to Warren Street where all the used car salesmen conned the punters and bought myself a little sports car, an Armstrong Siddeley. I hadn't had it a few days when I get a message from Harry Bryan would I go to Lyons Corner House at the Angel — they called it the Angel Café Restaurant. When I got there, there was Harry and Jock, and Harryboy Sabini was at another table. As I went over to Jock, Harryboy called over, 'Hello – you from the Hill? How d'you get here?' I said, 'I've just bought a lovely car'. I think I did actually say 'lovely'. I was so proud of it. He said, 'Would you like a day at the races? I've got the coupons', because, of course, petrol was rationed. He doesn't have to tell me to wear a suit and a hat because that was what we all wore back then; none of this no ties and windbreakers even in the Silver Ring.

He told me to pick him up and we drove to Newmarket which had just opened for racing again. On the way he takes out all these yellow telegrams, opens them up and starts making notes. You learn as you go along. Now, he was a commission agent and had the trust of the trainers to get their bets down. And of course he gets paid and he also knows for himself what horse is trying and which isn't.

When we get there and I've got parked Harryboy goes into the Members and talks to one or two people about the horses. This impressed me no end. I stay outside and when he comes back and we're walking along he sees someone coming towards us, 'This fella might stop and talk. If he does, you step aside'. The man said, 'Hullo Harryboy', and stuck his shooting stick in the ground and sat on it. Harryboy takes his hat off and keeps it off while they have a chat, with me standing a few paces away. When he's gone Harryboy tells me to put a few quid on a certain horse. 'It's the King's and it'll be trying.' The man he'd been talking to was either the Earl of Rosebery or Lord Derby, I forget which. The horse was Fisherman's

Yarn and it won in a photo-finish at 6/1 with Eph Smith up so it may have been the Earl of Roseberry because Eph Smith rode for him a lot. It was the first bet I ever had. I thought it was marvellous; a different world from a slum in Clerkenwell. Maybe it would have been better for me overall if it had lost. But after that I took Harryboy and his brother Joe racing whenever it was on.

I did a bit of work for Alf White and his son Harry, manning his stand at Epsom and Brighton. There's a picture of me and my half brother Bernard just before the two o'clock at Epsom on 21 April 1948. You can just see the names of some of the horses on the tissue — Sporty Boy, Clever Joe, Lionheart and Raffin. I think the race was won by Gordon Richards but I can't remember what he was on. People might think I was disloyal working with the Whites after they'd been enemies of Darby and the others in the 1930s but you've got to move on and anyway that was years before my time.

Bammy Russo was a floorlayer from Clerkenwell but he decided he wanted to open a book on the free course at Epson. He saved up a bit of money and I agreed to go in with him on it. I think we put a £100 in each. It all went wrong when we took too much on one horse. If it won we were done for and it did. Now in those days on the free course there were all sorts of people. There was Prince Monolulu, nice man, a big black fellow who always wore robes and feathers. Looked about eight feet tall. He was a tipster always calling, 'I got a Horse'. There were the usual religious cranks – spoilsports who tried to get people to stop betting. There was a fellow dressed up as a jockey who pretended to ride a horse and then would give out envees with tips in them and there was even a fellow who'd pull teeth. Anyway, that day there's this fellow who's a one man band. Drum on his back, mouth organ and so on. He keeps on plying 'Money is the root of all evil' and Bammy is really annoyed with him. He's done his dough and it mattered to hm. £100 wasn't any great harm to me. Anyway Bammy goes on and on about the money and so I get hold of this man with the drum and tell him if he comes over to Saffron Hill he can have a fiver which was big

London's racecourse gang of the twentieth century. The Cortesis and Sabinis pose together before they fell out. Derby Sabini is in the flat cap to the immediate left of the straw-boatered Enrico Cortesi. The formidable Bert Marsh, known as Pasquale Papa, is probably second on the left – JAMES MORTON

**Above:**

An original 1920 photograph featuring The Cortesis and Sabini Familes including Darby Sabini (3rd from left wearing cap). Darby and his brothers, HarryBoy & Joe who got Bert started on his apprenticeship at just 12. Darby would go on to become the boss of London.

# Bert with the Krays

**Above**

Ronnie Kray with Bert at the Stork Club, Soho

**Above (left to right):**

Sulky, Ronnie Kray, Bert, Bomber John, Buller Ward

**Above (left to right):**

Reggie Kray, Buller Ward, Bert, Red Face Tommy, Ronnie Kray

**Above:**

Reggie Kray, Vince Landa, Barney Beale, Bert Rossi, Ronnie Kray

**Above:**

Charlie Kray and Joe Pyle on the Set of "The Krays" in 1989 where Bert was assisting with technical advising.

**Above:**

Steven Berkoff as George Cornell seen with a bullet in his head. Director Peter Medak, Charlie Kray and Gary Kemp as Ronnie Kray in this never before seen photograph.

**Left:**

Bert here featured on the center spread of The Sunday People.

**Above:**

Bobby Warren, Tommy Falco, Bert Rossi, Billy Hill,
Ruby Sparks and Frank Fraser

**Above:**

Ronnie Kray, Teddy Machin, Bert,
Terry Downes (sparring)

**Above:**

Young handsome Bert (center) with his
Clerkenwell gang

# George Raft with Bert Rossi and friends

**Above**

*left to right*

Eddie Pucci, Ronnie Kray, George Raft, Bert Rossi, Reggie Kray,
Rocky Marciano and Charlie Kray

**Above:**
Shorty, Bert, Son Peter,
Rocky Marciano, Bammy Russo.

**Right:**
Dino Cellini, Meyer Lansky's
right hand man. Working
alongside Raft and Bert at
The Colony Club.

**Above:**

Bert with Willie Pep and his dear friends, The Powell Family.

**Left:**

A signed print dedicated to Bert by his friend, Willie Pep

**Above:**

Bert with his Wife Mary, Harry Hicks, Frank Fraser (right)

**Left:**

Jimmy Wicks, "Red face" Tommy, Henry Cooper and Bert

**Right:**

Bammy Russo, Bert and Bert's brother, Bernard.

*Epsom Downs racecourse, April 1948*

money compared with the pennies he was picking up.

That evening he urns up and I took him round outside Bammys' flat and off he starts banging the drum and playing 'Money, money, money'. The window opens and Bammy tips the chamber over him.

When I wasn't at the races I was working. Sometimes I saw more in one touch than straight people did in a year. You take that road or this. You have to take a risk but you've got your freedom. That's the chance you take. Some people can't bear the thought of going to prison, then they have to go straight. It's all a question of which packet you pick up. And some of that work was with Billy Blythe. We'd do half a dozen jobs together every year; fags, whisky, hijacks. In those days you could buy small houses for £1000 a time and we never looked at a job which wasn't going to bring us in a grand apiece.

Billy Blythe was a good staunch fellow, a soldier. He could have a foul mouth though , always effing and blinding. I accepted it because it was a way of talking with him while I was out with him but I didn't like it when he started in my house and I told him that. He never took no offence.

He was a fellow who earned his money. He would cut up the proceeds and go home and at six o'clock he'd go to the local pub and play darts. When I had a bit of money I'd buy suits and shirts or a car. Billy just lived the life of an ordinary working man.

Early on after the war I was getting pretty comfortable. One day when I'd been out with Joe Sabini and I took him home. He lived in Wood Green, a house with a lovely garden. He said the house next door was better and up for sale. He quoted me a figure. My father had just died and my mother and I were living in Barnsbury Road. When I got home she was cooking — she was a lovely cook, all Italian food, made her own pasta — and I told her I'd seen a house and I wanted her to come and look at it. She just said, 'No, no' and when I insisted she come and have a look she got annoyed. 'If you want to buy it, buy it'. 'Why won't you come?' 'You go out in the morning, you change your shirts, you go to the West End, come in a car. All these people know what you're doing. Now you want to buy a house. It could be three months and then the police come and arrest you and I'm left alone with no one I know'. And I never did buy it. You could see how she felt. My poor mother, she barely spoke English and until she died she couldn't read and write. She signed her name with an X.

It was 1952 that I took a tumble. Lorries had been my thing but then Cherry me and Billy Blythe did a jewellers over in Edgware. We hired a car, I'm not sure if it wasn't from Shonk. It could have been. We knew there was a small safe and we were after that. We found we couldn't pick it up. We got the rest of the gear and as we come out of the shop there's a policeman. I knocked him down but I was surrounded. The shop must have been belled up to the local station. Cherry and Billy got away and I got three years at Middlesex Sessions but it got knocked down to 18 months.

It was about this time I had a run in with the Islington Mob and Jimmy Wooder when he ran the Mob and they were friends with the Whites but now they were looking after things for a family the Phillipsons who were big bookmakers before the days of betting shops. They had a fellow Duza who was the governor then. Anyway, I'm working with my brother at Epsom and we've got a joint there and I decide to slip away and put a bet on a horse I fancied. So I went a couple of joints down and had a bet at the Phillipson's stand. 9/4 the horse was and I had £40 on it and I 'paid on' meaning I give them the £40. I didn't need to 'pay on'. Between ourselves you didn't need to pay up front like an ordinary punter. I don't think over the years Jerry Callaghan ever 'paid on' and he bet in hundreds if not thousands. The horse won and I went to collect my winnings and they give me £90. I was half way back to our joint when I realise they should have given me £130. The winnings and the stake back. So I go back and there's people waiting to put bets on and the fellow on the pitch says I've got to wait 'til they're dealt with. I say I want my money and this fellow Dusa told me to get to the back of the queue. I said again I wanted my money and he called me out. Said it was between us. Now who's there but that black fellow. Danish he was but he called himself Prince Monolulu. Always wore tribal dress and feathers which made him look about eight foot tall. He was a big tipster, used to call out 'I gotta horse'. When he sees what's happening he appoints himself referee and calls out, 'Make a ring, make a ring'. And the punters did. I laid into Dusa, I knocked the fucking life out of him and when I'd finished I went back and said, 'Now I'll have my £40'. If they hadn't give it to me I'd have pushed the joint over. That was the end of Dusa. If I'm in a fight I'd do anything. Knee you in the bollocks, nut you, butt you. No fucking Queensbury Rules. Anything to win. That's how you get a reputation. That's how you become a Guv'nor.

It wasn't all work. It was in the early fifties that Darby came up from Brighton to the Italian festival in Clerkenwell. I saw him in the Central and by then he knew of me from Harryboy and Joe. He said if I was ever in Brighton to look him up. So the next summer when there used to be a three day meeting in I think the August for the holiday crowds I went down for the races. I was staying at the Grand and I rang him up and he said, 'Come round'. I went round to his house and he said he was going to the pub owned by Tommy Farr who'd beaten Joe Louis for the world heavyweight title. Well that's what most people except the referee thought. When we go there who was sitting drinking but the great comedian Max Miller who lived in Brighton. He was so famous that when he played the Metropolitan in the Edgware Road and he overran they held up the Brighton Belle, as the train was known and which was the last of the night, until he got there. I think it ran at one minute past midnight but I may be wrong. The guard could see him getting out of a cab and he'd call out, 'Hurry up Mr Miller, sir, we can't hold her for much longer'. And if that wasn't enough, in comes the actor Laurence Olivier to join them. There I was with three of the most famous men in the country. I'm not usually lost for words but that afternoon I don't think I dared say a single one.

Funnily enough I cam across what must have been about Max's last recording. It was on YouTube and he was with Lonnie Donegan. The jokes were just the same 'I'm going out with a chiffonier'. 'What do you mean? A chiffonier's a tall thing with drawers.' That's right I'm going out with a chiffonier'. They still make me laugh.

Harry Bryan and Jock Wyatt were good to me. I was only a relative youngster but they had me in on three or four jobs when there was really no need. I suppose it was a question of their seeing how I used myself. I used myself properly and so they asked me again and again until I became one of the team. Not that I took part in everything they did.

It was just before Jock and Harry got their long stretches which finished them that I heard of what would be a nice touch. Rationing was still on. Lorries were fair game and very often the driver could be persuaded to drop his load. One evening I happened to be down in Fleet Street and I met a couple of fellows I knew in the Black and White milk bar which used to be on the corner of Bouverie Street where the old News of the World had their warehouses. It was the usual conversation, ' Got any interest in joeys?' Of course I had and so I gave the standard answer, 'If the price is right'. Then they tell me about the lorry they're going to do a jump up on. It was parked round the corner and I went and had a look. They told me the fellow parked it overnight in the same place every week and went off with a couple of brasses, so I realised immediately that this was going to be better than a few joeys and I said, 'Don't touch it. Leave it with me. There'll be a nice few quid for you'. And with that I was off back to Saffron Hill to tell Harry and Jock. On the way I saw Albert Dimes who was worrying that his wife Rose wanted a new carpet and he didn't have the money. 'Don't worry', I said, 'You'll have it. I'm working on a bit and I'll have the money all right'. Harry wanted to meet the driver so that we could put a proposition to him; far easier and safer than a hijack and I had a word with him in the milk bar. He was half inclined and so I said, 'Come out and meet the boys'. Out he comes and gets in the front of the car with me with Jock and Harry in the back. Did he want to be in on it? There's a bit of chat and it's clear he's going to go along with things but while we're talking Harry puts his hand on the headrest of the front seat. Now Harry always had three rings on his fingers, one and a half carats a piece but what was more he was missing part of one finger. Anyway it's all arranged for the following week. We'll get the keys and the lorry will go off to a slaughter. The introducers will get a whack; the fellow will get his – more than he'll make in a year so if he gets the sack it won't matter. Rose Dimes will get her carpet and Jock and Harry and me will have the rest.

It was Albert who told me to get the Evening News. There it was as a headline '£100,000 nicked', well not quite in those words but I could have dropped down dead. Some one else had nicked the lorry. Then Jock phones up. He's read the paper and can't believe it either. Two hours later he's on the phone again with even worse news. Harry Bryan has been nicked. It wasn't difficult to work out what had happened. The driver had been pulled in, that was only natural but he cracked early enough. 'Yes, someone had discussed his dropping the load'. 'Who was that?' And he tells them about Harry's groynes and missing finger and who do the coppers know like that? Simple really and so round they come to Harry who, for once, doesn't know a thing.

The coppers can't have been convinced he's done it. He's given them an alibi and its genuine but they don't leave things there. He has to find £500 in forty-eight hours or he'll get another pull. 'Don't take us for mugs. Sod the alibi. £500 or we'll put you on an ID and the driver will pick you out'.

Now where are we going to pull up £500? Harry's rings won't fetch that in a forced sale and so Jock starts making inquiries and blow me if it isn't Jack Spot's men, Teddy Machin, George and Jimmy Woods , part of the Upton Park mob, who've had the lorry. They hadn't bothered with the driver; they'd cased it and then just gone and took it. And so Jock says we've got to go and see them. He makes a couple of calls and we go over to a pub on their manor and he put's our cards on the table. 'Fair play to you and good luck nicking the motor,' but this is what's happened to us. 'We've got a problem'. Now they could easily have said our problem was not their problem. But no, to my utter surprise they pulled up the money which went straight to the law.

What the Upton Park Mob did for me and Jock and Harry was to stand them in very good stead when, a few years later, Jack Spot had to go.

But before then Jock and Harry went down and it was dead good luck that I didn't go down with them and it was all because I was late for a meet one morning in March 1951. And this was very unusual because I'm a good timekeeper.

I'd met Jock and Harry on the Friday evening when I went down to Kings Cross for a drink. It was something I did every Friday and this time Jock says did I want to come along with them on the Monday. 'There's going to be plenty of money in it,' he says, 'Be here 9 o'clock and we'll be off'. That morning I walked down from the Barnsbury Road where I was living to Jock's Place in the Cross and I was a few minutes late. It must have been five past when Madge, Jock's wife, opened the door. 'They've just this second left,' she says. 'Jock didn't think you were coming and there was no point in hanging around any longer. Tell Bert he's still in for his whack', he said. But they never came back. They'd walked straight into a police trap. What had happened was that Harry and Jock had got hold of a fellow who'd worked for Chubbs for years and had kept sets of keys for all the safes he'd made and he knew where they'd been sent. Harry and Jock had been at it for years. But the law tumbled them, kept watch, followed them to the job in Hampshire I was meant to be on and that was that. Harry got ten and Jock eight. Anyway the story was made into a film with Jack Hawkins as the clever copper, The Long Arm of the Law. Not much consolation for Harry and Jack though.

It was while Harry was in prison that Billy Hill went round to see how his wife was getting on. She asks him in and while she's making a cup of coffee for him he gets out his gun and starts messing about and cleaning it. When she comes back with the coffee the gun goes off and a bullet goes through Harry's wife's arm. Fortunately it was just a flesh wound but it shows how careful you have to be. There's been plenty of people who've got careless and killed their friends messing about with guns, showing people how they work, and done long stretches over it.

Johnny Furio was the first person after the war to set up an ice cream factory in London. He did it in Hammersmith and from the start there was trouble with a local firm coming in a couple of times a week causing his problems. He approached Bert Marsh and in turn Bert asked me and Albert to go over and help Johnny. He told us the men hung out in a café and so Albert and I went round. Just as we walked in one of them looks up and says, 'Hello Bert. What you doing here?' I was surprised he knew me but I said, ' The reason we're here is you're messing about a friend of ours. Now turn it up'. And they swallowed it. We went back to Johnny and told him he'd never see them again and there'd be no more trouble. He said he had to go over to Frith Street and he'd give us a lift. On the way he points out an attaché case and says there's a monkey in it for us. Albert is all for taking it but I had bigger ideas. I said no we couldn't take it. 'You're Italian, we're Italian.' When we got out of the car Albert says, 'Are you fucking mad?' I said, 'No you are'. 'What are you talking about?' 'When we was in Hammersmith did you see that queue? Who else sells ice cream? It must have been eighty strong'. I give it two or three days and then I approach Johnny. Will he set Albert and me up as ice cream distributors? He buys us some tricycles for the vendors to pedal about on — you used to see them all over the country before they brought vans in — and that must have cost him more than £500. We take a building in the Kings Cross Road. Of course we buy the ice cream from him and the vendors get it from us and we're in business.

But it wasn't for us. We were gamblers not businessmen. Albert liked going to the races and we didn't want the trouble of running a business. We had to be there at nights when the men brought the trikes in; wait 'til the last one pedals back. Next morning be there to send them out again. It was too much. We give it a bit under three months and then say to Johnny, 'We're not made for this kind of thing.' Will he take the trikes back and give us the money. And that was the last time I ever held what people would call a proper job.

Albert was like a brother to me but I've got to say he had no brains at all. He'd a temper and he'd tangle with the wrong people. One day I go up to Soho and Bert Marsh says, 'You've just missed it. Albert was here and he's done a silly thing. He's gone and slapped Harry Levene'. Now you don't do things like that to straight people and along with Jack Solomons, Harry Levene and his partner Mickey Duff were the top boxing promoters in the country at the time. I don't know what Harry had said to Albert but you don't slap people like him and Harry wasn't a big man. Albert could just have said, 'Fuck off'. Anyway Bert continues, 'Harry's going to nick him. You need to stop this.' So I ring up Mickey Duff who I knew and say, 'Look, I don't now what it was about and that's why I'm phoning you. Harry wasn't really hurt. Tell him not to take it any further because if Albert's nicked then Albert'll take it a stage in his turn. Get Harry to drop it out before there's extra trouble for all of us'. And that's what Mickey does.

A couple of weeks later Albert and me are at the Albert Hall for the fights and sitting at ringside with Harry are Scotland Yard's heavy mob, all shaking hands and laughing with him. All have been comped of course. I turned to Albert and say, 'Look at your old pal now.' I had that edge. Pull back rather than go steaming in. Albert didn't have it.

What I always tried to do was keep the peace or make it. There was no point in rowing amongst ourselves. We could do that with the law. But when people wouldn't listen you had to take action.

After the war, as I've said, I got to know Scobie Breasley very well. He was a commission agent by now and had offices in Holborn. For a time he was like an uncle to me. If I had a bit of stuff to sell, Scotch for example, he'd tell me which publicans would buy it and he never wanted a cut. He put up the money for one or two jobs as well. Anyway, I'm in Ted's café which was down in Little Italy one evening and when I come out there's Shonk. I could see he was all excited and I went over to him and he tells me he's bought a racehorse. I can't quite remember what it was called after all this time but I think it was Compact. Anyway it's running the next day, did I want to go to Epsom with him and his wife? 'I've got Gordon Richards to ride'. Now, Gordon Richards was the champion jockey many times and the number of races he won in the days before there were motorways and helicopters to get to different cards of an afternoon and evening meetings was incredible and he was riding against good jockeys as well; Doug and Eph Smith, Harry Wragg, the one they called the Head Waiter because he could time his challenge in a race to perfection, and the Australians such as Scobie Beasley. Do you know two years after the war Gordon rode 269 winners in a season? Just think of it.

Anyway the next day Shonk calls for me in his car. Chauffeur driven of course; he had an ex-Scotland Yard man doing the driving for him, and in the back was his wife. The horse was running in the name of Cyril Maynard which was what he then used for his bookmaking business. He'd moved on from Nick Gold. You couldn't have a betting office as Silvio Mazzarda could you? I'm properly suited and booted and with a trilby, of course. You'd as soon go out without your trousers in those days as you would without a hat. Hair all properly Brylcreemed. As I said before not like people turn up at the races these days. It was an occasion then, even at the gaff tracks.

It's a fine afternoon and Shonk sports a bottle of bubbly and then another and by the end of the second race his wife, well she's a bit tiddly. I wasn't bad looking in those days although I say it myself and when we go down to the paddock she's holding on to my arm and not Shonk's and it looks to me she's getting ideas. I can see him getting upset but what am I to do? I can't just push her off, can I? After that he cooled on me a bit. Never hostile but never as friendly. The horse lost of course.

The other thing was people often approached me to do someone on their behalf.

Of course, there's always going to be contracts. They go back as far as you can think of. Some people actually used to have a price list. There was a fellow in New York at the end of the 19th century called Piker Ryan who when he got picked up had a written list : $4 for a punching, $4 for both eyes blackened, $25 a stabbing and $100 up for what he called 'Doing the big job'. It was always said that Billy Hill here used to pay £1 a stitch and people used to look in the evening papers to see how much they'd earned the night before. But I think that was just a good story.

It was also in 1951 I got involved in the row between Mad Frankie Fraser and the Carters from South London and Tony Mella — Antonio Benedetta Mella was his real name . I still don't know what it was all about but Frank Fraser said it was over a long standing feud between the Carters and his in-laws, the Brindles, and that Johnny Carter had cut one of the Brindle brothers, Bobby. Whatever it was about Mella took the Carters' side against his own people. Mella had been a small time boxer and there were stories that he was being brought on by having carefully selected opponents but then when he went in with the Southern Area champion he took a bad beating. But he was a big man and one of the best on the cobbles.

Anyway I've just come out of the Central Club in Holborn and opposite's a waiting car. It does a U turn and there's shots fired at us. Someone said, 'That's Tony Mella'. I wasn't having that. What roused me was that I'd already warned him not to interfere and here he is a couple of nights later taking a shot at us. I went with Fraser and some others to his flat near Old Street and I said, 'Once you was friends with me'. He didn't say nothing. He knew it was on top. We cut him to ribbons and he got a bashing with a shillelagh which Billy Hill had give to Frank. Mella was tough as they come. He was game but he has to go down and he looks up at me, blood coming from everywhere and says, 'Bert, Bert'. That's when I said, 'That's enough'. We just left him. It was in the papers that the surgeon said that if he hadn't have been so fit he'd have died.

Next time I saw him was when I took my young son to the boxing at the Caledonian Road Baths. This would be about three weeks after we'd belted him. He had a trilby on to cover the bandages on his head and he had a crutch to walk with. He must have seen me come in. This was before the fights started and he made his way over – we was at the ringside. He hobbles around the ring and stops opposite me. I covered my boy up because I thought he might take a swing at him with his crutch. But all he did was look at me as if to say, 'Look what you done'. I felt I'd gone a bit too far. He'd never gone to the law.

A bit later I was doing a piece of work with Billy Benstead and another fellow who knew Tony. He said, 'I've bumped into him and he said he was skint. I said I was seeing you and he asked if he could come on a bit of work. I'd always respected him and as I've said after all he could have put us all away. I did think we'd overdone it and so I said all right. And from then on he became a very good friend.

# 6 : JACK SPOT AND BILLY HILL

A bit ago I started saying how I'd come to do Jack Spot and it all goes back a long time. It was just before the war that Spot – his real name was Comer or sometimes he used the name Comacho — came to the fore. Big fleshy man from the East End, he was a comer if you like. He started life with a game for mugs in Petticoat Lane on a Sunday. There were plenty of these things which are long gone now – like I've said the three card trick or Find the Lady, Crown and Anchor which you could fix by having a brake on the wheel, Spinning Jenny and Pick a Straw which is what Spot ran. In Pick a Straw there was a box with different coloured straws. You paid a penny or something like that and if you picked the one with a number on it you got a prize – of course all the good prizes had gone if there was ever any in the box in the first place. If you won a prize at these games it was what was called slum, cheap shoddy goods. But Spot was also doing a bit of protection trade on the free courses at the races. Anyway Spot liked his name because, he said, he was always on the Spot for Jewish shopkeepers who were being turned over by Oswald Mosley and his Fascists but it was really because he had a mole on his face or maybe it was a wart.

He had a big mouth did Spot. He was always going on about being Protector of the Jews and for all I know he may have been but, if he was, it would have been at a price. In that book about him Man of a Thousand Cuts he says he bashed up a wrestler Roughneck who was Mosley's protector in the Battle of Cable Street. Hit him with a loaded chair leg. Rubbish. For a start Mosley wasn't allowed to march the day of the so-called battle so Spot would never have got near him. The battle was East Enders against the police. Then Spot says he got six months for it. Rubbish again. What he got six months for was assaulting his one time friend Iskey Simmons at the Somerset Social Club in the City when Iskey refused to pay his weekly protection money, and that was much later anyway. But he traded on the Roughneck story all his life and no one came forward to say it was all balls. Not in his lifetime they didn't anyway.

That was just one of his stories. There was another about how he knew the American gangster Sam Clynes, who was said to be a former member of Murder Incorporated, and got advice from him. The advice included how to treat members of his team if they went to prison. Clynes suggested a weekly pension of £20 for wives at a time when a policeman's wage was between £9 and £11. Spot should have listened to him. He was a bad payer and that did him no good at all. Unfortunately all too often Spot failed to pay anything and in turn he paid the penalty for it. The Twins got cross with him over having to go to Manchester on his behalf once in their early days and not being paid properly.

After Clynes' death he said he had paid for a funeral service and a headstone. That was another load of bollocks. There was no such man as Clynes; it was a mix of James Hynes and Harry Kleintz. Hynes was certainly an American and he may have been shot when the gangster 'Little Augie' Orgen was killed. Later, together with Kleintz, he came to England where they did a robbery on a jewellers with that brilliant Australian climber , they allwent down for five years in June 1928 at Newcastle Assizes. There was further long sentences after a tie-up of a woman in Park Lane and Hynes died in Parkhurst in April 1943. Spot can never have met him. What is it they say in that film? Print the legend.

Then there's a story that while Spot was in Brixton he did Babe Mancini who was on trial for killing Hubby Distleman. I don't know if it's true. I wasn't there but this time I suppose it could have been. Distleman was Jewish, so was Spot. Babe was Italian, of course. And the second half of that story is was when he met Arthur Skurry of the West Ham Mob and that's how they became friends.

It's right backing for him did come from the Upton Park Mob and a real tough bunch they were. In the 1950s I had quite a bit to do with them. A lot of them were gypsies and there were big families such as the Bennetts. Now Arthur Bennett he was a hard man, everyone called him Porky. He got eight years Preventive Detention in February 1951 for slashing a wrestler in Ding Ah Ching's a café in Pennyfields in Limehouse. Before that in February 1948 he got six months for GBH when he ran his wife down with a car.

What Spot also did after the war was run a gaming club in the city for a man who would later become big in my life. Abe Kosky he was called. It was called Botolphs and they had Arthur Skurry who only had half an ear on the door.

After the war Spot set out to take over the racecourse pitches from the Whites who'd been running them. I don't know if Alf was still alive but if he was he'd retired. He'd had a son killed in the war and the firm was being run by another son Harry. Now Harry was what people used to call very 'hail fellow well met'. He was always smartly dressed, a very heavy smoker and drinker and a real pain when he'd been drinking. But what Harry wasn't was a fighter.

What had happened was that when we Italians were all interned the Whites had taken over control of the pitches and Spot wanted them. They were good money. He could organise which bookmaker had which pitch and his friends got the best spots. He could charge for the tissues, the chalk, the sponges, the same as Darby had been doing. But to do this he had to get rid of the Whites. And get rid of them he did. Billy Hill wasn't really interested in horses and so it didn't matter to him when Spot cut little Eddie Raimo at Yarmouth Races and moved in on the pitches there. In fact I'm not sure Billy wasn't on his toes in South Africa at the time over some furs.

After Spot did up Eddie, the Whites didn't do anything about it and once there was a sign of weakness in went Spot. With some of the West Ham Mob like Teddy Machin, Porky Bennett and other people, such as Monkey Bennyworth, he went to the Nuthouse, a club in Sackville Street off

Piccadilly, where Harry White was drinking along with a racehorse trainer as well as with Billy Goller and a few others. Spot was always keen to turn things into a situation where he could say he was acting on behalf of Jewish interests and he says to White, 'You're Yiddified', whatever he meant by that, and then he cut Billy Goller's throat. It was in the days when the death penalty was in force and Spot must have forgotten his own saying, 'You must never cut below the line here, cause, if you do, you cut the jugular – and the hangman is waiting.'

The story is that Harry hid under a table and that was the end of him as a leader. When Spot told the story to the Sunday Chronicle he called Billy 'Big Bill' to make it read better. He must have been the only person who called Billy that. Billy Goller nearly died. He had the last rites given him and Spot went down to Benny Swan's B52 Club at the end of the runway at Southend Airport and hid out.

Amazingly Billy survived but it was not until he recovered and was paid off that Spot returned to London. And so for a time Spot was Lord of all he surveyed. When he did come back he went to see Harry White and said he now wanted 30 per cent of his racecourse takings. What there's no doubt about was that later between them him and Billy Hill chased the Whites out of town.

But Spot had to be the great I am and he persuaded Abe Kosky to put up the dough for a robbery at Heathrow. Sammy Josephs, a fellow with whom Spot had worked previously, had discovered that cargoes were kept overnight on a fairly regular basis and they fancied getting into the bonded warehouse which contained nearly £250,000 worth of goods including diamonds and was due to receive a million in gold the next day. Naturally Spot didn't go on it but he had some of the West Ham Mob do the dirty work. Among them was Porky Bennett, Georgie and Jimmy Wood, Teddy Hughes, Franny Daniels and Teddy Machin.

I got all this over the years from Franny. In fairness the job had been well worked out and they'd maintained a twenty-four hour watch on Heath Row, as it was then called, for over two months . Dummy parcels were sent from Ireland and Franny, who was an authorised driver and was allowed in the customs sheds, checked they had arrived. Then it all went wrong. A fellow at the airport told his boss he had been offered £500 to dope the warehouse staff. In came the Flying Squad.

The plan had been to drug the guards at the warehouse and at first the raid seemed to go all right . The messenger with the tea was intercepted, and barbitone was dropped in the jug. But at the last minute the guards had been switched and replaced by members of the Flying Squad. The tea was put on one side and the three 'guards' lay on the floor seemingly drugged . Franny and the others went in, hit one of the detectives with an iron bar to ensure he was unconscious and then took the keys from his pocket. At that moment the other coppers attacked. Teddy Machin fell into a ditch, was knocked unconscious and as a result was never found. Franny held on to the underside of a van and, instead of being dropped off at the first set of traffic lights, as he hoped, was carried all the way to Harlesden Police Station, from where he made his way home. If you asked nicely he'd show you the burns on his shoulder still there many years later. My friend Billy Benstead also escaped. The next day most of the rest of them limped into the dock. They'd had a good battering.

Teddy Hughes received twelve years penal servitude with Sammy Ross one less. Jimmy Wood went down for nine. Jimmy's brother George , picked up eight. The saddest one of all, Alfie Room from Ilford, got ten. As for Spot the police could never prove that he was the organiser but they soon shut down Botolphs.

I say Alfie was the saddest story of them all because he went mad and a bit after his release he set fire to his daughter's wedding dress. After that he went for his wife with a knife at a newspaper stall outside the main gate of Ford's at Dagenham where she worked. He then swallowed a cyanide capsule.

That was really the beginning of the end of Spot as a gang leader and he turned back to the racecourses where thing went for him. Welshing by bookmakers was still rife. They would turn up with barely enough money to pay out on the first race and would be quite prepared to scarper. He'd done it hisself early on. According to him though, it was him who solved the problem at the request of the Chief Steward, the Duke of Norfolk.

Modestly he would tell the story that he had been recommended to the Duke by the northern racecourse inspectors he had helped at Doncaster who had put his name forward; sometimes thought he said it was a senior police officer, he was always changing his stories.

Spot helpfully explained that organisation was needed. The Free Side of a course had to be enclosed and a set number of pitches drawn up. These would only be allocated to bookmakers with a bank account with enough money to make sure they could pay out. As a favour to his Lordship, Spot would take it upon himself to make sure the allocations were straight. Oh, yes.

Later Spot claimed in his book everyone was pleased with what he'd done. 'You've made racing a pleasure, Jack. We no longer go in terror of our lives', he was told by small time bookmakers. If they paid him enough that is.Meanwhile what had Billy Hill been up to? Well he'd been on the run in South Africa over a fur job and that was where he'd tried to set up a nightclub or a spieler, one of the two. He was there with the boxer Bobby Ramsey who'd gone over for a fight. There was a set to with a local club owner and Billy came back here where his did his bird over the furs . And that was the last sentence he ever did.

It was while he was in the nick he repeated the stunt which Bert Marsh and Bert Wilkins had done before the war and probably lots of other people as well. He saved a screw from a seemingly out of control Jack Rosa. Rosa was awaiting a flogging and, at the time, the prison rules were that there could be no further punishment imposed on a prisoner in these circumstances.

So, the day after his flogging Rosa attacked an officer with a knife in the workshop. Bill intervened and was roundly condemned by the prisoners in the know who chorused that he was a bastard for saving the screw's life. Rosa apologised, claiming that it was the effect of the Cat which had sent him berserk. Billy was said to have given him £5,000. For his bravery, he six months knocked off his sentence. On his release in 1949 who's there at the gates to meet him and drive him away? None other than jolly Jack Spot. For a time an in partnership and I have to say they made a good fist of it. But it didn't last.

It was then Billy pulled off the Eastcastle Street robbery which has to be the biggest and best ever in Britain and in most places in the world because no one got nicked. And brilliant it was too. A post officer worker who had been steadily losing in one of Billy's spielers came to his notice and was approached for useful information. In return for writing off the money he owed, Billy got him to give details of when he delivered the mail bags.

After what the man said, Billy had a mail van followed every night for months from Paddington Station to the city. Then he did a brilliant thing. Out in the suburbs he rehearsed the robbery pretending he was shooting a film. Cars were stolen specifically for the raid. On the night of the robbery once the van left Paddington a call was made to the West End flat where Billy had lodged his men. Four men climbed into one of the stolen cars, a green Vanguard, and the other four into a stolen 2 1/2 litre Riley.

As the van turned into Eastcastle Street one of the cars blocked the driver's path. Six men then attacked the three post-office workers and looted the vehicle. They drove to Augustus Street in the City where the cash was transferred into boxes on a fruit lorry, belonging to Jack Gyp who was minded by Billy's man Sonny Sullivan and which had been left there earlier. Eighteen out of thirty-one bags were taken. At first it was thought that £44,000 in old notes was all that had gone but the full damage became known later in the week. The total was near enough £290,000. Think what would have been today. According to Billy the remaining bags were left because there wasn't any more room in the lorry.

There's only a few people in any city that can organise a job like that and from the word go Billy was No 1 in the frame but the police could never get near to putting it on him and he had enough on coppers himself to make sure he wasn't fitted up. No one was ever charged.

Who was on it and why wasn't I? First who was? Billy's new girlfriend Gypsy was said to be the driver. I don't know, I wasn't there, but she could have been. She wouldn't have been the first woman driver. Ruby Sparkes' girlfriend Lillian, who was known as the Bobbed Haired Bandit, drove him on jobs. Both the Sullivan brothers Slip and Sonny were on it although Sonny later said his brother wasn't, and so was Billy Blythe.

My old friend George 'Taters' Chatham was certainly there. Taters was a degenerate gambler as well as being one of the most skilled climbers of that and many another generation. He was said to have received £15,000 for his part. He was a good snooker player but not half as good as he thought. He used to play at the Red Fox in Hammersmith and these hustlers were coming in and taking his money off him. He gambled away his money within a matter of weeks in one of Billy's clubs and then was found trying to blow Billy's safe in an attempt to get his losses back . I remember the receiver 'Little' Stan Davis telling me Taters once approached him at the Epsom races to borrow £25 from him. He lost that and on the way home he hit the Epsom Post Office. Davis bought the stamps and savings stamps off of him. Taters always claimed that a South London thief Terry Hogan was the one who climbed into the cab in Eastcastle Street.

There was plenty of stories of the robbery over the years. One was that the man who had supplied one of the stolen vehicles was paid £24,000. He hid the money in his flat and while he was serving a sentence for something else members of his own team of car thieves dressed up as police officers, called on his wife, searched the premises and confiscated the money.

Back in 1952 Billy found that, just like Spot after the airport robbery, the police took reprisals. They might not have been able to pin Eastcastle Street on him but they were able to raid his spielers on an almost nightly basis. Eventually he handed them over to others. He was now also having domestic troubles. His wife Aggie was on his back trying to persuade him that with the money from the robbery he could actually become legit. He maintained that he owed a loyalty to the men with whom he had worked over the years. According to his autobiography he was still providing money for the wives of the men, such as the Wood brothers and Teddy Hughes, who had gone down over the airport robbery. That's what Spot should have been doing. And then there was his new girlfriend Gyp.

Why wasn't I on the job? For a start it was well known I didn't like these big, big jobs with too many people for comfort. A criminal's best partner is himself is one of those mottos I believe in and this one was mob handed. It's right to say nothing leaked out but it so easily could have done. A bit of careless talk here or there and in come the coppers. Loose lips give coppers tips. Second, if the truth is known, I was never that close to him — I was invited to the launch of his book of course — but although he put that first climbing job up for me I never really liked Billy Hill. He was a cold man, a bit like Bert Marsh. Also I'd blanked him on another job so maybe that was the reason.

You might think Billy Hill would have been satisfied with the Eastcastle Street job. And sort of retire on his laurels. When you think of what he must have taken he'd never need to work again but what does he do? Four years later he pulls off a gold robbery in Jockey Fields in Lincoln Inn. He sort of half mentioned it to me. Maybe he felt bad about my missing out on the Eastcastle job but when it come to it I was a bit busy at the time with something up in the Midlands.

It was a good piece of work though. It only took a minute. A lorry blocks the gold bullion lorry and a man does the snatch. Now, as I say the police only look at a handful of people for a big job, at least they did in those days when it was home grown talent so who gets a pull straight away – Billy. Now people can say he wasn't particularly likeable but no one can ever say he wasn't smart. He's put some of his money in a toy business in the Whitechapel Road. He took me round there one day. It was full ofdolls which called out 'Mama' when they were turned upside down and Teddy Bears which went 'A-a-h'. When the coppers went and raided the place that was all they found. Billy thought that was a great joke.

Of course he had an alibi. When he was asked what his alibi was he must have grinned like the Cheshire cat. The coppers can't have thought he wouldn't have a cast iron one. He knew exactly where he'd been. It was at the offices of The People where he'd been with the old and well-respected journalist Hannen Swaffer for hours. And who else was there? It doesn't take much guessing. None other than Billy's biographer Duncan Webb. They were both there at the party Billy threw for his book launch. That, so far as Billy was concerned, was the end of things. The gold was never recovered. Billy told me he'd heard it had been smelted down on the night of the robbery and buried in a garden north of London. He was always careful with his mouth.

In his later life Billy was the one who made the bullets and had other people fire them so to speak. He had a long quarrel with Billy Howard and there were stories that he made him fight a series of men to see who would run the smutter rackets in Trafalgar Square — you know, taking photos of tourists feeding the pigeons but with no film in the cameras. 'That'll be five shillings sir. Meet you back here at 3 p.m.' Billy Howard dealt with them all but then he came up against Tony Mella who was five stones heavier. Billy couldn't cope but I know he went to see Hilly in person a day or so later and he got a share.

One day I'm approached by Bert Marsh who says, 'Bill's (Hill) here. He's had some trouble with Howard. Would you do him for £500?' He wanted me to put Howard in hospital. I said, 'Tell him no way. Why would I want to do that? Billy's a friend of mine.' I respected Billy Howard. After all when I had my trouble with Riordan at the Angel those years ago he was the one who offered me help.

There's no doubt that as the partnership between Spot and Hill went on they started to fall out. Billy had made real money for people out of Eastcastle and then another snatch in Lincoln Inn Fields and men were starting to drift away from Spot to him. The other thing was that Spot began to be jealous. Billy had that tame journalist from The People Duncan Webb writing up how clever he was and how he was Boss of the Underworld and

JACK SPOT AND BILLY HILL

Spot didn't like it. So he had another writer Arthur Helliwell who wrote a bit about him in the Sunday Chronicle, not nearly as much as Billy got written about him.

Just about the last time they did anything at all together was what you'd call a bit of domestic business. It was over Billy's new girlfriend Gypsy who once nearly put a man's eye out in a club. That was another reason they fell out,

Gypsy was a good looking woman with a mouth and a temper to go with it. She'd been a brass and, now she was Queen of the Underworld, she didn't like being reminded of her past. Rita thought she was a cut above Gyp and when the four of them went on holiday to the south of France together it wasn't a success. So when in September 1953 she was approached by her former boyfriend, a Malt called Tulip, she persuaded Slip Sullivan to have him thrown out of a club known as French Henry's. In turn Tulip was protected by Tommy Smithson and Sullivan took a bad beating — Billy says his throat was cut but I don't know about that, I wasn't there — and Billy and Jack really didn't have a choice about seeing to Tommy .

Now, after cutting Sullivan, Smithson went into hiding, only to be given up by the Maltese he had been protecting. Told there was a peace offer on the table he was asked— ordered is maybe better — to attend a meeting at the Black Cat cigarette factory in Camden Town. He took a fellow from Paddington and at least one gun, a Luger. Once he was there he found Spot, Bill, Slip Sullivan and Spot's man Moishe Blueball. Spot explained to Smithson that they were simply there to talk and he handed over the gun. Just as Spot was putting the gun away, Billy slashed Tommy.

And then it's free for all. It was in the days when the death penalty was in force and Spot must have forgotten his own saying, 'You must never cut below the line here, cause, if you do, you cut the jugular – and the hangman is waiting.'

Smithson was cut over his face, arms, legs and chest. He was then thrown over a wall into Regent's Park and Spot sent Moishe to call an ambulance and drive Billy back to his flat. It was near enough another topping matter. The ambulance got to him just in time and the worst was Smithson lost a lot of blood and had nearly fifty stitches put in his face.

What he didn't do was talk to the coppers although they must have known who'd done it. The cuts were Billy's trademark, the sides of the letter V down each cheek meeting at his chin. Tommy was given a grand with which he bought a share in a drinker in Old Compton Street. According to some accounts although it seems unlikely it was Spot who paid the money but that the end of them as even a loose partnership.

By 1955 Spot had got control of most of the pitches on the free course at tracks like Epsom, Brighton, Ascot and at the point to points. He was starting being the big I am and we — that's Albert Dimes , Bert Marsh, me and other Italians —didn't like it. Albert wanted the racecourse pitches back himself. Spot started throwing his weight about at the Epsom Spring meeting. We'd expected trouble and we were tooled up. There was about eight of us just lounging around on the grass; me, some of the Falcos, Ray Rosa and a few others. I could see Spot along with Teddy Machin, who once took an axe to Jimmy Wooder, marching out of the tunnel to order the bookmakers about. 'You stand here, you stand there. Put that one there'. We just took no notice of him. When he come over to us he gave us a look and said, 'Leave this lot out'.

He'd bottled out and it made him look a laughing stock in front of the other bookies. It was after that Spot thought he had to do something to re-establish himself. He got hold of the Twins to look after him because he thought there'd be trouble. There was a story that we'd recruited Frankie Fraser and it's true Frankie was one of us but he was in Long Grove mental hospital at the time and they never let him out of an afternoon to go to the races that I heard of. Although they say they were there I never saw the Twins on the courses with him.

The real trouble came a couple of months later. Sheer madness on Spot's part. It was broad daylight with plenty of straight people about. Spot was in his drinking club the Galahad in Charlotte Street when he was told Albert wanted to see him and he went looking for him. Now Albert was a always good man with a knife. There's no doubt about that. It was always said he'd killed a man, Lawrence, in the East End just before the war. The fellow's body was found in a graveyard off the Mile End Road. I don't know what it was all about and really Albert was what you might call a bit out of his ground. Sensibly, it wasn't a thing he'd talk too much about. He'd just shrug his shoulders.

They met in Old Compton Street and, seeing Spot had a knife, Albert, who hadn't anything, ran away. Instead of letting Albert go and so lose face he chased after him. Now why did he do that? Just didn't think. Albert turned and they struggled for the knife. The fight moved into a fruit shop on the corner of Frith Street where they fought almost literally to the death until the Jewish lady fruiterer broke it up by banging Spot over the head with a brass weighing pan. He staggered to a barber's shop usually used by Albert where he collapsed and Albert was picked up by Bert Marsh and driven to the Charing Cross Hospital. Spot went to the Middlesex. Their injuries were horrific. Spot had been stabbed over the left eye and in the cheek, neck and ear. He had four wounds in his arm and two in his chest, one of which went into a lung. Albert needed twenty stitches in his forehead. He also had a wound in his thigh and a stab in his stomach. Both of them were charged with affray and grievous bodily harm to each other.

Once it got to the Bailey the trial was a fiasco. First the judge refused separate trials, then he agreed that the affray charge should be withdrawn. He invited the jury to acquit Albert on the grounds he had been acting in self defence but the jury refused. He then decided separate trials were the order of the day, Spot to go first. An 88 year old vicar Basil Andrews who seemingly happened to be passing and Christopher Glinski, a Polish war hero who was also in the area at the time both said, the taller, fairer man (that was Albert) was the attacker. Spot was found not guilty. The law knew that was wrong and no evidence was offered against Albert so the incident became known as 'The Fight That Never Was'.

Now although people watching the trial reckoned that Andrews was bent as a hatpin, the police didn't make inquiries while he was in the box. Usually what happened in those days was that the first question the prosecution would ask in cross examination was, 'What's your date of birth?' Once they had a date questioning would continue while a copper got on the blower to Scotland Yard and found out if there was a record. And if they had, they'd have found out that the Rev. Andrews had a bit of form. Apart from that he's been made bankrupt and the old rascal had lived with a brass for years. And not only that, the brass had been the principal witness in a murder trial back in the 1900s when a fellow Robert Wood was found not guilty of killing another tom down Camden Town way.

The police were not pleased with the Spot trial. A newspaper, I think it was the Mirror, got hold of Andrews and got a confession out of him. They also had a look at Glinski who was a first class conman and who went on to give evidence against the Richardsons. Soon Spot's wife Rita and two of Spot's men, Moise Goldstein and Bernard Schack, went into the dock charged with conspiracy to pervert the course of justice. By that time the Rev had found God again. Because he'd been on his uppers he'd been tempted and had fallen. His evidence had been false but now he was telling the truth about how he'd been given a few quid and been taken to Spot's flat and given the tale he had to tell. The three of them were found guilty. Rita was fined £50 but Moishe Goldstein received two years and Bernie a year less. In a separate trial Glinski was found not guilty of perjury and, typical, later he got damages for libel against some of the papers.

But that wasn't the end of things. Not by any means.

# 7 : CUTTING SPOT

I'd nothing really against Jack Spot until he set on Albert. He was a big mouth but he hadn't bothered me. In fact he'd sent me money while I was in prison over the jeweller's shop. That and a note to say would I come and see him when I got out. He wanted me on his side because so many of his men were drifting away from him and he thought if I come to him it might stop the rot. But what would you do if your brother had been cut to pieces? You wouldn't just stand by. And I didn't.

As soon as it happened I started putting things together. I was a bit of a diplomat. What had to be done, first of all, was to isolate him from the Upton Park Mob and what I did was invite them down to the Central Club. We had a few drinks and I put it to them that we were all thieves. Why did we want to get into a war with each other out of which only the coppers would benefit? I said that of course they would leave the club safely that night but would they have a think about things? They shook hands and off they went. A day or so later I got a call to say they would have no part of anything.

At the time Tony Schneider was another Spot man. He wasn't part of the Upton Park Mob. Four or five of us caught up with him at Tubby Isaacs jellied eel stall in Aldgate late one night. We more or less surrounded him. I said all I was interested in was Spot and I gave him the alternatives. He was petrified. He knew he could get cut and knew he could end up on the pavement so he says, 'I'm taking no part'. And that was all I wanted to know. He had a lucky get out. But after that we became friends and went into running junkets together. He had the money and I had the connections and we both did well out of them.

But that left Bobby Ramsey who'd somehow gone over from Billy Hill to Spot's corner. He was soon out of it. We caught up with him in Soho and gave him noughts and crosses. He was game. He never said a word about it, unlike Spot who when he realised he was isolated went crying to the police for protection. Fat lot of good it did him.

How did I know Spot was going to be outside his flat off the Edgware Road that night in 1956 ? I had an insider in his camp. He was another who came over to us. He's not going to double me because he knows I'll hurt him badly and Spot's not going to protect him. His instructions are to let us know when Spot leaves his flat. Nipper Read in his book says the man was Nathan Mercado who used to bet as Sid Kiki. I don't suppose for a minute he's alive now but still I'm not saying if it was or it wasn't. You can work it out from there. The call came and we went down from the Central Club mob-handed in a couple of cars. There wasn't the traffic in those days and you could easily move around London late in the evening.

Spot said that he'd been attacked by about twenty men that night and he named Billy Hill, Albert Dimes, the Gilliam brothers, Bobby Warren, Frank Fraser, Billy Blythe, Tony Falco, Johnny Rice, Charlie Mitchell, the dog doper from Fulham, and me along with a few others. What is right is he was given a bad hiding, cut to ribs, blood all over the pavement, Rita shrieking. He needed about 70 stitches at the end of it. Rita made a statement that she saw Billy Hill hit Jack with the shillelagh she had given him. She was right about some of us but Billy Hill wasn't there though.

In fact it soon became clear that Johnny Rice, Billy and a couple of others had cast iron alibis from straight people and couldn't have been involved. Johnny Rice said he was with Billy Hill most of the day and took two friends to the Mayfair Hotel along with Albert. They were two car dealers from Manchester.

After we did Spot we all came back to the Central for a drink. I never thought he'd grass us up. But then the copper Tommy Butler started pulling people in —Frankie Fraser, Ray Rosa, Bobby Warren and some others —and he charges some of them. I thought Butler would be satisfied with Frank and a few more but it might be sensible to go away until things calmed down.

I was sensible but I was also foolish. I said to Billy Blythe, 'Are you coming with me?' Him and me and Billy Hill took the train to Heysham near Blackpool and then Billy Blythe and I got a boat to outside Dublin where Billy had a nice bungalow. In those days trials at the Old Bailey took place within a few weeks of an arrest, so what I reckoned was that I'd stay away for another month or six weeks until it was over and then come home. I never reckoned Butler would be so vindictive to come after Billy Blythe and me when he's already got bodies.

Then who should turn up but Gypsy? Well, its Billy's bungalow and we can't really say 'No' can we? Anyway she wants to be out every night dancing but we didn't want to show our faces. Fortunately she soon gets fed up and pushes off. I didn't know why she come out in the first place.

But after she'd gone that's where I was foolish. I give Mary a bell and say hop on a plane. That's fine and she comes over but they must have been watching her or been watching Gypsy. One day Billy Blythe's out doing a bit of shopping and he rings the doorbell. I answer it and it's, 'Bert, I'm sure I'm being tailed.' Now I's not difficult to spot someone tailing you particularly if that someone doesn't mind you knowing. We go to the window together and I look out and sure enough I can see three or four heads and I know it's on us. I say to Mary, 'Get a coat, we're off'. The three of us walk into the street taking nothing out of the house and at the end there's the main road. I tell Mary, 'When we get to the corner we're going to make a run for it. You just walk on. There's nothing they can do to you. Tell them the truth. You come here for a holiday with me and you don't know nothing more'. And that's what we did. We made a run and got on the first bus we could and that took us to the seaside. Now while I'd been over there I'd made some friends and one of them was a man, Des Cooney, his father Andrew was a top general in the IRA, back when it was a proper established army in the 1930's. Anyway when we get to the seaside we book into a boarding house and I go out and make a call to him.

'Where are you?' and I told him. 'Is there a picture house?' Yes, I told him there was and he said he knew where we were and he'd come and get us. Now, this is again where I'd been foolish. We were exposed. We didn't have a lot of contacts and I thought it would be best to get us back to London. Frank and Bobby had been weighed off by now but there might still be something which could be done. What Des said he could do was get us back on a fishing boat, drop us off somewhere near Dover. We would be put on the boat the next morning.

That night we're in a pub with Des, and Billy goes off to make a call to Billy Hill to say what's happened. He's away a long time and I can't understand it. It can only take half a minute to say we're on our way so I go to look for him and there he is listening. 'What are you doing Bill?' I ask and he hands me the receiver. What do I hear but a woman saying, 'Keep them talking as long as possible'. I said, 'Put the fucking phone down Bill' but that moment there's something like a fire bell goes off and the place is full of fucking Irish law with guns. 28th June it was.

Next morning instead of being on a boat we're in the dock at the Dublin High Court with a brief telling the judge the extradition warrant to get us back to England is no good. What has happened is that Billy Hill has given Pat Marrinan, his tame barrister, a few quid to come over and get a solicitor to act for us. Of course, Pat should never have done this. It was against all the rules of the Bar taking instructions from someone who wasn't a solicitor and he wasn't half made to pay for it later.

The warrant Butler had for our arrests was all wrong. The judge said it either had to have our surnames and Christian names on it or if the police didn't know our names — which they did — there had to be a detailed description. All that it said about me was that it was a man in his thirties, about 5' 6", well built with dark hair which the judge said could apply to thousands.

He threw the case out and said we were to be released but before we could leave the building, Butler had got a new warrant sent over. Pat whispered for us to make a run for it but I knew we were caught and told Billy not to try. I don't suppose we'd even have made the street. The place was full of Irish coppers and one with braid and a stick was directing things.

They drove us across the border to Belfast. Billy started struggling in the car and that didn't help because the law brought it out at our trial but I just sat quiet. And then they flew us back to London. Billy had a brief called Gane, a fellow from Richmond, and I had him as well. There was an identification parade at Paddington. Well there should have been but we reckoned we were being fitted up and we wouldn't stand on it so they just produced Rita who of course said it was us. I said there and then I'd never seen the woman in my life. There was some other men but they didn't identify us. Later Spot gave backwards and wouldn't say who'd done him and after I'd been nicked he even told a man in the prison synagogue I hadn't been there but it was Rita did for me. She identified me looking through the window of my cell door.

But that was it. I had about forty quid on me when I was nicked in Ireland and the coppers confiscated it. I wrote to a man McIver who was now in charge of the case asking for it back. I didn't get it and I wrote another. I can remember it today, I wrote, 'Mr McIver what have I done that you're persecuting me?' but I didn't get a reply or my money. I then asked for a lie detector test or a truth drug but they were never going to give it me.

Two weeks before my trial I was in my cell in Brixton laughing. I was going to show up that bastard Butler at the Old Bailey. I was going to walk out.

It's a long story how I knew I was going to do it and it went back to years earlier when I was knocking out forged petrol coupons while they were still rationed. No coupon, no petrol and so they were gold dust. One of my customers had a garage north of London and Cherry Titmuss and me drove in one day to give him his quota when I could see him talking to another fellow who looked like a copper to me. My client started walking over and I told Cherry not to say a word. 'Got them?', asks the man and now I'm wary. 'No, Jim they weren't ready. I'll be back about four this afternoon'. Then I asked him, 'Who's that fellow?' And he told me it was his brother, Ted. 'He wants to talk a bit of business with you. He's got a bit of a problem. And he's short of money'. 'I thought he was a copper,' I said. 'He was, ex DI but now he's a head of security in a warehouse'. 'There's a caff round the corner', I said, 'send him round in ten minutes'.

There he told us the story. He was Head of Security at a department store educating his son privately but he was having trouble paying the fees. Anyway he told us there was cash in the vault where he worked and how the job could be done. We went over there and had a look round. There was a place in the basement we could hide until everyone went home. There was only one night watchman. I remember it was December and dark and so a couple of days later Cherry and I went round and parked the car. There was no wardens and no electronic surveillance in the streets in those days. We were down in the basement masked with silk stockings and gloved up when we heard the nightwatchman doing his rounds. I remember he was a Scot. I whispered to Cherry to let him come to us. 'As he comes in I'll go for his top half, you get the legs'. And that's what we did. I give him a tap and we wrapped him up like a sausage. Then it was easy except there was so much to carry away Cherry had to go and get a suitcase from one of the floors to put it in. When we were going I got a cushion and put it under the man's head, threw a blanket over him and told him we'd call the law when we were well away. I wasn't going to leave him on the stone floor all night. He was just doing his job same as we were. And that's what we did. We stopped at a telephone box at Blackfriars Bridge and I dialled 999 and give them the details. We sorted out the security man's share, took it to him a couple of days later and he was well pleased. 'Thank God, Bert', he says.

He put another job up to us once. Two or three years later I'm in Old Compton Street with my wife Irene and we're going to the theatre when I hear a voice, 'Hello, Bert'. I turn round and it's Ted. There he is in a dark suit, white shirt, bow tie. 'Can we have a word tomorrow? I may have a little something of interest for you'. And a little blag is what the little something is. He's security for some theatre and he goes to the bank in Tottenham

Court Road with the manager once a week with the takings. All I've got to do is push him out of the way, snatch the bag and be off. The trouble is that all this has to take place in broad daylight in Soho and you know how crowded that is. Dozens of straight people all around you and some of them might want to have a go, like that fellow D'Antiquis who'd got shot in a robbery there a couple of years earlier. People could get hurt so I had to swallow it and say no thanks.

Now it's 1956 and I'm thinking what to do about the Spot trouble. And who do I think of but Ted the Security Officer. I know he's living in Portsmouth and so who better for an alibi. Cherry goes down to see him and he's up for it. The story is that on the night Spot got it, Ted and I had had a minor accident in Portsmouth at a time when I couldn't have got back to London to cut Spot. 'And look here's Rossi's name and address he wrote down when we exchanged particulars'. You didn't have to give an alibi in advance in those days and so here would be an ex-DI putting me miles away. Old Rita's got it wrong. She'd already identified Billy Hill at the Magistrates Court and now she's got it wrong again. I wouldn't even have to go in the box. As I say I'm laughing. And when I get a not guilty I'm going to call out that Butler's a crooked copper.

A few days before the trial Cherry goes down to Pompey again to see Ted and tidy up the ends and what does he see outside the man's house? A funeral. Ted's gone and died the week before. Just fell over with a heart attack.

After that it was all downhill. I was defended by Malcolm Morris who went on to represent Timothy Evans when Christie fitted him up over the deaths of his wife and baby. Now no one couldn't really shake Rita even though she'd had this conviction for conspiracy and she'd made all these statements which she contradicted, like saying there were twenty men. She said she'd been shaken up at the time and now she was sure she was right. As for Ginger Dennis who was in the dock with us she said he'd worn a mask and it had slipped and straight away she'd called out, 'I'll recognise you again'. And she was a good looking women with a nice accent. The jury lapped her up.

I told the jury I'd been at the boxing at the Empress Hall which was in Earls Court and I'd then gone back to the Central to settle a bet. There was a whole lot of verbals against e . Butler said I'd said I told Blythe I knew Hill would give us away when he knew the law was getting near to him. Now how could I have said that? Billy Hill had already been seen by the law weeks earlier and cleared. When they asked about why I wouldn't go on an ID parade I said that knowing about Rita from past experience I knew it wouldn't be fair.

I'd told the police I'd never met Ginger Dennis. But there was a visitors' book for the Astor Club in King Street, Brighton — it was known as the Bucket of Blood — which showed that Frank Fraser, Ginger and me had all signed in on the same day and all of us had given the same address in Brighton. That didn't help.

Billy Blythe didn't do himself any favours either. He was calling out that the coppers had framed him, telling the jury the law had taken an oath on the Bible and God should lay a curse on them for it. It never does any good that sort of thing. Quiet and respectful goes down a lot better. When you've had the not guilty then you can let fly.

After the jury was out an hour or so they come back saying they couldn't agree. The judge leans forward and says they must go and try again. So what happens is they come back with a Not Guilty on the s. 18 charge —that's grievous bodily harm with intent to cause grievous bodily harm. For a moment I thought we was out of it. But then they say guilty on the s 20 — that's just causing grievous bodily harm. Now how can that be? The man's been cut to ribbons by a gang if the pros is right. How can that be anything less than a s 18? They might even have stuck an attempted murder on us.

Anyway it's clear the judge is going to give us what he can — seven's the top and he gives Billy a five, but he's got a conviction for cutting a copper anyway ten years earlier and another for wounding a couple of years after that. And he's got to give me less because I haven't anything for violence and, when it comes to it, not much in the way of convictions at all, so he gives me a four. We appealed of course but it went nowhere.

The story doesn't end there. I got sent to Winchester and while I was there I ran into a couple of fellows, Raphael Levakoff and Nat Flower whose other name was Bloomberg. By this time Spot had been in Brixton charged with slashing Tommy Falco outside the Astor Club in Mayfair. They told me that while he was in the prison synagogue Spot had said that if he was acquitted of slashing Tommy he wouldn't appear against either me or Billy. He's told Nat, 'One of them is not guilty'. Nat asked him, 'Which one?' and he said 'Rossi'. Nat had asked why he was going against an innocent man and Spot had said, 'To hell with him. He is a pal of Albert Dimes and he's a member of the gang. He was not anywhere near my flat that evening but because my wife has given a statement to the police I can't tell them otherwise'.

I got all this together and put in a petition but Spot said that although he knew Levakoff he'd never met Nat and that was really an end of it. Of course they both had form so who was going to believe them anyway? But it was worth a try.

Setting Jack Spot up for slashing Tommy Falco wasn't one of Billy Hill's best ideas. In fact it was a really foolish one. The original idea was that a fellow called Victor Russo should be given £500 to allow himself to be slashed and the blame put on Spot but he give backwards so Tommy agreed to be done. There were to be a couple of witnesses to say as they'd been leaving the club with Tommy, Spot had been waiting for them and he give Tommy a few cuts. It was stupid because the law knew from the start it couldn't have been Spot. They had been watching his flat day and night out because Rita had said she was scared. So unless the copper on duty had been off having a slash so to speak or had gone to sleep there was no way Spot could have come out of the flats without being seen. They still let him go on trial though and he got a not guilty. But Billy still make sure after that he got run out of London. Spot opened a club in Paddington but it was broken up and then torched while I was inside. Billy Hill and the Twins were involved in that. After that Spot went back to Ireland with Rita.

What would have happened if Spot had gone down for a couple of years over his attack on Albert? Would he have had to be punished? I think he would still have had to be taught a lesson, either while he was inside or when he come out. He knew it was on top.

As for Biily Blythe, poor man never came out. He had a duodenal ulcer which burst while he was in Walton, that's in Liverpool, and he died in the hospital there in February 1957. He had a wonderful send off. There was twenty Rolls Royces, and £1000 worth of flowers all over the pavement in Myddleton Street where he'd lived. Albert and Billy Hill went, of course, and so did the cat burglar Ruby Sparkes.

In June that year poor Pat Marrinan got struck off for helping us in Ireland without being instructed by a solicitor and I was brought from prison to give evidence against him when the lawyers wanted him disbarred. They had armed police round the car that brought me because a load of fellows came up from Saffron Hill to see me. I wasn't interested in escaping so I sent them off to get some fizzy drinks. When it came to giving evidence I said I hadn't heard Pat say anything about our making a run for it. But they had it in for him. He tried saying he'd been used by Billy and that he'd been struggling at the Bar with a wife and young family but it did no good. They'd had a tap on Billy's phone and had heard him talking to Pat a few times. Billy had even got him a flat in the same block. After Pat got disbarred he went back to Ireland.

I did my time, got full remission and was given money for the London train. There on the station at Waterloo to meet me was Mary and Tony Mella who'd brought her along.

'What do you want to do Bert?' asked Tony. By then he's got half a dozen clip joints where mug punters sit around with a hostess for a couple of hours and then find they've got a bill they don't want to pay. It hasn't changed much. I read in the papers that a few years back the Council was sending out messages to tourists, '£5 to get in : £500 to get out' and that would have been cheap in some places.

Why didn't I go in with Tony in the clip joints? I didn't really like the atmosphere so he said he's got space why didn't I take it? I did and I ran a bookmaker's office over one of his joints for a while but to tell the truth I didn't like Soho. It ran for a bit but it was like a lot of clubs and spielers. You take premises and see how it goes and if after a while it's not making you money you drop it out. I was more for the racetracks and the fancy nightclubs. Soho was seedy, so after a bit I dropped it out. I liked The Garden more.

But by then I'd met Ronnie Kray.

# 8 : RONNIE KRAY IN PRISON

When I was in for Spot and I went to Winchester the first screw I saw I thought I recognised. Where could I have seen him and then it dawned on me it was the former boxer Vince Hawkins who'd fought some good men. I'd seen him at the Albert Hall beating Ernie Roderick for the British title about ten years before. I thought 'That's handy' and that I could get a bit of gear in through him so I propositioned him 'Can we do any business?" And what does he say but 'What would you like?' I think I'm on a winner and I say, 'Snout, couple of things' 'No, problem, ' he says, 'I'll put you down to se the Governor in the morning'. I'd gone and chosen a straight screw. I thought that was it but he was a decent fellow; he never reported me.

I couldn't eat the food in that nick so I made arrangement with people who worked in the kitchen to smuggle stuff like corned beef and bacon out to me. I had a pot of Brylcreem and when I'd finished it I cut a slot in the lid and then I got a fellow who worked in the chapel to get some white spirit and a wick. I got a couple of tall books and I set it up so I'd made a small stove in my cell for cooking bacon. Then one night I'm cooking just before lights out when the cell door is opened. A screw had come round with the evening cocoa, well that's what they called it. 'What's that smell?' And I thought, 'I've been nicked' but he just said 'You better get rid of it.

That was a success but what wasn't a success was when Tony Mella had a parcel of stuff — salami and olives and things — thrown over the wall. The idea was it could be hidden in a panel in a bathroom in the deputy governor's quarters but he discovered it. So I'm brought to see the Governor and I could see he was enjoying himself.

'Rossi, do you like salami?' I knew what had happened and said 'As much as anyone, sir'. 'And you're keen on music ? ' So I said the same thing, and it goes on, 'And olives?' 'And cigars?' because Tony had put a couple in my package. 'Well', he says, 'I've got pleasure in telling you, you're not going to enjoy them'. At least he couldn't prove it was me and so I was never charged over it. But I never got any favours after it. I was hard put to get what I was entitled to.

It was in Winchester that I first met Ron Kray and he was the brother I had most to do with over the next ten years. And it wasn't always for the better as far as he was concerned. Once you're in the nick if you're sensible you get on with it, do your time and get out. You don't want trouble. In those days you just lost remission if there was even a sniff of it. As we were both Londoners I teamed up with Georgie Cornell who came from the East End originally but had married a girl from south London. His name was really Myers. And we used to walk round the yard together. I had been put in the mailbag shop and I'd been there about nine months or so when this fellow Ronnie Kray is brought in. He was 22 at the time and I'd never heard of him; he was from a different part of London. Don't forget we're talking about the middle 1950s. Clerkenwell and the East End were countries apart. But he knew me and so now there was the three of us Londoners. He was also put in the mailbag shop. As I'd got friendly with the screw in charge, I told him I'd been doing the mailbags for nine months and it was driving me mad. Could I go to mattresses which was a couple of steps away up on a platform? That left Ronnie in mailbags. After a week he says, 'Can you get me up there with you?'

The screw was a Geordie, not a bad fellow and I ask him and he says yes. Next thing Ron asks if he can share a cell with me — I had one on my own —and I say a very definite 'No'. Things were all right for a couple of days and then he starts going very odd. I said to him there was a good film showing on Sunday, was he coming?

'I'm not coming to the film on Sunday'.

'Why not?' I wondered what's going on here.

'I know why you want me to come to the film on Sunday?'

'Why?'

'Because you've arranged to have it put on me'.

What on earth is he taking about. But he starts rabbiting on bout how I don't like him. I don't want to lose remission but he's got a long sewing needle like an icepick and I'm thinking things might erupt and I'd have to do him.

'I thought you was my friend', he says.

'I am your friend.'

I've got my own needle handy and I'm watching his hand. He was obsessive.

'Look Ron, I've had enough. I'm going to have to hurt you.' I thought there would be a reaction but suddenly he changes tack and goes the other way saying over and over, 'I thought you was my friend'. Suddenly I was called down to see the Governor. I'd ordered a painting by numbers kit and it was about that. There was six or seven of us waiting to see the Governor and one of the doctors passes by. Since leaving the mailbag shop I know I have a nut case acting strange on my back and I said, 'Excuse me, Doctor' and I told him about Ron. 'I spoke to him two days ago and there was nothing wrong with him,' was the reply. I was very respectful. 'I think you should look at him, sir. Don't forget I reported it to you'.

I go back to the shop and I'm standing there in dreamland when a screw comes up to Ron, calls him out and takes him to the hospital. A bit later I'm called over there and the doctor asks me, 'It won't go further than this office but is Kray into you for bacca? The reason I ask is that a week ago he had glasses made and when he was shown a tray of spectacles he asked if he could be allowed to show them to you. He says a warder brought them to you and you chose his glasses for him. I thought it was funny at the time and that's what makes me think he's afraid of you'.

I said there was no way was I dealing with bacca or that he was into me for some. The doctor appeared satisfied and when I asked what was going to happen now he told me he was going to Broadmoor. I got a message to his brother Charlie telling him what was happening.

When I came out from the Spot sentence Ronnie Kray was already on the streets. I was having a drink in the Central when who comes in but Ron and the fixer and go-between 'Red Faced' Tommy Plumley. After a bit I go to the toilet and Ron follows me in and gives me £200 saying, 'Take that, I appreciate what you've done', which was good of him. I don't know if he meant I was the one who got him into Broadmoor where life was a lot easier. But he was still mad as a hatter.

A bit after I came out I noticed a fellow who was partly crippled wasn't in the Central club as usual and I asked around where he was. I was actually with Ron in Soho when another fellow told me that Tommy Falco, who came from the big family in Clerkenwell and had been involved in setting up Jack Spot on the GBH charge, had given him a slap and a kick. When I heard that my blood was up and I said to Ron, 'I'm leaving. I'm going to the Central. I want to see Tommy Falco; find out what's happened'
'I'll come with you'.
'No, it's my row.'

But along he came and who's there but two of Tommy's brothers who had no idea what I was thinking. It was 'Hello Bert' but all I said was, 'Where's that fucking brother of yours? He took a fucking liberty. If he's not about you'll do' and I started a ruckus. I admit I was out of order and it looked as though there was going to be a real row, with me on the wrong end of it, when all of a sudden there's a couple of shots. There were thirty or so men and women in the club and Ron's pulled a gun out and started firing. I said to him, 'You're fucking mad Ron', and he sort of simpered, 'I thought you was in trouble'. I went back to the Central next day and apologised. Later people said Kray was shooting up the place trying to take over the pitches at the point to points after Jack Spot was done, but it wasn't that at all. This was in the late 1950s and Spot had been done years before.

# 9 : THE KRAYS

People often ask me how many people do I think the Twins killed or had killed. Colin Fry in one of his books says they had killers come down from Scotland on contracts and the total may have ended up around thirty but I don't believe it. Of course we know about George Cornell, Frank Mitchell and Jack McVitie and there was a story about their friend Mad Teddy Smith and another about a rent boy — but thirty? For a start there's not enough faces disappeared in the years the Twins were running Whitechapel. And if there's contract killings it's generally got to be faces who are killed. We'd have heard of them. If they were straight or even half -straight people there'd have been an outcry. Why hasn't someone put down their names? Of course, there was one fellow who drove for them, Jimmy Frost who they were said to have killed, but he turned up years later. He'd been up in Newcastle and there's stories that Mad Teddy Smith skipped the country before they got to him and died in Australia a few years ago.

I know the title of this book says I was 'Mentor to the Krays' but if I were Tony Mella, with the way he mangled up words, I'd say I think they were 'unmentorable', if there is such a word. Goodness knows I and others tried hard enough. They had good people around them as well, people who knew what they were doing. People like Leslie Payne and Freddie Gore who were two of the best Long Firm fraudsmen of the time. But did the Twins learn how it should be done? No, of course they didn't. Would they even listen ? No, of course they wouldn't.

Now running a Long Firm Fraud, or LF as it was known, in the 50s and 60s was an easy way of making money. What you needed was premises, preferably on a High Street, a bit of start up cash, a bit of time, and someone to run it. You started off buying easily sellable stuff such as chocolates or cleaning material, things like that, the sort of thing you could knock out quickly. You paid cash for it, and the next time you asked your supplier for a bit of credit. You settled that up and did it again and then you expanded. Now A, the person you'd been dealing with, would give a reference to B saying you were straight. In turn you'd settle with him and he'd give a reference to C and so on. Then when you'd got enough credit you'd have a bust out, sell everything at bargain prices and scarper. If you got it really right you would clear the stuff out and then have a fire and claim on the insurance as well. That's what the Richardsons did when they accidentally blew up half of Mitre Street in the East End. In those days the police weren't really interested. An LF was more for the Board of Trade. You'd probably changed managers a few times and anyway he'd ordered the stuff on the blower so there was no question of him being recognised and you sent the last manager off on a cruise with his wife. Of course if you did LFs really, really right they could be vast, like a spider's web running over continents.

But did the Twins have the patience? No, of course they didn't. They didn't have to do anything themselves, just check up from time to time and see Payne and Gore weren't nicking from them. And of course they wouldn't dare. They weren't heavies. But no, the Twins wanted the money NOW and so all the ground laying and hard work was wasted. Things just got wound up before the goose was popping the golden eggs, and they didn't do it just once, they did it time and again. I don't know how Payne stood them for so long. He had a wonderful scheme going for them in Africa but that all went wrong as well and he got nicked with them trying to get stolen bonds out of Canada, and somehow they blamed him for both those.

Leslie Payne, and he ought to have known as well as anyone, thought that the Twins had around an average of thirty people on their payroll at any one time. They'd be given £20 cash each a week, that's a bit under £300 nowadays, as well as being taken out to clubs such as the Astor where of course they may not have paid full whack but a bottle of champagne could easily have been a tenner. Payne thought it cost them around a £1000 a week for starters in those days.

And then in their booze and drug-filled brains they decide Payne's going to the police and so they get Jack McVitie to go along with another member of their firm Billy Exley to shoot him at his home. Now although McVitie was decent enough robber in his day he's off his head on drugs by this time and so he takes the Twins' money — £500 I heard — and when it's Mrs Payne who opens the door McVitie loses his bottle and runs off. Is that the sort of man you want to have working for you? Same with Alf Donaghue. If you shoot a man do you expect him to be your best friend if you give his wife a bunch of flowers and him a few quid?

Another thing they didn't do was check the people they were dealing with properly. Take that Alan Bruce Cooper who was the one which really brought them down. He was meant to have been close to Angelo Bruno, who I got to know later, but who did he work for? Well himself for a start but then he was the secret contact of that copper John Du Rose. When Nipper Read nicked him what does he do? He says you better ask Du Rose about me and Read goes spare when he finds he has been his man. Cooper had even put his own father-in-law away on a drugs charge.

They claimed they were close to Angelo Bruno and did a deal to launder stolen bonds through him but there again they told the same story about laundering bonds through the Montreal mafia. Then they say they had a deal with Tony 'Ducks' Corello of the New York Lucchese family. If they did, dealing with the Twins was just about the kiss of death. Poor old Angelo was killed and Tony Ducks went down for something like 100 years. He was another who kept himself to himself and for years avoided prosecution which is how he got his name. He 'ducked' out of things. That was until the government had tapes of him and he got the 100 years. That was in 1987 and he died three years later in the Springfield Medical Centre. He was 87.

I never mixed with the men who were part of the so-called Firm. They really weren't my sort but I liked Bill Ackerman who was with them for a time. He was a great charmer. He wasn't really a player. A good card man who had a spieler in the East End and the Twins started leaning on him. He spoke to me about it. They didn't know he knew me and they didn't realise quite what a good card player he was either. I had a word and from having to pay them they started to pay him looking after the spielers they had an interest in.

As I say he had charm and a half and he charmed some girl into going to Las Vegas with him once. While he's there there's a fire in the hotel His wife who's back here finds out and wants to know if Bill's all right. She rings up and the receptionist says, 'Oh Mr Ackerman's all right. He and Mrs Ackerman have just walked past on their way to dinner'. That's how he come to be divorced.

Bill Ackerman was forever going on about earners. 'Bert, any earners?' he'd say. I was with him once in Bournemouth when he starts up, 'Any earners?' ''There's money all around you, I said. ' What do you mean?'. 'Look at those trees. You could cut one down, take it home and make five million toothpicks out of it'. That kept him quiet for a while.

I don't know how Bill wangled it but he once got a ride on Sinatra's private jet. He couldn't stop talking about it for weeks. I had to put an end to it. 'Well,' I said. 'I slept in his bed'.

People were always having trouble with the Twins. Not Cornell trouble but trouble. There was a fellow Mickey came from Bloomsbury. Now he was a nothing, a nice boy who talked like Jimmy Cagney but he wasn't into villainy. He and some friends go out one Saturday for a few drinks and end up in the Regency.

Next morning I got a call. 'Have you heard what happened to Mickey? Ronnie cut him last night'. So down I go to see him. His wife lets me in and Mickey's still in bed, bandages all over his face. From what he said Ronnie had taken a bit of a liberty and he's afraid Ronnie might take it further still. So I went to see him. Ronnie's got a bit of a different story. 'Mickey got a bit saucy. He's a nothing and I fucked him off'. I said, 'You should have told him to take a walk. There's the door, hop it. You didn't need to do what you did. Mickey's worried you're going to take it further.

You're not are you?' And he got the message. 'No, that's the end, Bert'.

One day in Hatton Garden, Matty Constantinou asked me if I could do anything with a load of snout. 'We had a lorry load offered. Do you want to buy it?' I said I could put it in a warehouse and then knock it out. It was easy as pie and into the slaughter it goes for the night. Next morning I go round and we've had a tumble. It's gone. Someone's nicked it. So Matty's friend George Meisl and I find out who the driver was and go round to this dirty old block of flats where he lived. He's having his dinner. It's, 'Hello, Bert'. He knew me but, there again, most people did. I came straight out with it, 'Where's my snout? You must have drove it out.' 'I can't tell you', he says. When I said he was going to put your coat on straight away and take me to it,' he says 'You know what they'll do to me.' I was tooled up and I showed it to him, 'I'm going to do that to you now.' He says, 'I put it in a safe place'. We all went round to another slaughter and I took it back. That evening I get a call from Ronnie Kray who says, 'You beat me to it.' I tell him 'That snout was mine and I took it back'. 'I didn't know it was yours Bert', Ron says. You could never leave things hanging in the air with him. You never knew which way he'd jump so we agree on a meet at their club Esmeralda's Barn in Knightsbridge the next morning at 11 o'clock.

Ronnie was beginning to try my patience and, with him, things could be off in a hair's breath. So what I did was take along three close friends, Cherry Titmuss, who had a gun with him, Ray Rosa and Jimmy Watson. I tell them if I'm not out in fifteen minutes I think things will have gone off so come in. Ronnie's there on the second floor. ' Hello, Bert, sit down'. I said I wasn't going to be staying. 'No, sit down'. Now I didn't know if he was tooled up but it had to be likely. Then he almost begins to whine in that high pitched voice of his, 'I didn't know it was yourn Bert.' He taps me on the knee, 'I've always wanted to be your friend'. I knew then he was going to swallow it and I said, 'Well you know now,' turned round and left. I never heard no more from him about that but it wasn't the last time Ronnie got up my nose.

The next time it was over Tony Schneider — Anthony Isidore was his real name and he was ironically known as Uncle Tony because he was a moneylender. After I warned him off about siding with Jack Spot I'd met him again through George and Matty. Now, there was a good businessman. Tony'd buy and sell anything and of course he was buying snide jewellery off Matty and George. He'd been given the green light from Jack Spot in his heyday and he'd expanded his business so that his became a top class and straight affair. He used to charge a lending rate of 50 per cent. It was through me he linked up with the Italians in New York. There was a rumour that Peter Rachman had put properties in Tony's name and when Rachman died he found himself with all these houses and he went from there.

I'd been running junkets with Henry Shapiro bringing gamblers over from the States and now Schneider had the idea we could do the reverse and send the Brits over to Las Vegas. He's putting that together when I get a call from Ronnie, 'We'd like to be involved'. Now he's got me going again. I'm not having it. Tony wants to go to the law but I tell him he can't. 'Calm down, Tony. Leave it to me. They're getting to be a fucking nuisance. I'll have a word and tell them to drop it off'. So off we go to the Kray's house Vallance Road. Now generally there was no problem going there. I never heard of anyone being hurt there. You usually tea and biscuits from their mother. I read, however, of one of the Teale brothers being raped by Ronnie but that was a domestic not business. But Ronnie was mad, full stop. You could never be sure so Schneider has a gun with him. Once we're there in the sitting room there's both of the Twins, it's 'Hello Bert,' sit down, have a cup of tea'. Same old routine. I say to him, 'I understand you phoned Tony. Do you need to be in the junkets? He's my partner.' And Ronnie says, 'He's an old friend'. I said, 'Don't give me old friend. He's my partner. Leave it out. I don't tell you I want to be in something you've got going.' And again Ron backs down, 'We didn't know you was in it'. Every time it came to a confrontation they dropped it out. They knew what would have happened if they'd tried to do anything to me.

Funnily I never had much to do with Reggie. He had a mean streak and Tony Schneider was one of the victims of his cigarette trick. He'd offer you a cigarette and then a light and as you were bending down he'd punch you and break your jaw. He thought that was very clever. Reggie worked the same stunt with that bent struck-off lawyer of theirs Stanley Crowther. He was in the Regency one night with his boyfriend and Reggie asked him to stay behind. What does he do? Breaks the kid's jaw. How can you expect people to be loyal to you when you do things like that? And, of course, at the death Crowther makes a long statement to the law about their long firm frauds.

Ronnie could be stupid as well. He was another who couldn't think things through. He and his brother Charlie come to me one day and he tells me he's hurt somebody and he's going away. 'Don't phone me at home' and he's about to tell me where he's going. He wanted me to know where he'd be. I said, 'Don't tell me. You know how to get in touch with me. If it ever come on top and they capture you you'll blame me.' That was just a stupid little thing, but to go and shoot someone in a pub like he did with George in view of straight people that's just sheer madness. If you have to do someone don't do it in broad daylight in front of people. Give yourself half a chance.

I'd got to the stage when I really was going to kill them. I was fed up with them. They kept coming to me. Would I go to Manchester with them? Lean on some clubs there for pensions? They had this idea of having all Britain in their pockets. Common sense told me they wouldn't last two weeks in the North. Two weeks; they didn't last two minutes. They were more or less met on the station by local officers and put on the next train back to London. They wanted to be gangsters and show offs at the same time. The people at the top, people who'd got Scotland Yard tied up, were sensible and quiet and the Twins weren't either of those things. I'd rather be tied up with the others.

Charlie was the sensible one of the three of them; an ordinary fellow really. You could have a conversation with him. Ronnie was always the dominant one. He came to me one day, would I like to go halves with him in the gambling at the Regency? Why not? It was mostly dice with a bit of kalooki. But I only lasted a month or so there. Gambling and drinking don't go together and the Twins would come in late at night with their followers and they'd all been on the piss. Throwing their weight around. Even though the tables were taking around £500 a night for the house I couldn't stand it. They were spazzatura. That's the Italian word for rubbish.

I got a call from Charlie one morning. Would I pop down to the Regency. Of course, I would. When I get there I haven't been in the place three minutes when there's Ronnie rolling around on the floor fighting someone. Well I steamed in, got the fellow off him and give him a couple of smacks. The fellow runs off into another bit of the club and when I'm talking to Charlie there's a few shots. Now Ronnie's shooting at him. I couldn't stand with that. That was it for me.

They couldn't understand when Mickey Duff opened the National Sporting Club for boxing of an evening why they'd been blocked for membership/. Mickey told them he wasn't having gangsters and they said, 'Well you're having Bert'. And Mickey says, 'Bert conducts himself properly. I'd have him round my house for Sunday lunch'.

We all heard soon enough about Georgie Cornell. Things like that go round like wildfire. I think it was Freddie Foreman who told me over the phone. I didn't want to know; they were a bunch of lunatics. Ronnie was always on to me to tell me when he'd hurt someone. It was as if he wanted my approval. 'Well done, Ronnie. Good boy.' Well, he wasn't going to get it. Same again with Frank Mitchell. We all knew they had him off Dartmoor. I can't think why the law didn't. Why didn't they just sweep them up? Then again I heard soon enough he'd gone missing. Same with McVitie. They were open secrets.

By the time they were arrested people were seriously fed up with the Krays. One thing was they'd turned on so many people. One of them was the blagger Billy Gentry. I don't know what he'd done to offend them but they wanted to iron him out and they sent some of the firm to find him. Albert Donoghue came back and said he was nowhere to be seen but they were disobeying orders. Albert knew where he was perfectly well.

After the Twins were nicked Detective Inspector Henry Mooney, who was Nipper Read's No 2, came and wanted me to give evidence against them but I wouldn't. I told him, 'They was always all right with me'. Any misunderstandings we'd soon cleared up. I wouldn't have said anything even if they hadn't been. Then Mooney said they happened to know I'd given Ron the gun which he'd used on Cornell. I said, 'Rubbish. They've got more guns now than I ever had'.

Then when it came to it the Twins wanted everyone else to take the blame. Donaghue was to take the blame for Mitchell, Barrie for Cornell, and someone else for McVitie. Ronnie Bender claimed they chucked him to the wolves. He was another who was staunch for too long. He was right when he told a journo after he came out, 'Legends? No, just a pair of fame-hungry psychopaths'.

Mind you, sometimes Ronnie could have a good heart. When I was living in Gee Street near the Barbican I was having trouble with a neighbour — pompous woman — over my little girl's poodle. She'd rung the council to say the dog was yapping and disturbing her. 'They're Italians, you know'. So now the Council was on to me saying the dog had to go and I was given a month to get rid of it. I had to go out one morning and so I told my daughter, who was nine or ten at the time, not to open the door if someone from the Council came. When I come home about six in the evening there was £15 on the table. I asked her where she'd got this and she said Ronnie came round and she wouldn't open the door to him. When he convinced her who he was and she said I'd told her not to let the landlord in, he pushed a roll of notes through the letterbox. He thought it was that I couldn't pay the rent.

Ronnie used to phone me several times a week. 'Bert, what you doing this evening? Come to the pictures'. I think his favourite film was that Hitchcock Psycho with Anthony Hopkins. He'd keep telling me the plot and then saying in that whine of his, 'Do you know what part I like best, Bert?' It was like a child, he just repeated the same things time and again. 'You know at the end of the film Anthony Perkins is sitting outside the doctor's room on a stool when a fly lands on his arm and you hear the voice, "I know what they're thinking I'm going to do squash it. I wouldn't hurt a fly". And he doesn't. That's what I like best'. I don't know if he got it right but that's how he told it.

I never went to see Ron in prison but I did see him in Broadmoor. It was back in October of 1989 and I was asked to do some technical advising on the set of the Krays Movie with Charlie Kray, the one directed by Peter Medak with the Kemp brothers. You will see a never seen before picture that my Jimmy took while filming the blind beggar scene, and if you look closely you can see the make-up bullet wound on actor Stephen Berkoff's forehead. He was a lovely fella and I got on with the Kemp Brothers really well, they only lived around the corner about 2 miles from me in Clerkenwell Islington.

So, just before filming started, I had a call off Ronnie. Now me and my Jimmy, we used to go and see him quite a lot, you see Ronnie was always being offered an earner from the inside, and he knew he could trust me as I trusted my great nephew Jimmy.

We did very nice out of some of the stuff offered our way, but nothing messy needed to be done, to be honest with you 9 times out of 10 it was just a call or knock on a door with a friendly message to pack it in. It paid nicely. I'm not going to tell you we did this person or did that to another person because the right words from us put a plaster over the cut.

Anyway on this occasion we both went to see Ronnie, and at this point he was in Broadmoor. The first words out of his mouth were "You can tell that fucking Peter Medak he's not using machine guns in the movie!".

My Jimmy said to him that this is going to be released to a big US audience, you can't go around shooting people with handguns, it won't have the appeal, they want to see machine guns for that dramatic and exciting effect. Ronnie nodded and said "Oh yeah, ok then".

We probably spent another hour with Ron before getting up to leave, but just as we started to walk away he shouted "You can tell that Peter Medak, no machine guns!".

I looked at my Jimmy, rolled my eyes up and muttered under my breath "he's still mad as a box of frogs". But I still kept writing to him.By the end his writing was so bad he had someone print out the letter as well. At one time he wanted me to take up a diet of garlic pills. Another time said he was living off raw eggs and honey. It didn't do him much good. He died within a year. He always thought he'd get out. He was going to have a big party and me and my friend Billy Jones were to be the first people invited he said. In 1974 he decided him and Reg were going to keep their names out of the papers in future and he wrote to me saying I should do the same. What did he think I'd been doing all my life?

# 10 : SOHO

Looking back, in a funny way in the old days Soho was like a patchwork quilt. All bits and pieces which didn't overlap but were side by side and made up a whole. There were the straight businesses like the old Italian shops such as Lina in Brewer Street and I Camisa and Parmigiani Figlio in Old Compton Street. The wrestlers Paul Lincoln and Ray Hunter had their 2I's Coffee Bar on the opposite side to the Admiral Duncan more or less next door to I Camisa and it became a great place for teenagers. Tommy Steele and Cliff Richard more or less started out there.

You'd be surprised at some of the people that we would bump into. Back in the day Lucian Freud and Francis Bacon used to hang around in Soho, and often came to one of my gambling speillers in Mayfair. I don't know how much you know about art, but they used to come around and try and sell work for 30, 40 quid a pop. One painting in particular by Freud was called Fat Sue, the woman in the piece was paid about £10 for being his model. You know the one, the big fat woman lying on a sofa with her tongue hanging out. Well, he tried to offer me this for about £30 but I declined. That painting only went and sold for £35 million a few years ago at auction.

Some of his paintings he just gave away, cast-offs, painting he didn't want to keep because he didn't like them or made mistakes. A lot of these cast-offs ended up in the hands of a landlord at the French House. He was sitting on millions but didn't realise it at the time. You know what he ended up doing with them? He burnt the lot. Priceless pieces of art up in smoke just like that.

There were the girls, of course. Really that was what Soho was known for. Most of them walked the pavement in those days. They each had their own little strip and it was nailfiles and scissors out if one girl got onto another's patch. Girls' beats were jealously guarded by their pimps. By the end of the 1940s if a girl changed hands the buyer paid the vendor a percentage of her earnings for an agreed number of months in return for him making sure that there was no trouble from girls on the next beats. And what you won't believe is that after the war and well into the fifties the girls all wore hats and gloves.

One of the girls was killed a bit after the war and I was sorry when I heard about it. Rachel Fenwick or Ginger Raye we called her. You'd see her around the place often in a spieler called the Bees where I often played cards. At one time she'd run a club La Romaine in Wardour Street. I remember her saying she'd married a black American dancer but he'd left her and gone to Paris where he died. She had a boyfriend who had lunch every Sunday and he stayed the night. But that didn't stop her working. She was a nice woman for ever giving sweets and money to kids and was always talking about giving up the game but so many of them do. Talk about it, that is, rather than actually give it up. She was slashed to bits at her place in Broadwick Court one night. The law never found out who killed her.

The Messina brothers were still running the majority of the girls there after the war and up to the '50s. They'd been trotters during the war and one of them, I forget which, built a sort of secret cupboard built in his flat so he could hide in it if there was ever a raid by the law. Then in the '50s that newspaper fellow Duncan Webb decided to have a go at them. You know the stuff, 'London's most evil men', and after a bit questions began to be asked in Parliament. Webb was a funny man, great friend of Billy Hill and he wasn't averse to going with a brass himself.

The Messinas had been under siege from other Malts as well, such as a fellow Amabile Ricca who was shot in Carlisle Street. A couple of brothers got a few years for manslaughter for it. We knew who they all were but, as I say, they didn't really bother us. They had drinkers they used and they wouldn't normally come near ours.

I'll tell you though of a man who was a sort of bridge between us and them, the Malts that is, and that was Tommy Smithson. Now I liked Tommy. He was an ex-fairground fighter. He come from Liverpool and he was always getting the rough end of things. But no one could say he wasn't game and couldn't fight. Scarface they called him because he was getting cut all the time but Albert and I called him Mr Loser. He was what you would call dapper and liked silk shirts. He had a girlfriend called Fay Sadler who was a good class hoister and had been involved in the Pen Club Shooting when the club manager Selwyn Cooney got killed and one of the Nash brothers from Hoxton nearly went down for murder. Tommy'd been in the Merchant Navy until the 1950s and when he come out he found things had changed. The Malts had control of clubs and cafes in the East End and he decided to set up his own protection racket looking after them.

I'll tell you the other thing he did and that was work a spinner with Tony Mella around the dog tracks but they fell out and, as I've said, Tony cut him not as badly as Jack Spot and Billy Hill did. The other thing about Tommy was he was a loner and you can't be a loner in our business. You have to have friends.

Then there was the street bookmaking from before the war until there was licensed betting shops in the fifties. When he came out after his sentence over Montecolombo, Bert Marsh never went back into crime but he remained friendly with Jim Wicks. Bert was a leader but he was never a criminal. He and his mate Sebastian Buonacore, who we called Vesta, opened up betting on the corner of Greek Street. If you wanted a bet down in Soho it went through Bert Marsh. He still ran it even after the licensed betting shops came in. You'd think that street corner bookmaking would go once there were betting shops about but don't forget with a bookmaker it was cash down at the time of the bet and there was tax to come off winnings. A street bookie might give a good customer a bit of credit and there was no tax in the pound to come off of the winnings.

As for his mate Bert Wilkins, he was more of an entrepreneur. When the Americans went home after the war they left behind Jeeps and other heavy stuff and he started buying them up in partnership with George Dawson who became known as the 'Orange Juice King'. That ended in late 1959 when George went down for six years for fraud. I think it got cut to four. I once went on his yacht and he had this football made up of old fashioned white fivers squashed together. By then Bert Wilkins had set himself up in the nightclub business and he owned the Nightingale in Berkeley Square. His nephew was Joe who was a big man in Soho running clubs and escort girls. Joe did a lot of time over one thing and another. He survived a shooting — by the Krays so the story went — over an escort agency he was running in Beak Street.

There were also independents, people who used to prey on tourists such as people who ran corner games. In those days it was difficult to get to see what was called a blue film and men would take say ten shillings and tell the punter, 'Go and wait in that doorway round the corner and I'll be with you in five minutes'. As a come-on he might have postcards showing explicit sex scenes 'from the film'. If their luck was really in the punters saw a film made in Scandinavia showing a woman undressing or some overweight Swedish women playing volleyball in the distance. But more often their luck wasn't.

Then there were the two queer pubs the Golden Lion in Dean Street and the Fitzroy off Charlotte Street. By the 1970s the Golden Lion had been taken over and its place taken by The Compton which was previously the Swiss pub. There were clubs like the Colony in Dean Street run by that woman Muriel Belcher. And next door to that was the Caves de France which was run by the boxer Primo Carnera's brother. I don't know if his mother had a sense of humour or didn't have much imagination because she called him Secundo. Those were places where we wouldn't go.

There were plenty of Soho characters about in the 50s such as the artist Francis Bacon who was forever hanging around the York Minster. What I never did was drink in pubs and clubs like the Premier in New Compton Street which was where villains and coppers used to meet to do a bit of business. There was another down Fleet Street way where a couple of coppers were found one night rolling on the floor when one was trying to tape the other doing a deal. If there was business to be done then I left it to people like Frankie Alberts and 'Red Faced' Tommy Plumley. If you wanted business done it all depended on what area you were in. If you were in the East End you went to someone different to a man you'd go to if you lived in Shepherds Bush.

Some people said Frankie's name was Holbert or Holpert but we always called him Alberts. I don't even know if that was a moody He was a bit of a mystery. He said he was a JP, that's a magistrate, and that was how he could help with the police but I don't know. That copper John Symonds who went down over the Flying Squad troubles in the 1970s said Frankie was done for selling pornography just before he died but I never heard that. Doesn't mean to say he didn't.

And then there were the drinkers and the spielers. You only needed a 7/6d licence to open a drinker. Although I never really liked Soho, I ran clubs and spielers there and it was good money. The usual house cut on betting was a shilling in the pound of each kitty and a kitty could be as much as a couple of hundred and more a time. The great thing was to keep the cards flowing so the house got more and more of the pots. And bits of work came my way. I'd do any sort of work I if I fancied it. Here's an example. Peter Hogg was a fellow who had a lot of machines in the West End and one day someone comes to me and says people from Fulham are threatening him. 'If you can do something about it here's a share in it for you''. I make some inquiries and the person from Fulham is Charlie Mitchell who was running long firms for the Twins so I go to him and say, 'Leave it out Charlie' and he agrees. So now I've got a share in machines. And that's how things came to me.

A man Albert couldn't stand was Tony Mella who'd became a friend of mine. This was well after I cut Tony and we'd patched things up between us. One day Tony invites me and Mary round to his house in Stamford Hill for the weekend. This was well after we'd had our own trouble. While we're being shown around Tony's wife moves the pillow in their bedroom and I see a gun underneath. 'Are you in trouble?', I ask Tony. 'It's Albert,' he says. 'Everytime I try to talk to him he just cocks a deaf 'un. You know what happened last time. That's what the gun's for'. I can't let this go on. They're both friends of mine. 'Leave it to me' and I contact Albert to meet him downstairs at Peter Mario's in Gerrard Street for a bit of Italian food.

I said to Albert, 'How do you find Tony?' 'I don't like him.' 'Why not?' 'I don't like him. He's got every joint'. And he had. Tony had taken over almost all the strip joints and near beers in Soho. Albert was envious and this was him being a bit communist. 'I don't want nothing to do with him'. I said, 'You've got to be mad – he's with us'. 'He's not one of us. If we have a row with anybody would he be with us or against us?' 'He'd be with us', I said. 'He'd put up money for the law or for the defence.' 'He'd give it you but would he give it me?' asks Albert. I said, 'Do me a favour and say hello to Tony'. Next time I saw Tony I asked if he'd seen Albert and he said he hadn't. 'When you do I think he'll be all right', I said. This was when Tony said Albert was a capitalist when he was winning and a communist when he was backing losing horses. 'Albert thinks like a Russian. When he's skint he thinks everyone should share and share alike'.

This isn't being disrespectful to Albert but he didn't know when to leave well alone either. He was quite happy to be called Angelo Bruno's man in London. And he shouldn't have been. He was getting his name in the papers far too often. Albert had introduced me to Angelo when he was over and we had a meet at his hotel but I didn't get my name in the papers. That would be around 1960 and I did a bit of work for him over here and a couple of times in the States.

It wasn't Albert's fault he was in an accident when he was in a taxi. He got a lot of money when he injured his back but when he was cross examined in court he had to say he hadn't paid any tax for years and the next year an MP called him a 'squalid small time hoodlum'. Instead of just taking no notice he goes to see the man at the House of Commons who in turn refuses to see him and that got in the papers as well. Then he got named when that brilliant conman Charles Da Silva went down over a swindle when he sold a non-existent fishing fleet sight unseen to a Yorkshire farmer. Charlie was said to have got £4000 from the deal and Albert double.

Then he gets his name in the papers when an apprentice jockey has a spell in prison one year over the Zetland Gold Cup at Redcar. He has a barrister go and make a statement to the judge saying he's not involved and of course that's reported as well with the judge making snide comments about him.

Poor Albert got cancer and he died in November 1972 in Beckenham . The Twins sent a wreath from prison that read 'To a fine gentleman – From Reg & Ron Kray'. The family weren't having it at the funeral and got rid of it. What was also said but what I never believed was that Albert tried to use National Labour Party members against people like Spot and the Jewish 43 Group in the late 1940s. For a start that organisation was gone by about 1950. And we were never anti-Semitic. There's plenty of times the Jews and the Italians have worked together in what people call the Underworld. It was money not politics with us.

But the king of the near-beer joints was my old pal Tony Mella and there's so many stories about 'The Al Capone of Soho', which is what the News of the World called him when he died. One of them, and it's the one I like best, is that someone shoved a bayonet up his arse and left it there. The metal cauterised the wound and it healed. Don't ask me how. Then there's the story that that dwarf Royston Smith who hung around the Twins gave him noughts and crosses. I'd have know if that was true because, dwarf or not Tony, would have done him. He'd already cut Tommy Smithson in Rupert Street after he'd had a falling out with him.

All credit to him, Tony had built himself up while I was away over Spot. By the beginning of the 1960s he had his fingers in a lot of pies. He was in the dirty books racket with a fellow Reggie Power who finally gassed himself over a girl. After the war, at first shops were discreet with a front section and the dirty books kept behind a curtain. Prices for them which were generally didn't have pictures ranged from £20 upwards. Postcards from Paris did a good trade — 10 for £1 at a time. Of course the shops could only operate if they had the go ahead from the law. By the middle 1950s the bookshop owners were paying the police up to £100 a week and they had to pay another £25 if they were allowed to stay open until 10 p.m. which was when they did most business.

Then Tony started the near beer joints where mug punters got charged to drink with the girls and he was fairly ruthless about recruiting. If he saw a good looking girl – and give Tony his due his girls were the best looking in the joints – he'd just commandeer them, no one would stand up to him. There's no doubt he was a big man and, no disrespect, he was something of a bully. But he never bothered me. We weren't in the same line of business. I was never interested in the girls or in porn.

In fact Tony and I had a nice little casino going, nice plush drapes and everything; dice, kalooki, chemmy, poker and klobyosh or bela as it was sometimes called. It was a bit like piquet. You took out the 2 – 6 cards and set up sequences and then took tricks. There was even a four handed version called Barlinnie Rules, so you can guess where that originated. Anyway our club wasn't in Soho, it was the whole of the second floor of a building we had in Stamford Hill. A lot of the local Jewish community turned up and there was never any trouble. Tony saw to it that the local coppers were all right.

But here's an example of how Tony treated his friend Alf Melvin. Alf used to settle up in Soho of an evening, collecting the rents. One evening he puts his head round the door. Tony's playing and I see Alf and say, 'Come on in, have a cup of coffee'. No, he said, he wanted to get away, his wife was waiting at home. He just wanted a quick word with Tony. Now Tony must have seen him but he won't leave his chair so I go over and say, 'Alf's here and he wants to get home'. All Tony says is, 'He can wait. I'll come when this shoe is finished'. He always treated Alf like that, as some sort of skivvy.

Alf had been his strongman when he was taking over the clubs in Soho. Although he was older than Tony, Alf idolised him. It was a bit like George and Lennie in that book Mice and Men except George never treated Lennie as badly as Tony did Alf.

There's no doubt that Alf got a good living off of the clubs and he saved his money and that was when the trouble came. His wife wanted him out. She didn't like him in Soho until all hours mixing with the brasses. She always waited up for him and she worried if he was even later than usual. So Alf tells Tony he wants out but Tony knows he's got a man he can trust and he doesn't like it, says he's got a good job why leave? And Alf says, 'It's my life' and things like that and adds his wife doesn't like it. That's when Tony gets nasty and says something like, 'Your wife should remember when she was selling toffee apples off a barrow'. Now what you should never do is make a remark about someone's wife like that but for the moment Alf lets it go.

I was in the Hatton Garden club when I got a call from Georgie Russo. 'Bert, there's been trouble up here in Soho at the Bus Stop, which was Tony's main club. I thought maybe there'd been a fight but he went on, 'There's all the law around. Something's gone wrong. I think there's been a shooting.' Then a few minutes later he rings back, 'I've got bad news, Tony's dead and they're fetching out another body'. I knew it was a waste of time going up because if the law was there, well the law was there and there's nothing can be done. I said to George to come and tell me what had gone off. What had happened was Tony had kept on belittling Alf in front of the girls just because he knows he can and then that day he makes that one remark which is just too much. They kept a gun in the club and Alf picks it up and shoots Tony. Then there's this awful moment when he realises he's murdered his best friend. His world's over. There's no topping but it's twenty years away and so he just puts the gun in his mouth. He'd probably been planning it because there was a note in his breast pocket to his wife saying he couldn't go on as he was. Tony made it into Frith Street before he died on the pavement.

I'm going to go to Alf's funeral, 10 a.m. on a Friday and then guess what happens ? Tony's wife rings up and says his is the same time on the same Friday. Alf's is in the East End and Tony's is South London. Now what can I do? I can't go to one and disrespect the other. So I thought I'd leave it out and I told both girls I was very sorry I couldn't come and they understood. I heard there was a lot more at Alf's funeral than at Tony's. The wives sent a wreath to each other man's funeral and the girls who worked for Tony split themselves up between the two. But there's no doubt quite a few people were pleased to see Tony go. Of course, it was the end of the club in Stamford Hill.

People like to say that Bert Marsh or Billy Hill or Albert and me were the Kings of Soho but we weren't. The real Kings were people like Ken Drury and Wally Virgo at Scotland Yard. They'd had their hooks in the place for years and they made fortunes out of it. That was another reason I didn't like the place.

Frankie Alberts was their man. That's what I knew him as but other people said he was called Holpert and that he was a lay magistrate. I don't know about that. Every Friday night he'd go to the dirty bookshops and draw money off them. Then he'd take it back to Scotland Yard. If you had a raid then they'd take your stock and sell it on to Jimmy Humphries, who ran strip clubs and bookshops and was well in with them. That's how Drury came a cropper. He went to Cyprus all exes paid by Jimmy and his wife Rusty who was a stripper and the papes found out. .

But the biggest villain in Soho was another copper, Harry Challenor, known as Tanky. He was a terror. Bent as a hairpin and everyone knew it on both sides of the law and no one did nothing about it. He'd been in the military in the war and he had a 'good' one. Got the Military Medal or something like that. Then he became a copper and he was moved to Soho.

Within a matter of weeks he had smashed a 'protection gang' who were extorting money from strip clubs. It did not matter that the men said that they had been beaten and said they had weapons planted on them. They were not believed. Nor were other complaints.

From then on, Challenor was the self-appointed scourge of Soho, and that's what his superiors wanted from him. No one minded him standing on a table in the charge room singing a popular song of the time, 'Bongo, bongo, bongo, I don't want to leave the Congo', walking home from West

End Central to Surrey every night, and his calling anyone and everyone 'Me ol' darlin'' as he gave them a clip. Nothing mattered so long as the arrests and convictions kept on coming. It was said that in the witness box he could make Soho sound like Chicago, and he described fighting crime in London as, 'like trying to swim against a tide of sewage'.

If he'd stuck to Soho characters there's no knowing how long he would have lasted. In the 1960s, juries and magistrates were not inclined to believe defendants, especially if they were people like us and the officer in the case was a decorated war hero. But he pushed his luck and planted bricks on straight people in a demonstration against the King and Queen of Greece, outside of Claridge's hotel where they were staying. And one of those arrested and given a clip by Challenor was a Donald Rooum, who was a member of the National Council for Civil Liberties.

Challenor told Roumm he had found a brick in his pocket and was charging him with carrying an offensive weapon. Sensibly Roumm refused to sign for it as part of his property, and after he was kept in custody overnight he handed over his clothes to his solicitor at the first court hearing the next morning. No brick dust was found in his pocket and he was acquitted although Rooum never got his costs.

That was the end of Challenor although it was tidied up as best the law could. By the time he appeared at the Old Bailey, charged with three other coppers with conspiracy to pervert the course of justice, he was found unfit to plead and sent to a mental hospital. Stress. The other coppers, all younger and junior to him, got three years' imprisonment. Challenor was only in a few weeks and he then came out and worked for the solicitors who'd defended him.

But if the law had put a stop to him and others like him earlier then there wouldn't have been the Ken Drurys and Wally Virgos there were later.

Until, I should think, the late 1950s Soho was all Italian, little shops and businesses. Now it's half Chinese. There used to be that big Italian restaurant Peter Mario's at the Leicester Square end of Gerrard Street. Billy Hill and Albert and me we all went there and we'd take visiting American boxers but that's become a Chinese now. It all come about after a Scot Frankie McGovern who spoke a bit of Cantonese let some Chinese have a room in a club he had for gambling in Gerrard Street. The story was he'd won it in a poker game. And from then on that part of Soho below Shaftesbury Avenue gradually become Chinatown. But there again they never bothered with us. Just kept themselves to themselves, and we didn't bother them either.

# 11: THE CLUB IN HATTON GARDEN

It was in the 60s that I had a club in Greville Street in Hatton Garden, the jewellery district near Clerkenwell. The whole building belonged to an Italian property dealer who had a restaurant on the ground floor. He let the first floor to Matty Constantinou and George Meisl for their jewels business and since the top two floors weren't being used they said I should have it as a club. A spieler really. There was tables for cards and dice and Mary ran the tea bar at the back. I brought in a television for the racing and I'd take the bets on that. The top floor I and Mary had as a flat. It suited Matty and George. I was a bit of protection for them. They did a bit of fencing and there was always the chance someone would try to rip them off.

Where there's jewellery there's got to be villainy. They go hand in hand through history. Look at the Great Pearl Robbery back in 1913, well before my time but it was still talked about when I was in the Garden. Cammi Grizzard was a big name and he put it up. It was said that once when the law come round for a search he was having dinner and he put the stolen jewels in his pea soup.

Hatton Garden's had it's fair share of jewel thefts and I was never surprised when the coppers came knocking after one. Some of the jobs were well executed and some were just amateur night stuff. One which went off just before Billy Hill did the Jockey's Fields bullion robbery in 1954 was when Abe Cobden had all his stock taken by a young fellow Bert Clark along with a woman Thelma Hoad- Johnston and another jeweller Charlie

**Above:**

A genuine headline in the NY Daily Press as a welcome to Bert upon
his arrival to New York City. Thanks to the Gambino Family.

**Above:**

Bert with Lord and Lady
Docker, Albert Dimes,
Bammy Russo

**Left:**

Bert with Billy Hill and
Lady Docker.

**Above:**

Tony Burns, Frank Fraser, Bert Rossi, Tommy Wisbey, Ambrose Mendy
and friends

*Photograph taken at a boxing event in the*
*Repton Club, Bethnal Green*

**Above:**

Alex and Anna Steene with Bert

**Above:**

Alex Steene, Jersey Joe Walcott and Bert

**Above:**

Berts Mafioso associates Meyer Lanksy ( Top Left ), Nicky Scarfo ( Top Right ),
Angelo Bruno ( Bottom Left ), Carlo Gambino ( Bottom Right )

**Center:**

"Big" John C. Berkery

**Left:** Big John C. Berkery Wedding attended by Philadelphia Mob Boss Nicky Scarfo sitting in the middle. Salvatore (Salvie) Testa sitting 2nd from the right. Salvie was the son of slain mob boss Phil "The Chicken Man" Testa, who was killed in 1981 from a nail bomb, after taking over from Angelo Bruno. Salvie was killed a few years after in 1984. Both allegedly on orders from Nicky Scarfo.

**Above:**

"Big" John C. Berkery's Wedding. Attended by Raymond Martorano, Johns 2nd wife, Big John, John Simone, Angelo Bruno

**Above:**

Big John, John Simone, Angelo Bruno

**Above:**

Faceoff of 2 great friends Carlo Gambino and Bert Rossi.

**Above:**

Bert With "Big" John C. Berkery and friends in Atlantic City

**Above:**

Abe Koski and Lou, the nephew of "King of Soho" Tony Mella, with Bert (Right)

**Above:**

Bert on his first trip to New York City.

**Left:**

A photograph of Bert in 1955, at just 23 years old.

**Right:**

Bert with one of his best, dearest friends, Cherry.

**Left:**

Bert with best friend Albert Dimes

**Right:**

Bert With "Big" John C. Berkery, in Atlantic City.

© BERT ROSSI
 NOT TO BE COPIED OUT
PRIOR WRITTEN
PERMISSION

**Left:**

Bert with old Clerkenwell friends Mad Hay and Nelly Sabini

**Right:**

Another of Bert With "Big"John C. Berkery and Joe, a Capo of the Gambino family in Atlantic City.

Ady. It was the time old trick. 'Show my fiancée the rings' and while he's getting the trays out someone comes and chloroforms him. This time they didn't put enough on the pad and Abe comes to and sees them rifling the safe. He must have put up a bit of a fight before he went under because he's managed to scratch Clark. Abe runs out into the street calling robbery and Clark, silly fool, instead of getting away he stays and rinses his face in a basin. He then runs up some stairs and is caught on the roof. He got three years early the next January, and the day after Thelma and Charlie are found in the Pack Horse Hotel, Staines where they had registered as Mr and Mrs Lewis from Cambridge. They'd taken an overdose. She was meant to be a big jewel thief, known as Black Maria or The Black Orchid, but this time she hadn't picked her team too good. She'd had a life all right. According to the papers she was reputed to have 'killed' three men, something on which she remarked, 'I didn't kill any man. Any man who died just couldn't stand the pace'.

Funnily her old man was a struck off solicitor who'd been a motor boat racer before the war and he was doing a ten for fraud at the time. He'd set up as an estate agent and was leasing the same flat to different couples at the same time. And the flat didn't exist either. People were so desperate after the war to get a flat they took it without ever seeing it. You may think that's funny but people still do it. I knew a couple who went to Spain where they'd bought a house without ever seeing it or even going to Spain before. But they were lucky. At least it was there when they arrived.

There was a good blag in June 1973 when an old man William Trenner got done for a load of jewellery when he was on the way to the diamond exchange in the Garden. I don't think anyone was ever done for it but the story was George and Matty had a share. Not me.

A bit away from Hatton Garden in 1980, two Chicago-based gangsters armed with a handgun and a hand grenade stole jewellery valued at £1.5 million from a jewellers in Sloane Street. Mafiosi Joseph Scalise and Arthur Rachael, who took a matter of seconds to get the jewels, were nicked eleven hours later in the States and sent back here where they got nine years.

Their haul had included the 26 carat Marlborough diamond, worth £400,000 at the time, which has never been recovered.

Now if they'd been from New Jersey or Philly I'd have most certainly been asked for advice. They couldn't have gone about things in much more of a wrong way. For a start there's no way Jerry, which is what Scalise was known as, should have been on any robbery. He was born with a deformed hand – missing three fingers; just a stub with a thumb and little finger. Not difficult to work out who that is. Then they travelled on the same plane, stayed in the same hotel, the Mount Royal at Marble Arch. They dressed up as sheiks with false beards. That was all right but they rented a car in their own name and someone took down the licence plate. And these were serious men in the Chicago Outfit.

I'd have told them bring the gear here. They'd have got their money and gone home sweet. As it was they flew back to Chicago together and were picked up more or less as they left the plane. At least they did mail the Marlborough diamond somewhere. They give it to a taxi driver in a package. They had that much sense. The nine years didn't teach them, Jerry did another stint in a cocaine sting and then in 2012 he picked up 100 months which I work out as eight and a half years. What he'd done this time was along with Rachael again was to try and burgle the home the widow of Angelo LaPietra, 'The Hook wh'd been boss of the Chicago Outfit. I'm not being disrespectful but was that a sensible thing to do? He'll be nearly eighty when he comes out in a couple of years time. And I don't suppose the Mob is very pleased with him either.

Then in 1993, the jeweller Graffs' Hatton Garden workshop premises was robbed of stuff valued at £7 million. The blag was put down to a group that was known as The Rascal Gang because of the Bedford Rascal vans they used.

The last and biggest was in April 2015 when the Hatton Garden Safe Deposit Company, an underground safe deposit vaults was burgled. The burglary occurred during a period in which both the Easter Bank Holiday and Passover coincided. Lot of bird was handed out over that and who knows what has never turned up. The Mastermind certainly hasn't.

Another of the things which went on in the Garden was doctoring second hand and tax free jewellery. In fact it was new stuff being sold without Purchase Tax. To my knowledge no one ever got pulled but some people had shaky nights.

There could be some big games at the club with the pots running into thousands. Most often I'd just take a shilling in the pound but sometimes I played. There was one fellow come in the club. He came from Manchester and was called George so of course he was known as Manchester George. He played cards a few times and he was always a winner so I thought I'd make some inquiries about him. I rang up a pal in Manchester, gave a description and asked if he knew him and what sort of a name he had. 'He's called Manchester George and he's a sharp'. So now I was on my guard. One day around midday I'm more or less on my own when he comes in and asks if I want a hand of rummy. I open two fresh decks and we play for £100 a side and he wins. I've been watching his hands and I can't see anything wrong. He says double or quits? So now there's four hundred on the table. He wins again and he's about to pick up the money when I put my hand over it. 'Look,' I said, 'You can search me and then I'm going to search you'. He starts blustering saying I can't do that. 'All right, then I'll count the cards' And there should be 104 but there's only 100. 'Out', I say. He starts again saying he hasn't got them but it's all bluster. 'Out and don't come back'. I'd have been justified giving him a smack but I just kept the money.

All sorts used to come into my club and most of them were good thieves. One of them George Chatham — we called him Taters because he was always complaining about the cold — was described in the Guardian as the 'Thief of the Century'. Strong and agile, like a monkey and fearless with it; everything you'd want in a climber. Now I've gambled enough money away in my time but Taters would leave a card game when he was losing, go and do a job, fence the jewels and be back at the tables losing it all again in a couple of hours. People say he stole £30 million in his lifetime but that may be a bit over the top. It was certainly a lot. One of his best was in 1948 when he stole the Duke of Wellington's sword from the Victoria and Albert Museum. My friend Mikey Harris told him about it and he expected a cut from it. Taters roped two ladders together and broke a window 40 feet up. There was a guard in the room and he waited until the man was at the far end away from the swords. But he never profited from it. One of the swords had an emerald collar and the other was gold with blue enamel and diamonds. He prized the stones out and gave them to girlfriends or lost them on the horses and cards. When Mikey went round for his share Taters told him all the jewels had been paste.

Taters copped a couple of big sentences in the middle 50s While he was on remand for burglary he broke out of Brixton. That was in the April and by the time he was found in the September he was charged with a big safe breaking at a jewelers in regent Street He picked up five for the first burglary and another ten for the second. The judge was having one of those days when he says things for the papers telling Taters he'd chosen to make himself an 'enemy of society'.

The people he'd turned over was like a Who's Who itself — Maharajah of Jaipur, Lady Rothermere, Madame Prunier, and Raymond, the society hairdresser they called Mr Teasy Weasy . When he did the place of the Countess of Dartmouth, who became Raine Spencer , he fell off her roof and spent six weeks in hospital. Wasn't nicked over it though.

Then there was Cherry Titmuss — I remember him coming in the club and showing me the best piece of jewellery I've ever seen. It must have come from Italy. It was unmarked but it was pure gold, a chain of thorns with Christ head emeralds, five troy ounces. There were emeralds for the thorns and diamonds for the eyes. I wish I'd bought and kept it. He'd also got some Italian cartoons. They were genuine and they were beautiful. He showed them to me but I said no, I couldn't do anything with them.

One of the best jewel thieves of his time, Peter Scott, was a funny man. Funny in the peculiar sense that is. He was very good looking and could pull women just by looking at them. But he had his kinks. Instead of doing a simple screwing job and getting out, he'd stand in people's bedrooms watching them. He married a model, Jackie was her name, and then he drew a long sentence on the Moor. She was desperate to get pregnant and she used to drive down to the Moor in a white van with a mattress and have it off with him while he was meant to be on a work party.

He had a feud with the other top class man Ray Jones who liked to be called The Cat. Probably, no disrespect to Taters, Jones was the best climber as such there was in the business. Maybe not the luckiest or the cleverest but the best climber. Both him and Scott claimed they stole Sophia Loren's jewels when she was staying in the Norwegian Barn near Edgware making that film with Peter Sellars in the 60s and they both kept going on in the papers about it saying they'd done it. Jones also claimed to have given one of her rings to his wife Anne, who wore it for 15 years until someone nicked it from her. He must have been mad; he actually walked into a police station in the 90s and confessed but by then no one was really interested.

Jones' best bit of work was an escape he did from Pentonville at the end of the 50s when he and a mate climbed to the roof over the main prison landing but then as Ray was climbing down he fell, smashed his kneecap, and broke his ankle. But he still went on, climbed another wall and then fell again in another jump and broke his other leg. But you've got to credit it him, he continued on and then he fell through a skylight and knocked himself unconscious. He used to say he came to when a couple of screws found him, thought he was dead and went off to look for the other fellow. So he dragged himself across the Caledonian Road and begged a group of men to give him a lift. Now he was lucky, there were a lot of villains in the Cally at that time and he chose lucky. They took him to a flat he knew and he managed to stay out for nearly two years. It was in the Guinness Book of Records. He always reckoned Peter Scott grassed him up but I don't know, I wasn't there.

They were all climbers but another firm I bought a lot of stuff off were dips and hoisters. They called the Kangaroo Gang. They were Aussies all right but they weren't really a gang, more a collection of individuals who came and, when the going got a bit warm, went and they worked together.

They'd steal to order and they once took a chimpanzee out of Harrods when it had a zoo on the top floor. Just put it in a pram and pushed it out. On the surface they were a charming bunch but you didn't need to cross them. The sort of leader was a fellow Duke Delaney who was as good a thief as any I've ever met. They had some wonderful ideas about distracting shop staff — this was before CCTY mind — one would piss against the counter while the other gathered round to watch. I never knew their real names. There was a girl with them who they called Ma Barker. She wasn't the prettiest but she had a good figure and when she took all her clothes off in a shop in Bond Street you can imagine what sort of stir it caused.

One of them whose name I did know was a fellow Tom Wraith. He had a flat in Marble Arch and he lived there with his girlfriend Grace O'Connor the former wife of a big Sydney crim who'd been shot in one of the gang wars they had over there. There was also another bird on the scene and somehow the girlfriend copped it. The law spent sometime looking for her and they thought she's maybe been buried in Hyde Park but they never found the body. Tom went back to Melbourne and he got topped by another girlfriend who took a tomahawk to him. I heard he'd become a heroin addict by then.

There was always a load of waifs and strays coming into the club thinking I was an easy touch for a few quid or a dinner and I suppose Mary and me were. I didn't like lending money to the punters. I'd rather they stopped playing but one day a fellow comes in with Sammy Kanter and drops his money. Sammy says will I lend him some. I don't even know the man but Sammy says if I give him £300 and he doesn't pay me back the next day I can have a van he's got worth three grand at least and I can have the log book as security. I have a look at the van outside and I'm always going to get my money back so I lend it to him. Next day Sammy comes in and says 'You're never going to believe this but he's topped himself. The van's yours'. How could I take it? The man had borrowed £300 done it and reached his peak. How could I take a three grand van off his widow? Serves me right for lending it in the first place.

There was a fellow used to come in who we called Arthur Askey. You could have put him on an ID parade with the comedian. He was always well dressed but he was what we called a fiddler. He'd walk into the club and say, 'Shall I make the tea?' What he wanted was a couple of quid at the end of the day.

One day we were talking about the Victoria Sporting Club, a casino which had opened in the Edgware Road. It was a nice place and at the beginning, before the law changed, they'd served the better punters free drink. Arthur was all for it. Could he go? Did they let women in? We told him yes to both; the wives usually sat together and had a few sandwiches and a chat. One evening we're there at the dice table, about eight of us and in comes Arthur and his wife. He comes over to us and the croupier recognises him as the comedian straight away. 'Move over, make room for Mr Askey'. Arthur says he wants to play a 9/4 chance. That's forty pounds to win ninety if the man throws the number he first threw before he throws a seven. Couple of throws later he's bust and the croupier is asking Arthur for the money. He's digging around in his pocket and eventually he finds two pounds and hands them over. 'No,' says the croupier, 'It's another £38, Mr Askey'. Arthur thinks he'd been betting in shillings. We said to the man, 'He don't play £90 to £40; he bets in shillings'. The fellow had to wear it but it was the end of Arthur's evening.

There was another fellow who used to hang around Mary and me. We called him Lou the Bandit. Lou Canasti his name was. He had a crippled leg, maybe it was a club foot which was quite common in those days. and always wore a homburg hat. I think he got out of bed, got dressed and came to the club. We fed him for years in the flat we had upstairs over the club, breakfast dinner, tea. One day, just to wind him up a bit, I said to Mary, 'That Morrie Meisl (George's brother) is driving me mad. I've had him up here making out he's dropped a six carat diamond and I know he hasn't. I suppose he's thinking of getting the insurance for it. £600 or so he'd get'. Morrie had said nothing of the kind, I was just winding Lou up. I keep on about the stone so Lou can hear and then one day just before Mary calls him in for his dinner I've dropped a zircon I had with me where he can't miss it. Sure enough when I come in for dinner it's gone. I don't say a word but I noticed he'd gone and got a book on diamonds out of the library.

Another time he was there before the day of Tony Nappi's funeral. It was about nine in the evening and I said 'Lou, what time's the Mass for Tony. You can speak Italian. Ring up the church.' 'He says he can't do that. It's nine o'clock. I can't do that'. He's been brought up that you couldn't disturb a priest in an evening. So I think I'll wind him up a bit. I ring up and say 'Is that the Italian Church?' He thinks I'm through to them but I've just rung the club downstairs. Then I say into the phone, 'What do you say? I think you're being very rude. What's your name? Sister Bridget, you say. I'm going to report you. And I put the phone down. 'She said I was a bit late honing up'. I said to Mary 'You go downstairs ring up. Say you're Sister Bridget, cry a bit and say you're being sent back to Ireland.' So she does this and Lou can hear every word. Now he wants to go down to the Church to plead for her, and off he does, When he comes back he tells me he's rung the bell and the priest answered. 'I've come to see you about Sister Bridget'. And the priest says 'We don't have a Sister Bridget'. But Lou says 'I know you have. She's being sent back to Ireland and she's very upset'. He thinks he's speaking to a nut case. But Lou continues and so the priest says 'Very well, in the circumstances I won't send her back'. And Lou is all over him with gratitude. When he comes back to me he's so proud, 'I've saved her' he says. He had a good heart. I never told him it was all a joke.

He was always on at me to get him on a job and again just to wind him up I told him about a midget who collected the takings at Hampstead Heath Fair at Christmas. All a fanny. 'It'll be easy,' I said. 'Three in the morning, he's on his own and he takes it to a caravan. You're very lucky, Lou. I'm going on that and it'll be a walkover'. 'What happens if he won't let go of the bag?' I say,' Then I'll give him such a whack I'll put him on the ground'. He thinks it over and then says he doesn't fancy it. 'Well,' I say, 'Maybe you're right, you're just not cut out for it.' But it's the last I hear from him about wanting to go on a job.

You learn things as you go along. Coming from where I did I never knew anything about jewellery and nor did a lot of us. There's a story that Ruby Sparkes when he was young got his name because he didn't realise he was handling rubies. He thought the stones was rubbish and threw them on a fire. But I learned. I was never an appraiser but I had some idea of what was what. George and Matty would point things out to me but I would never price stuff for anyone. That wasn't my job. I was better than some though. My friend Alex Steene, the boxing promoter, now he was a joke when it come to looking at jewellery. I remember going to his place in St Martin's Lane and he was proudly showing me a gold chain he'd bought for his wife. I forget what he said he'd paid for it but good money in those days. It wasn't even gold. Even I could see that. But I never told him. Now, there was a man who loved looking like a Mafioso. He could have been that fellow Robert De Niro kills in The Godfather Part Two, all big cream suit and dark glasses. When he sat ringside he couldn't understand why people were looking at him.

I think Alex started his working life on a fairground at Hampstead Heath and went on from there. When I took him to Italy with me he was an embarrassment. We were in this restaurant waiting for Dino Cellini and the moment he arrives Alex is on his feet hugging him, giving him a kiss like in the films and saying 'All right Dino; all right boy? ' He didn't even know the man. Dino looked over his shoulder at me as if to say 'nut case'.

It was while I had the club that I gave away a bar of gold. A fellow who worked for Billy Smart's circus came to see me. I knew who he was and I bought bits and pieces from him from time to time. 'I've got a bar of gold'. He wanted cash of course. I asked him how many carat and he said 'Nine'. So I took it to a fellow Joe Benjamin in the Garden and he pays me. I take a bit off the top and give the rest to the circus fellow. He's back within the week. I thought he'd got something else but what does he say? 'It was 18 carat'. I'd given a bar of gold away for half the price. I don't know if he thought I was going to swallow it myself but I just said, 'What you fucking telling me for now? It's gone'. I didn't go and see Joe about it. All he would have said was 'No, it was nine carat'.

I had all sort of clients. Most of them were in the life, but one of them was a dentist. He'd buy from me and sell the stuff on to his patients. And you won't necessarily believe this but it's true. Charles Forte, that's the founder of the catering firm, comes to me one day to buy a crooked diamond. He's going to give it as a present to his sister or someone in the family who won't know it's bent. Why would a billionaire want to buy a crooked diamond? Because he's a billionaire is the right answer.

Another man I worked with was Morrie Spurling, who was called 'The Egg' because he was bald as a coot. He worked with Brian Kutner, a fellow they called The Swan. Good thieves they were. They were good people. Now, in his day Morrie was a world class thief. He worked all over Europe and South Africa but in the end his last job was in Thirsk, a small town in North Yorkshire. It wasn't his lucky day. He got stopped there for not wearing a seat belt. Then he steals some gold chains from a shop and is caught on the security camera. That might have been all right except the copper who stopped him for the seat belt had a look at the video and recognised him. At least he got a suspended sentence. After that I think he packed it in. He was on sticks by then anyway.

In those years I had a good thing going. I was moving three/four kilos of cocaine a week, making a thousand a kilo with a fellow Steff. No problems, I could move it with people in Manchester, Leeds, Birmingham. And then I get a call from Italy. Another fellow Enzo is in trouble with the mafia there. Different lot from the Americans. He's a friend of Steff. Can I help out? Again, no problems until Enzo gets big ideas. He can get hold of a really big parcel so could I move it? But it all goes pear shaped. Him and Steff went back to Italy and they're caught with it before they get it to me and I think they got twelve each. But they were staunch. My name never came into it. But, of course, that was the end of my £3000 a week.

One day a young fellow Cecil, Jewish, South African comes to the club and asks if he can come in. He's been told to look me out. He keeps coming in and over time opens up. It seems he's on the run from South Africa where he's wanted. Now if someone comes in and he says his business is with banks then I'd try and put him in touch with the right people; same if he says he's a clerical man. I never took anything from it. This fellow was a conman and one day he tells me he's been and conned the wrong person, relieved him of some money and he'd done it to a medical fellow who's got connections.

Next thing I know is Joey Pyle who's a really big name in South London comes to see me one day. We don't talk on the phone. I always got on well with Joey . In the early 1950s he'd been involved in the Pen Club shooting when Jimmy Nash, the brother they called Trunky because of the size of his nose got five years for assaulting Selwyn Cooney. Jimmy was lucky. He got a not on a charge of killing him. So was Joey. He got a not guilty as well but he got 18 months for the assault. After that the law had it in for Joey. There was one trial after his place had been searched when the law was looking for Freddie Sewell who was wanted for killing a copper in Blackpool. They didn't find anything about Sewell but they said they'd found a gun and ammunition and Joey was done for possessing a gun and some ammunition and that if the jury found Joey not guilty it would mean the officers had committed perjury but he got a not guilty all the same. They could get him on anything so they started objecting to clubs getting a licence if they thought he'd got an interest in them.

Joey knew the fellow Cecil was in my area and he had a bit of work to carry out on behalf of this doctor. It wasn't life and death, just a bit of hospital. What was my connection with Cecil, he wanted to know. I said, 'He's on the run and he's skint. He's only trying to make a living. Don't give him a belting. Leave it out'. Joey looks a bit doubtful and tells me he's been given £1000 to do it. Now I can understand why he doesn't want to drop it out. 'Can we work something as one boss to another?' Anyway we settled on Joey going round to Cecil's flat but instead of giving him a beating he'll splash him with pig's blood. Then Cecil would go off to Brighton, keep out the way for a bit and the doctor will think he's had his money's worth. So I got hold of Cecil and told him to listen carefully. He was to make sure he opened the door that morning around 10 o'clock and he wasn't to tell his girl what was happening. Just let her see him covered in blood. But that's not enough for Cecil. He was a good talker and he says he can't go to Brighton because he's skint. I said, 'Listen, you can do it my way or you can go missing. Do you understand?' I also say to Joey, 'Look, you keep £900 and I give the kid £100. That way you don't have to do anything'. Joey's happy, the kid's happy and I suppose I am. I'm still not sure I wasn't conned about his having no money. Anyway Joey knows I owe him one.

And that one came over the fighter Lennie MacLean who wanted to have a go in with Roy Shaw who was top of the unlicensed boxers at the time. There'd always been unlicensed boxing in Britain, unlicensed didn't mean illegal it just meant it was outside the control of the Boxing Board. It was bare knucke, knock down and kick stuff and it went on a fairs between gypsies and in back rooms in pubs of a Sunday morning but now in the 1960s. It was getting big with heavy betting and serious money changing hands.

Now Roy Shaw, there was a nice man. He'd done a lot of bird and when he come out for a long stretch he was in his forties and the Board wasn't going to give him a licence so he fought a few fights at fairs and then there was the chance of a bog, big fight with a fellow Donny 'The Bull' Adams who reckoned he was the top man at the time.

I'd known Lennie for some years. He was just another kid in the neighbourhood as far as I was concerned a well-set boy. He borrowed a bit of money off me once - repaid it on the nail of course and another time he came to me asking if I could get him a job on a club door. My friend Jimmy Spinks from the Hoxton mob was his great Uncle and Bobby Warren was an uncle himself. Anyway, he come to me one day and said he'd heard Joey Pyle was promoting these unlicensed shows and there was this fellow Roy Shaw who was top dog. Lennie fancied himself. Could I get him a match? It was easy to arrange. I knew Alex Steene who was fronting for Joey Pyle who owed me a bit of a favour. I think Lennie lost the first time round and then did Roy up over the ropes in the second. I didn't go to the fight or any unlicensed fights for that matter. It wasn't boxing to my mind, just brutal.

What you have to be careful about is knowing who sent someone to you. That's why poor old Charlie Kray came a cropper over the drug deal which got him twelve years back in the 1990s. If someone get's in touch they should give you a name straight off saying, 'Tommy recommended I get in touch with you'. Then you should get hold of Tommy and ask if that's right. Of course there may still be problems. Tommy may be under the cosh from the coppers and being made to place someone, but it's elemental to make inquiries in the first place. And if Tommy is under the cosh you are likely to have heard stories anyway. But to have someone ring up and say, 'Bert I hear you're a good man, the right man for this'. Well, it may be flattering but it's foolish not to take precautions. And if they don't give you a name then you should ask who they know so you can make inquiries, otherwise it should be, 'Thanks, but no thanks'.

Charlie just never bothered. Whether it was because his boy Gary had just died or he was desperate or just wanted to be big I don't know but he let his guard down and that cost him dear.

There was another time the law tried to slip one in to me and, like the time with Jock Wyatt, I got out because I missed an appointment and that wasn't something I did often. I've been very punctual all my life. If I say I'm going to be somewhere then I'll be there. There was this fellow Chuck came in my club and, as you do, we got talking. Then Alfie Haynes, a very good conman from South London gets hold of a bundle of travellers' cheques. That's how Alfie earned his living. Chuck says he could get rid of them abroad but I wasn't going to give a bundle like that to someone I'd only known a few weeks so I said I'd meet him in Cologne, where I had a jeweller friend, on the following Monday morning and I give him the fare to go over there. He was to go to the jeweller and say he was a friend of Bert Rossi and he'd be welcomed. Now I fully intended to go over that morning but somehow I missed the plane. I'm still at home trying to organise another flight when I get the call from the jeweller. 'Bert? Are you still coming over? I don't know what's happening. 'What were the police doing here this morning? As I opened up there were the law. They asked me if I knew a Bert Rossi from London and I said yes, he'd be walking thought the door any minute. Eventually when you didn't show they went away.'

I asked him had there been anyone else there and he said, 'No, only the law'. Chuck hadn't turned up and he was the only man who knew what was going on. I hadn't told my jeweller friend anything but that I was coming over to meet Chuck. Believe it or not Chuck turned up at the club a couple of weeks later. 'Oh, hello Bert'. I took him outside, gave him a right belting and threw him down the stairs. Sometimes it's better to be born lucky than rich.

Of course it wasn't just in Soho the coppers had their paws in things. Every time they raided Georgie Meisl they copped money. It was a way of life. Once summer I was arrested after a night at Harringay dogs. I'd bought some curtains from a man at the Central Club and there they were on the floor of my flat. He'd had some rolls of cloth from the railway. Down the station it was the usual, 'Can we do some business?' In those days one in ten would say 'no' and nine would say 'yes'. Then it comes to a figure. This time it was £200 which was a lot of money when the dogs was still running at Harringay. 'When?' 'Tomorrow'. I said I was making a book on the Derby at Epsom and he said he'd come down with a colleague. I met them behind the joint and handed over the money. He gets a day at the races and if anyone ever asks, the entry in his book is, 'Meeting confidential informant'. I never got the curtains back. I suppose he hung them up himself. That's how it works.

It was through George and Mattie that I got to know Abe Kosky and later Angelo Bruno and Santo Trafficante and a load of others from the States. If there was no action in the club I'd leave Mary in charge and spend a good part of the day with them. Really what I was doing was minding them because they had quantities of jewellery, straight and not so straight, going through their hands. If they had clients they knew and could trust I'd leave them to it and go back up to the club. Otherwise I'd hang around. One day they're behind their desks and I'm on a chair when a man comes in. They look up and say, 'Hello Abe' so I know they know him and it's business so I go out back upstairs. This happened for the next few days. It turns out that what he's wanting is five carat and upwards stones. Now these would cost two grand each and more back in those days. After one of his visits, George told me the man – Abe Kosky was his name — asked who I was. 'I told him you were the guy who did Jack Spot'.

Now it turns out Abe Kosky was a big man in the game and well respected. I remember him taking me to the Dorchester one day. It was full of Jewish businessmen and he was like a Messiah. It was handshakes all round and 'Hello Abe,' 'How're you doing Abe?' as we were shown to our table. Over time he told me a good bit about himself. He'd started life running a café in Whitechapel and had done a bit of receiving before moving on to the gaming clubs and then to putting up robberies. I never saw any girls in his flat but he'd been married at some time because his daughter married Eric Miller, the head of the big property company Peachey Properties. Miller was said to have topped himself on the Day of Atonement 1977. A lot of people didn't believe that, however, and said he'd been done.

Abe had also had the Botolph Club in Aldgate which was run by Jack Spot and, when that was closed after the Heath Row fiasco, when a lot of good boys went down, he organised a Friday night Faro game at premises in Northumberland Avenue. Apparently there were huge sums on offer at this game which was run by a fellow Hyman Goldfine who was known as Raffles and another man, Joseph Leighton, who was something of a mathematical prodigy. Spot was the minder and it was his responsibility to make sure winning punters got home safely. Spot was also his bagman and each week he'd take the money to the police to make sure the game stayed open.

Next time Abe comes in he catches me on the stairs. 'Are you doing anything tonight?' I told him I wasn't and he said, 'Come and have dinner with me in Isow's'. Now, Jack Isow's was a smart restaurant in Brewer Street. Back in the 1930s Jack had had a bad name with the police but by the 50s he was well respected.

Kosky doesn't say nothing about business during dinner, just a chat about clubs and boxing and racing, and I'm wondering what it's all about until once dinner's over we go to his mansion flat off Russell Square. He had a whole floor. He offers me a scotch and cigar to which I've always been partial and then he comes out with what he wants. 'I'm going into business with some Americans It's going to be a very big club. I can't be there all the time. I want you to represent me here'. And that's how I got in with other branches of the Mafia.

# 12 : MAFIA DAYS

Next thing is Abe drives us over to the Club and one of the first people that he introduced me to that night was Dino Cellini who was Meyer Lansky's representative , a man I got to know as a friend. Lansky grew up with Bugsy Siegel in New York and went on to be the financial brains of the Mob, moving money all over the world. It shows that Jews and Italians could work together perfectly well. If you see The Godfather Part 2, Hyman Roth is near enough Meyer Lansky. Except for his death that is.

Now, in books on the Mafia you don't read too much about Dino Cellini but there's no doubt he was Meyer Lansky's man in London, man all over the world really. He was born in Steubenville, the steel town in Ohio, and what he was was brilliant with dice and cards particularly in the days before cards were dealt from a shoe. He could deal from the bottom, top, half way, anything. He could just about make them talk. I always thought I was good but I wasn't in his class. The Mafia learned about him and started to use him as what was called a mechanic or a bust out man, someone who was brought in by the house to break a punter's winning streak and hustle people who the house thought had a load of money to lose. It wasn't long before he was used by Meyer Lansky to run his casinos in the Bahamas and then the Riviera Casino and Tropicana Club in Havana. Dino also had a school for croupiers in Cuba and later ran one in London. Teach them how to deal, to recognise cheats, cheat themselves and, almost just as important, how to keep a game speeding along. Don't forget time is money. The house has a percentage every time the wheel spins or a shoe empties so the croupier has got to keep the action going without the punters thinking they are being pushed. The more spins of the wheel you get in an hour the better it is for the house. And the same with throws of the dice, a good croupier has to clear up the losing bets on the table between each throw and you don't want him taking too long over that.

Of course, what they had to do was find premises and the place which I thought was ideal was a place in Berkeley Square, a big white building not far from the Mayfair Hotel, five minutes from Piccadilly, if that. and that's what I told Abe and Dino. At the time was owned by the Tolaini family who had originally had a restaurant in Dalston and I knew them well from Saffron Hill. Then they'd opened the nightclub the Latin Quarter in Wardour Street — which was where David Knight got killed by Tony Zomparelli one night in 1970 — before they opened this very smart place in Mayfair. Some people had thought it was too small for a smart club and casino but I could see it could be brilliant. Not too large and impersonal. Castro had booted the Mafia out of Cuba and they was on the look out for places in London and ideally all over England.

There was only one place where gambling was legal in America in those days and that was Nevada. What the Mafia saw over here was the opportunity of not only laundering money but sending people over on gambling junkets. So far as the casinos here were concerned they'd get the expertise from the trained croupiers and they'd get the benefits of the junkets.

So I introduced Abe and Cellini to the brothers. There was a bit of discussion over the price of course but it was soon settled and the brothers came away with a nice profit. The club was to be called The Colony Club.

I used to go down to the Colony about eight in an evening, have some supper and I'd often stay until it closed. It was a wonderful place in those days. Absolute style, more dinner jackets than suits, girls all dressed up and ready to go. The girls from the Astor would come in after their show and the icing was the old film star George Raft as the host. Of course, George was well past his best by then. He had a toupee and the story is that he had to put on a corset to keep his stomach in but he could still dance the Charleston and he could bring the women to their knees.

I remember one late afternoon taking a drive home I got talking to George Raft, and we ended up talking about Bugsy Siegel, or Benjamin has he liked to be called. He told me that Bugsy had asked him to lend $100,000. Now, you have to remember back in those days $100,000 was a lot of money, even if Raft was the highest paid actor in Hollywood. I said to Raft, did you ever ask him for it back, and he turned to me and said "how could I Bert? He was a cold hearted killer".

Raft was a big star in Hollywood, long before Frank Sinatra was heard of, and Raft dated a young girl called Ava Gardner, who Frank would end up with later down the line. Well one evening, Raft went around to Ava's, and her sister was there, both getting ready for a night out. Suddenly the door bell rung, and Ava asked Raft to get it while she finished getting herself dolled up. Well, Raft opens the door and see's standing before him, Howard Hughes, the same Howard Hughes who made it big as a film producer but also put tens of millions into Las Vegas. He owned some of the casinos over there, but the poor bloke ended up dying in a plane crash in 1976.

And the punters who were there? Who wasn't? The management made it a point to ensure visiting American stars were there and at one time I think the whole cast of the Dirty Dozen were all in the club one night or another. I used to play dominos with Telly Savalas of an evening.

It was while he was at the Colony George got an invitation to do a cameo role in that James Bond spoof Casino Royale which they were filming at Pinewood studios near Windsor. He just had to get shot a bar or something. Would I like to come on down with him and be an extra for a day? I didn't fancy it. I didn't want myself on screen so I said could I bring the old boxing champion Jack 'Kid' Berg instead. That was all right. I just watched and during breaks George introduced me to people. The cast was a wonderful one: David Niven who was James Bond, what a nice man. Peter Sellers, Ursula Andress, Orson Welles, William Holden. It was like being in Hollywood on Thames. What was good for the club was that while the film was being made and a bit afterwards they came in of an evening.

Dino was always there and as I got more friendly with him and he started to trust me he told me more and more about things. What had happened to bring the Mafia over here was when the Betting and Gaming Act became law in 1970. Now there was never any real intention that casinos should open all over the place it was meant to be all about old ladies able to play bingo but open they did and through the doors came the Mafia. They were under pressure from Bobby Kennedy and they had to find some way of laundering their money through legitimate businesses.

It was interesting — educational more like — to hear and see how the Mafia worked; how they'd compromise someone. It was Henry Shapiro who told me this story. Henry was the son of old Gurrah Shapiro, who founded Murder Inc in America along with Louis Buchalter and who was executed way back in 1944.

When the Mafia were trying to establish themselves in casinos over here there was one fellow who was dead set against them. Article in this paper, article in that, all saying how gaming was an evil thing. So what do they do? They invite him over to Las Vegas to see how casinos operate. Gave him the treatment; wined, dined, taken to a floorshow where there's plenty of good-looking girls on the stage. Just in conversation someone in the party says, 'John, which do you think is the best looking?' And he says, 'the second from the left' or whatever. Bit later when the show's finished some of the girls come into the room and who should be among them but the one who's second from the left. She's passing the table when she's invited to sit down and have a drink.

Henry was staying at the Lancaster in Lancaster Gate and I went to see him in his room. 'Come on up Bert'. I thought it was some tom he was wanting to talk about. It was but another sort of tom. He opens his valise and takes out an envelope and shows me a picture of the showgirl bent over a chair with John having her from behind. They'd made sure his face could be seen. He wasn't so keen on shouting out about stopping casinos after that.

I'll give you another example; a story I heard from Dino. An MP, I forget his name, at the time was also very much against casinos, and the Mafia had a pickpocket put a packet of cocaine in his pocket just before he got on a plane from New York. When he landed he was pulled out of line and searched. When it come to it the customs found nothing. He must have taken his jacket off on the plane because the packet had fallen out but just think of the defence, 'I didn't know it was there'. How many times has that been heard? 'Oh yes, sir. Six months please'. Even if he didn't go inside he was ruined for those days.

You didn't often get London faces in the Colony but you did get American ones. That was where I met up again with Angelo Bruno, the head of the Philadelphia Mob and Meyer Lansky himself. You wouldn't think either of them was killers. Bruno was known as The Gentle Don and you'd never think he was head of an organisation like that. On the surface they're quiet, unassuming, polite. It's interesting how people like Bruno with no great education could make their way to the top. They're very nice fellows, very polite; if they've been given the OK they like to talk to you, feel you out for themselves. As for Lansky he must have heard of me through Abe Kosky and Dino and checked me out with people like the boxing promoter Jack Solomons. He phoned me up one day from his hotel, 'Come over and see me'.

People like Bruno weren't dangerous until you upset them, then you've picked the wrong person. In business they're totally different. They weren't dangerous if you didn't upset them. But if you do they switch off and you disappear. They may have been called criminals but they only shoot a man if he is a rat. If you double on them then you suffer the consequences. If you double with people of their calibre you've got to be an idiot. I've known people who've been invited to Las Vegas, all smiles and a good time and then they just haven't come back to London no more.

Dino told me one day that once Lansky asked Abe Kosky to do him a favour. There was someone of theirs over here in a bit of trouble and Kosky got the charges dropped. Angelo said how much and Kosky named a figure which they thought was over the top for what he'd done so he was invited over to Las Vegas. Wined and dined. Abe saw reason and it was all sorted out but Dino said if he hadn't listened his grave was already dug. I knew who I was dealing with. I played the game. I'd been tried and tested.

The first thing is someone has to OK you and then it's a question of talking 'What line of business are you in?' and so on. Do they think you'll stay stumm if the law gets to you. If they do and they like you, you're more or less invited into their circle.

I had a friend — British he was — who was called over to help out on a couple of occasions. One time one of their men had borrowed money and although he had it to repay he wouldn't. He thought he'd doubled them successfully but you can't. He was found dead in New Jersey. Why did they have someone over from England? Well that person would be a stranger and could get close. The man knew it was on and as a result was going to be careful about people he knew. They all had cast iron alibis for when it went off. They may get pulled in but they're in the clear. A job like that would be well into five figures and expenses.

The Mafia didnt mess around let me tell you. I remember I got a call from New York in 1983, they said "Bert go to the normal phone box and we will call you in 15 minutes." So off I go to the phone box, no questions asked, just like I had done on and off over the past 20 plus years. So the phone rings "Bert hows things in London?" Ok I said. "Listen Bert, we need some outside help with a job over here." In my stomach I knew what was coming next. "Bert would you like to take a job on with our mutual friend and get rid of Roy? He's becoming too much of a risk." They were talking about DeMeo. Now this was difficult because it was my turn to do them favour. The only problem was, no one wanted to take the job because Roy was a complete physcopath known for killing nearly 40 people. Besides that he was protected by his own crew, a crew of killers. It would be hard to get to DeMeo and I know a few high profile people who decided to stay away from the job.

This was a very difficult decision to make but on this occasion I had to decline aswell. The thing was you have to understand that I was approaching my mid 60s and I had young grandchildren that I wanted to watch grow into adults and hopefully help them in whatever they wanted to do with there lives. And as someone who has gambled all my life you don't always come out smelling of wine and roses. I can tell you that it was 50/50 as the wages for the job were life changing to some people, so that shows how big it was. In the end the job was handed to one of his own crew and the rest is history.

I always played with my own money at the Colony. I never shilled. And if I lost I lost, not like the story Frank Sidone told me of Frank Sinatra who used to go to the tables on his way to breakfast in a casino hotel and have a $100 chip on red or black. If he won he pocketed the money and if he lost he said put it on my account. He kept on doing this doubling up and after four or five mornings of loss the manager tumbled. He asked for the money and Sinatra gave him a clip. Everyone thought he was out of order and Angelo Bruno wouldn't talk to him for a long time. Passed a message telling him to fuck off. This was over the phone and so Sinatra went to the restaurant and went over to the table where Bruno was sitting. Angelo looks up and says, 'Who told you this is a bus stop?'

I always liked Frank Sinatra. Dino introduced me to him at the colony. I know people said he could be difficult to put it mildly, and of course he took liberties and fell out with Angelo Bruno but he was never anything but pleasant with me. What I liked was the way once he'd met you he knew your name, or at least he knew mine. It's a trick of course being able to remember names but so many people in show business act as though they've never seen you in their lives no matter how many times they've met you. With Frank Sinatra it as always 'Hello Bert, How are you doing.' That sort of thing. I was in Las Vegas one time when there was a knock on the bedroom door. I'd ordered room service but when I went to open it there was Angelo and Frank and Sammy Davis saying come backstage and see us after the show tonight. I don't know where Dino was. I thought that was a really nice gesture.

Another man I liked was Ed Pucci who was Frank Sinatra's bodyguard. Now he was enormous, giant of a man . Not many people remember the story of how Frank jnr got kidnapped and had to be ransomed.

It happened in 1963 when Frank jnr was 19. He was snatched out of room 417 at Harrah's, Lake Tahoe and Frank paid something like a quarter of a million dollars. The fellow who was the mastermind, Barry Keenan, was said to be legally insane and he and the other two fellows got those long American sentences like life plus 99 but they were soon released. There must be something in the insanity bit because Sinatra offered a million dollars and Keenan said he only wanted a quarter. There was a story that it was all a publicity stunt but I don't believe that for a moment.

After it was all over Frank sent him along to London out of harm's way and Ed came with him. There's a picture of me and Ed along with the Twins and Charlie at Al Burnett's Stork Club. You can see what a big man he was.

Of course some people in the club were rowdy and upset the other punters and had to be asked to leave. I walked in one night and it was 'Hello, Bert' as usual but there was also an unusual amount of noise coming from over on a dice table. Now there's often an amount of noise at a dice table with people calling encouragement, as opposed to roulette or blackjack where all you hear is the ball spinning or the cards going down, but this was excessive and people were telling me they were unhappy. There's this fellow calling out all the usual stuff, 'Baby needs new shoes' and rubbish like that. There's a lot of people at the table but all you could hear was him. Dino says will I have a word so I went over. Dino doesn't tell me who he is. He's a big man with a couple of buddies with him and a brass he's picked up, low cut dress; he actually rubs the dice on her tits for luck before he throws them. As you know dice pass in turn when the fellow craps out and I was betting 'out' meaning I didn't think he's get the first number he'd thrown before he threw a seven. Anyway he eventually loses; the dice pass to me and I pass them on. That's when he turns on me, 'Why don't you play? Have a bet.' Then just as suddenly he turns nice, 'What's your name, where you come from?' I tell him it's Bert and I'm Italian. 'Same as me,' he says and now he's taken a liking to me. 'We're going back to the Hilton for a party. Why don't you come along?' It's then Dino marked my card. 'Don't, go, Bert. Don't you know who it is? It's Roy DeMeo'. He was one of the Gambino's top executioners. He had his own crew. I don't know how many people he killed before he was done himself a few years later sometime in early 1983, but it was thought to be over a hundred.

He hung out in the Gemini Lounge in Flatlands, Brooklyn and the victim would be lured through the side door of the lounge and into the apartment in the back portion of the building. Usually it was DeMeo himself, with a silenced pistol in one hand and a towel in the other, who would shoot the man in the head and then wrap the towel round it to stop the blood.

Then another member, very often it was Chris Rosenberg before he was taken out in 1979, would stab the man in the heart to prevent more blood from pumping out. They'd take the body into the bathroom, take off his clothes and let the rest of the blood either drain out or congeal . After that Roy's crew would place the body onto plastic sheets and dismember it, cutting off the arms, legs and head. The bits would then be put into bags, placed in cardboard boxes and sent to the Fountain Avenue dump in Brooklyn, where so many tons of garbage were dropped each day that it would be nearly impossible for the bodies to be discovered. This was called the Gemini Method, after the lounge. At one time there was a plan by authorities to excavate sections of the dump to locate remains of victims. But then they had a touch of the seconds saying it was going to be too costly and anyway unlikely to turn up any real evidence.

It was DeMeo himself who did Rosenberg following a narcotics deal with a Cuban drug cartel that Rosenberg stole from. He killed him as restitution. The story is that Roy was killed at Patrick Testa's place in East Flatbush by Joseph Testa and Anthony Senter after a deal with Anthony Casso who was known as Gaspipe. Before that, I had met Roy again when I was in New York and he was nice as pie but I never went near the Gemini and it could have been nasty for me if he'd turned round against me in the Colony that night. This is what people like him are like. Totally unreliable. Give you money one minute and kill you the next for looking at them the wrong way, or what they thought was the wrong way. That's why they never become top, top men.

The Colony Club used to attract many high profile stars but I remember the once when I was in there with Dino, and I noticed this woman at the bar, real beautiful lady who could turn many a head. I said to Dino "who is that at the bar?" He turned to look at me and said "Well thats Giancana's girl isn't it!". I said "You what, the Giancana, as in Sam from Chicago?", he said "Yeah sure". Well, after that we got introduced to him and ended up on a table with him at the Colony Club having dinner. I met him twice there, and we used to have a general chat.

Like I said, we met loads of stars at the club. There was the American comedian Bob Hope, the legendary American actor Paul Newman, and even Warren Beatty who starred in Bonnie and Clyde, and later he went on to play Bugsy Siegel in the 1991 film Bugsy ended up paying the club a visit while he was over here. They were all at the Colony, but Sam stood out.

Sam was a courteous man; boss of the Chicago outfit but no side at all. Expected respect but he gave respect as well. He often used the name Sam Flood and what he did was share Judy with John F Kennedy and I'm not sure by the end she didn't prefer Sam. After the Colony Club Sam started to slide a bit. He'd been too high profile going out with women like the singer Phyllis McGuire; she was one of the McGuire sisters. He did a bit of time for refusing to give evidence at a Senate hearing and then he went to Mexico with his bodyguard but he got deported. More or less physically dumped over the Rio Grande. Then his bodyguard gets shot and finally someone does Sam. June 1975 it was He's just out of hospital cooking sausages and someone put a couple in him and then half a dozen more. Now that's making a statement . Looks like it was someone he knew. There's so many names put up. The fellow who was his driver Butch Blasi. Now he's one who could certainly have got in the place. Then's there's Ant Spilotro and Harry Aleman, who bribed a judge to get off a murder rap once. There's been so many suggestions why. Of course Harry and Butch and Spilotro are all dead now and I don't suppose I'll live long enough to find out who it was. Then there's why. Maybe it was because he wouldn't share his money properly. More likely it was because He'd been due to go before a committee investigating whether the CIA and the Mafia had been in bed together over the plot to kill Jack Kennedy and they weren't sure he remain staunch. People have said it was on the orders of Tony 'Batters' Accardo or Joey 'Doves' Aiuppa.

Now Batters was a fortunate man. The worst he spent in jail was one night. Fortunate, but he was a dangerous man as well . In 1978, when he was in Palm Springs , his River Forest home got turned over. A bit after afterwards, seven people were found strangled and with their throats cut. The law it was on Batters' orders. By the time he died he was well in his eighties and he was just about respectable. He's got legitimate businesses all over the place. Restaurants, travel agencies, hotels, you name it.

Joey Aiuppa got his name when he was done for transporting doves. Apparently out of season you could only have 24 doves at a time but when the FBI raided his car they found over 500 frozen ones. He got three months for it. I'll tell you another who got done for dealing in birds and that was the grass Vinnie Teresa. He claimed he was no 3 in the New England outfit and then he went and gave evidence against Meyer Lansky. It was the usual excuses - someone stole his money, wouldn't support his wife and threatened his children while he was away one time. I think he got five years in Seattle over smuggling birds into the States and then he picked up another ten for dealing in cocaine.

As for Joey Doves he got done for skimming in Las Vegas and he went down for 28 years. He only got out a year before he died in 1997. He was 89 just a few years younger than I am now. One of the other stories about Sam Giancana's death was that Aiuppa had Johnny Roselli do Sam over not sharing the profits from Mexican gambling. Now Johnny Roselli was another who ended up badly. He was found stuffed in a 55 gallon drum near Miami in August 1976. There were stories about skimming and here was also a story that he'd been the one who'd shot Kennedy from a storm drain in Dallas and maybe that was how he had to go. They never found out who did Johnny but I can say for certain on that occasion anyway it wasn't me.

Back in 1971 I also had the pleasure to meet Frank Costello. I actually met Frank in Madison Square Garden at the Frazier vs Ali fight and he was by far one of the smartest people I had ever met, even though he was into his early 80's and had retired from 'the life' long ago. I remember saying to him, if there is anything I can do for you, any favour you need London bound then you know where I am. Sadly, I found out that less than two years after the Frazier and Ali bout, Frank had passed away in February of 73

There was so many stories about the Krays and the Colony that I don't believe any of them. Stories that they wanted £300 a week protection but Dino thought they wanted £3000 and gave it to them. That they'd all settled on £1700 a week. If that had happened I'd have heard of it. Ronnie couldn't have kept his trap shut. He'd have been on to me on the blower within twenty-four hours. I don't believe they had any sort of pension from the Colony. Do you really think you can interfere with the Mafia? They may have had a one off payment at the start because it was easier rather than take them out but if they'd really been a regular nuisance the Mafia would have had someone over from America, boom and back on the next plane.

And as I got to know the Americans better they started using me. I was happy and it didn't clash with what Abe wanted me for.

The first time I went to America for the Italians it was just a delivery job. I had to take a packet and pick one up. Near the Zoo in Philadelphia was the handover. The man's already waiting when I get there and I'm early. We exchange the packets and I'm off. I never ask what's in the packet and I certainly don't look. Maybe there was nothing, just a test. If it was, the money would have meant nothing to them. In fact I think it was something they'd do quite often. Just test you out. What you don't do is ask questions. They'll tell you what they want you to know and nothing more. In fact my Great nephew Jimmy Andrews, he had a similar experience many years later the first time he was over there. Had to meet a man in Central Park. The fellow takes one look at him and says, 'I recognised you by your shoes. They gotta be English'. He could have said that about me. I was very proud of my shoes and I still am. I've got 30 pairs even at my age. Its funny because I see my Jimmy as a younger version of me and just like me he will take our secrets to the grave.

It hasn't been easy for my Jimmy though, he fell out with a lot of family and friends, and lost a lot of money through relapsing into gambling, including 3 lovely houses. At the 11th hour when all hope was lost his beautiful mother Kathy reached out to me, and that's when I intervened. You might laugh as I know I was getting into my mid 80's, but I was still the sharpest pair of scissors in the box. I started to get my Jimmy back on track with getting him a few jobs here and there, both in the UK and in the US, and everything was starting to shape out. He had even started to carry on writing his own book that he had been working on for quite a few years, about his own life.

Then all that hard work over 2 -3 years I had put in, got wiped out. Back in 2011 he was involved in a near-death car crash and after spending over 4 months in hospital and a further 3 months at home convalescing, he went he off the rails again. He hit the drinking and gambling yet again, and I'd had enough so I left him to it. But then at the beginning of 2015 I gave him one last chance to get his act together. I told him that if he let me down again we were finished. I said to my Jimmy, "you should stop drinking as its ruining your life, and all the good family, friends and relationships you have in it".

I don't think he realised how loved he was but he really upset so many good people who wanted to help him, but it all just fell on deaf ears. As far as I could see the booze and prescribed medication he was on was a lethal cocktail that he shouldnt have got involved in.

Anyway, that was then and this is now. He put his book on the back burner and got involved in this book about my life story. I'll tell you now, it really put the fire back in his belly, and i'm proud to say he has been off the booze since June 20th 2015.

At first a lot of the work was collecting money the mug punters lost on the junkets. Then Henry Shapiro and me would organise trips for punters here to go to the States. Then Tony Schneider took over with me. They'd go to Las Vegas, lose more than they had with them and got credit. Then once they were back here it was time to pay. Same in reverse when the Americans came here and lost, they had to pay back home. And then there was always stuff they wanted to buy to take home to their wives, a sort of penance for the brasses they'd hooked up with while they were here and the money they'd lost or even won. And of course most of them did pay but a lot of people who came on junkets lost more than they intended and decided when they got back home they needn't. They were rats welshing on their responsibilities, but you can't run a business where people run up credit and then welsh, can you? And sometimes I'd be asked to go to the States to do something similar that end.

I'd be given the address, go round and see them, knock on the door very politely and say, 'You know you owe the money, you know you've got to pay. Get on the phone to the people at the casino and work something out.' And that's what they'd do. Of course, sometimes they gave backwards and I had to go and see them again and let them know if they didn't honour their word they'd have to go to hospital. Often they'd have a shop or a house and if needs be they'd sign that over. Of course I got a cut of what they paid up.

And gradually I became their man in London. Would I look after someone when they came over? Bert's Italian you can trust him. Show him around. And it grew. People would ring me up and I'd go and meet them at the airport or the Hilton which was where they generally stayed. They'd have to give me the name of the man who recommended me and I'd check back of course.

I'd met Carlo Gambino, through Angelo at the Colony. Carlo was leader of the Commission and he must have taken a liking to me for he took me fishing a couple of times in upstate New York. I don't remember catching much. We should have used dynamite. I did a bit of work for the Family. That didn't come from him direct but he must have authorised the capos to use me,

Sometimes if they wanted to distance themselves from something or other it was a question of delivering packages. What people don't realise there was a fair bit of low level kidnapping and maybe the people who was paying the ransom didn't want the lower ranks to know they'd paid up or what they were doing. If you're not there you don't know just how accurate things are but take the kidnapping of Gambino's nephew, Manny. The people who done it had already got $150,000 for the safe return of Frankie Manzo, who was what they called a capo with the Lucchese family, but they wanted $350,000 for Manny to go home. His brother wouldn't or couldn't pay and offered $40,000 and Manny was found in a dump in New Jersey. That was one story. The other was they paid the ransom but he was killed accidentally. I heard the man who was top dog of the kidnappers, fellow called Jimmy McBratney, copped it at Snoopy's bar in Staten Island a year or so later. I think it was John Gotti who went into Snoopy's dressed up as a policeman and Jimmy was shot. He was probably lucky. I heard that a long and nasty death had been planned. I don't know what Jimmy and his mates had thought they was doing tangling with the Gambinos.

The Yardies here did the same thing. Don't try and kidnap the top man but niggle at him through getting someone a bit lower, one of the lieutenants. And of course it wasn't always between families. It could simply be a bit of bloodletting between members. Sometimes the people in the States would tell you what was in the package. It was depending how they were thinking and what they wanted to be let known. The top men were like chess players. What's the best move five or six moves down the line? But more often they wouldn't tell you and you certainly didn't open it to have a quick look. You reported back when you'd delivered and the fellow who took the package would as well. Just a bit like a personal bank transfer really.

Then one day I got a call from Philly. There was a Jewish fellow Dave in Brixton on a serious charge, could I do something about it? A man with tip top monetary connections. I went to see him, got him a top solicitor and he got bail. He had to report twice a day to Savile Row police station.

He had no chance of beating the charge and so it was a question of his getting out of the country. He wanted to go to Leeds and get a private plane. I said, 'Dave, that's not a good idea. Once you're in the sky you can be monitored. Train and boat are much better.'

I took him to an Italian barber and had his hair permed and dyed and then I went and saw people in Waterloo and got him a false passport. Next it was, would I go with him? I spent couple of days having a look at the passport controls. Now Dave spoke with an American accent and I'd got him a British passport. This was long before terrorism made things difficult and most of the time the officer didn't even look up to check. But he did every now and again. It was much easier if there were two of you. You didn't stand out and it give the man who was on his toes someone to talk to and look natural for the few seconds at passport control. I'm eating and apple and Dave has a sandwich. No one ever looked twice at him. As soon as we passed the fellow I said ,'You're home'. I went with him as far as Paris. It was just a question of holding his hand.

But as soon as we're in the compartment a porter brings our bags and Dave wants to give him twenty quid. And we're talking about thirty or more years ago. 'Give him a fiver top', I said. 'You're just drawing attention to yourself'. I stayed with him to Paris where he paid me off. We shook hands and I got the next train back.

If you were on bail for a long time the police didn't really worry too much about you missing a signing on. After a time very often you just had to wave at the copper in charge of the desk at the station and he noted you down. It was only if you missed four or five on the trot that they started to think. By that time Dave was long gone. While he was here he done me a great favour. He introduced me to an Iranian princess, well that's what she said she was.

Once he was home he rang me to thank me for my help and then he phoned a second time. He had a bit of business for me. I had to go to a travel agent and pick up a ticket for Switzerland. 'If we pull this off you'll never have to work again'.

I flew over to Geneva and went to meet him at this hotel on the lake. He's waiting in the lobby, gives me a hug, sits me down for one of those small cups of coffee and says, ' You see those people?' I have a look and there's two men sitting on a bench with the newspapers. 'They're with me. While you're here you mustn't talk to them or recognise them. What we're doing is waiting for a certain fellow to come over.' I realise he's done the early work for a snatch. I thought it would be a ransom job but from what Dave said the man wasn't going to go back to wherever he come from. He'd tell me nearer the time what was to happen. We waited about ten days but the man never came and I flew back home. I got paid for my time of course. I never knew exactly what it was all about and I did have to work again.

Funnily enough, I did hear of Dave again. About 18 months after I last heard from him, Tony Ferrante from Philly, phoned me up about nine one night. I didn't even know Dave knew that group. 'Why are you ringing me?' 'You gave him help. We think he's about to be pulled in and he's going to open up. What do you think?' You can't teach people to be staunch. They either are or they aren't. I thought he was 100 per cent, but I couldn't say if he was going to remain staunch. I'd have bet my life on Cherry and Billy Blythe but I couldn't vouch for Dave. I never heard any more and it wasn't for me to make inquiries.

It was through Dino and the others that I met the Irishman John Berkery who very early on did me a really big favour. Now John was a fellow with many interests. The police in America said he'd been head of the K & A gang, an Irish mob of housebreakers in Philly and that in 1959 he'd been involved big time in the burglary of a coal baron, Pottsville's John Rich, which netted around half a million dollars. They said the burglary had been set up by a nightclub hostess and both she and John went down but they won retrials. By that time one of the witnesses against him had been weighed down in concrete and chains and dropped in the sea and another had been shot. Nothing to do with John but the prosecution didn't bother to go ahead with the case. That was before I knew him. Years later he went down for 15 years when he was convicted of being involved in P-2-P which was a drug used in the manufacture of Crystal meth. He was on his toes for five years before they found him in Florida. A good bit of the time he'd been in Europe.

One day out of the blue I get a call at the Hatton Garden club from him, 'Hello, I'm a friend of Eddie' and he gives the man's second name. Now I know who Eddie is all right. He was a hitman for the Philadelphia Mob and I knew John was his friend. It was the usual thing, John had been given my number. 'He's one of us, say hello to him'. We went out together a few times and got on well. At one time he was managing a boxer who was on the Ali-Oscar Bonaventura bill but the fellow got talked into going with Ali's manager Angelo Dundee.

How the favour came about was that one day I was at the club when my friend Billy Jones brought a fellow in to see me. He had a case with him and when he opened it up there were two or three hundred American coins, all gold; they had an Indian in feathers on the face. And they certainly weren't straight. I took them down to George Meisl and he put a figure on them. He thought they were worth £9000 but the fellow wanted eleven and he wouldn't budge. I give him the coins back and off he goes with Billy. Half an hour later Billy's back on his own. He tells me he's set the fellow up for a meet with another buyer in a hotel in Bloomsbury. The fellow had a Mercedes and I got the keys to the boot. When the fellow comes for the meet Billy tells him to leave the coins in the car and go inside. I just waited till he'd gone, and then so were the coins. It was up to Billy to explain to the geezer he didn't know what had happened to them.

Now John's in London and when I meet him I show him the coins. For obvious reasons I didn't want to put them about here and he has a look and gives me a figure that he thinks they'd be worth in America. It was quite common for jewels and coins to go round the world in a matter of hours. I remember when Duke Delaney and the Australian Kangaroo gang did a jewellers in Zurich they had Little Stan Davies come over and take the diamonds to Montreal that night.

This time there wasn't the same urgency but if the coins are worth so much more in America the next thing, therefore, is for me to go over with them. I took a friend of mine Solly, a Hatton Garden jeweler, with me. I told him I'd make it worth his while. We had a stopover in Maine where you had to refuel in those days. We had to leave the plane and go through customs and Solly and I went into the little restaurant at the airport for tea and something to eat. We're called to re-embark and I walk back to the plane and then comes Solly but he hasn't got the briefcase. I'd left it with him and as he was coming out, the customs had got hold of it and kept it. The only thing Solly had was a receipt. After everything I'd lost the fucking lot.

Once we got to the hotel John was there and while I was unpacking I told him the story.

'Give me the receipt,' he says and he goes and makes a telephone call. He comes back and says, 'You can go down tomorrow morning and pick the case up. There'll be nothing to pay but give the man $100. That was the amount of clout he had. I did just that and sold the coins in Philly.

But it wasn't long before the press and the politicians in the UK turned against Angelo and Dino and the rest, saying it was Mafia front money coming to this country and one by one they got their marching orders. In early 1967 George Raft was the first and in fact his orders weren't marching, they were just not to come back. Next Angelo Bruno got banned and instead went to Nice where he had a flat. For a time there was some thought Dino could stay but then he was also told he had to go. The BBC had featured him in a 24 Hours programme about George Raft saying Dino was connected which of course he was. He wanted to sue them for libel but he finally went in March that year. He rang me up early in the morning the day he was going. Would I go with him to the station? 'Of course', I said. Photographers everywhere but I stayed in the background.

He ended up going to Rome to set up some gambling operations over there. One time I took Alex Steene and his lovely wife Anna on holiday over there, beautiful place is Italy. But, that wasn't the only time I went to Rome, I went to see Dino a few other times to see him about work and to check how things were going. Alex and Anna were none-the-wiser.

# 13 : PHILLY, PARIS AND FLORIDA

When I was in the States John Berkery used to take me round with him when he was doing business. I just went along for the ride not as muscle or anything. I remember one day we drive up to this half-finished hotel in Philadelphia, it was one of the chains, I don't know if I ever knew which. There were piles of carpets being laid, painters here and there, 40 people still digging up the grounds to lay the flowerbeds. Anyway John goes to see the manager and we sit in his office and have coffee and John asks what's happened to one of the kiosks in the hotel's shopping mall. 'That's still open for letting,' says the manager. 'I've a friend who'll be interested', says John and it was marked down for him straightaway. . I said to him later, 'You couldn't do that in England'. All he said was, 'Why not?' and explained the manager had to do business with the Mafia over there, otherwise it's trouble with the Unions. There can always be a fire somewhere, sprinklers turned on, flooding. John wouldn't do it but that's the fear.

One of the people John introduced me to while I was over there was 'The Major' or 'The Maje', a black guy from Little Harlem in Philly. Benjamin Coxson was his name. I don't know how you'd describe him – you name it, car thief, civil rights activist, drug dealer, entrepreneur, man about town. He tried once to run for Mayor of Camden, that's Philly not here. He looked a bit like Don King, the boxing promoter, but his hair didn't stand up like a wave of electricity had gone through it.

I'll tell you who he was great friends with and that's Muhammed Ali. There was a story Ali owned the house in Camden where the Major lived which he called the White House but I don't know if it's true. I do know from what I was told that when Ali couldn't get a fight over refusing to fight in Vietnam the Major spent a lot of time trying to arrange where he could box and eventually Ali fought Jerry Quarry in Atlantic City in August 1970. For a time he was certainly Ali's business partner.

One of his best deals – not with Ali this time – was buying a bar for $600 and then turning it into a really smart club before he sold it on to John Berkery's friend, the nightclub singer Lilian Reiss.

The Major was sort of the same rank as John but like John he reported to Angelo Bruno on behalf of the Black Mafia there. I'm with him one time and he says, 'Bert, I've always wanted to get a new Rolls Royce, could you arrange to have one shipped?' No great problem. I said to my son, 'D'you want a week in the States?' and he took it over and took it to Philly. I don't know if the Rolls is still going but the Major isn't. He was literally executed around June 1973. Four men broke into his house, tied him up and then lined up and shot him in the back of the head in a home invasion; him and his girlfriend and a couple of her children. Another boy was left tied up in another room but he escaped and sort of hopped down the street to a neighbour to give the alarm. The Major's girlfriend survived but her daughter Lita died. One story was he'd doubled someone over a drugs deal but I heard he'd been killed because he'd had a couple of other Black Mafia bosses shot a bit earlier.

I know that after the Major was shot Ali said his hands were clean which was a bit of an odd thing to say. I don't think anyone was convicted but a member of the Black Mafia, Ron Harvey, the fellow they thought had been one of the shooters, died when he was in prison over something else .

Harvey had been involved in a terrible brutal murder earlier that year. He and some of his crew broke into the Washington, D.C., townhouse of the Muslim basketball star Kareem Abdul-Jabbar, looking for one of Abdul-Jabbar's friends who was living there and who'd offended them. The friend, Hamaas Abdul Khaalis, was a leader of the Hanafi sect of Muslims in Washington, and he had said Elijah Muhammad, the leader of the Black Muslims, was a false prophet. Neither Abdul-Jabbar nor Abdul Khaalis were home that night, but the Black Muslims still went ahead and killed seven people, five of them kids.

A bit happier story, I was taken to a Mafia wedding once. All the men in tuxedos and envelopes handed to the bride, a lovely looking girl . There must have been six hundred there, all of us sitting out in the sunshine, all the men kissing each other. It was just like The Godfather. I was introduced to everyone around. 'Bert, this is Vinnie, he's in the numbers game. This is Tommy, he's my uncle; he's in the Teamsters'. Jimmy Hoffa was there, very pleasant and unassuming, but his trouble was he wouldn't move over, let someone else be top man for a bit.

I was with John another time when we and Georgie Meisl went over to dinner at the home of an Italian fellow. He owned a restaurant where we'd had a couple of meals and John had introduced me as a 'paisan of yours'. Next time we were in he says to John, 'I've told my wife, fetch Bert along'. It was a wonderful house, all marble and gold and around nine o'clock I hear a great whoosh outside. I look out and there's a swimming pool lit up in blue with a fountain at one end. I said, 'I don't mean to be rude but how much did the place cost?' And he said, 'Half a million dollars.' It would have been £5 million here at least. Him and George start talking about jewels and he tells us he's bought a diamond for his wife which she doesn't like. 'How much is it worth?' he asks. George whips out his glass and starts looking at the blackness which is how you value a diamond. 'Something in the region of $7-8,000 dollars.' 'What would you give me?' the man asks and then says, 'Give me $6,000.' Of course, it's come from a screwer.

Now the problem is coming back here. I've got it shoved down in my jacket pocket. Mary is coming to pick me up but it's then we're pulled by the Customs. Forty years ago there wasn't the security there is today and I can see Mary waiting with a friend. I say to the officer, 'My wife's here. If we're going to be long I'll go over and tell her to go home and I'll get a cab.' And that's just what I did. I palmed the diamond, put it in my mouth, give her a long kiss and she takes it. Twenty minutes later we've been searched and are on our way. I think they knew we'd been with the Mafia. I wondered if somehow there's a mark on our passports. But of course all it takes is a phone call while we're in the air.

Then another time John picked me up and said, 'You're going to meet a fellow who knew Al Capone'. The fellow now has a lobster restaurant and outside there's a stand, all shellfish, crabs, lobsters, scallops, the lot. John goes in to see the Governor and introduced me to a man called Mac who's doing the shelling. He's the one who knew Capone. ''Bert,' he said, 'what you read about Al you can disregard. He was a stand-up guy. A good guy. In the depression he put his own money out to run a soup kitchen and although people say it was just for publicity he'd help small guys who were down on their luck'. And he goes on to tell me how he and Al and a load of others are in a Turkish Bath in the depression when Al sees a stranger and calls him over. 'We all get talking and the fellow's English, comes from Liverpool. Al asks what the man does and he tells him he's making hooch. He'd got in trouble in with the law in England and had scarpered. Al says 'Well I can use you' because he's peddling hooch round Little Italy and he always needs a new supplier. Anyway he give him $100 and tells one of his men to go round the next morning to have a look at the hooch. When the man arrives there's no fellow and no hooch visible. Now Al's afraid someone's been slipped in on him so he has the man picked up and wants to give him a good slapping until the man tells him that his mother had given him her last £10 to get him out of England and with Al's money he's wired her $60. And he produced the receipt from Wells Fargo showing he's sent it to her. And so Al gives him another $60 and takes him on'. Al must have been a fellow like me. Got a lot of heart.

Of course, not every bit of business would go your way and there was no hard feelings if everyone had been square. Once I went over to Philly when Bruno was doing his contempt sentence. An Irish firm had done a diamond job and John Berkery wanted to know if I was interested in purchasing a parcel. I went over with George Miesl. The deal was in a hotel room and George had a look at them and put in a figure taking into consideration the risk we'd run to get the stones back to London. but there was a couple of other firms also looking them. One thing I do remember was that Frank Sindone was with us at the hotel and I remember as we all were walking down the corridor with the Irish he said to me so everyone can hear. 'Bert, if you're not happy with anything, let me know'. It was a quiet warning to the Irish not to try to mess me up. When it come to it one of other firms made a better offer. You put a price on things that you think you can make a profit on.

It was when I was at the Ali fight with Frazier that I met Frank Costello. John Berkery had invited me and Albert over and Matty Constantino and George Meisl were there as well. There was about ten of us in a restaurant and Frank Sindone, who's very friendly with me and was minding things while Bruno's away doing time for not answering questions at a Crime Commission, says, 'You don't want to see the prelims do you Bert?' Now, that's a statement not a question. I can't say, 'I do want to see some six rounder with a pair who couldn't knock their mothers over', can I?

I remember we drove up to a bar in Little Italy and Frank Sindone calls the bartender over and says to tell Frank I'm here. The bartender looks at him and says 'Frank who?' Sindone looks back and says, 'Costello. Don't fuck me about'. He expected the barman to stop what he was doing and get straight on the blower. The barman comes back and says, 'I've spoken to his wife but he's already left for the fights'. When we got back to the boxing we found we'd been moved to ringside on Frank Costello's say so. What a nice gesture that was. Afterwards we went back to his apartment. You wouldn't think that a man with that background would be interested in someone from London but you'd be wrong. They were always on the look-out for a new face that they think will be beneficial. So they can say to people going over, 'Your man in London is Bert Rossi'.

Costello was the man they called the Prime Minister. Of course that was towards the end of his life. He's survived an assassination attempt by Vincent Gigante, the one they called The Chin, and done the decent thing and refused to identify him. After that he'd retired from top spot. Vito Genovese had taken over but Frank was still regarded as The Man. We talked generally and about the boxing that night. It was an honour to meet him.

Not every bit of business would go your way and there was no hard feelings if everyone had been square. Once I went over to Philly when Bruno was doing his contempt sentence. An Irish firm had done a diamond job and John Berkery wanted to know if I was interested in purchasing a parcel. I went over with George Miesl. The deal was in a hotel room and George had a look at them and put in a figure taking into consideration the risk we'd run to get the stones back to London. but there was a couple of other firms also looking them. One thing I do remember was that Frank Sindone was with us at the hotel and I remember as we all were walking down the corridor with the Irish he said to me so everyone can hear. 'Bert, if you're not happy with anything, let me know'. It was a quiet warning to the Irish not to try to mess me up. When it come to it one of other firms made a better offer. You put a price on things that you think you can make a profit on.

There's been times when I'm sure someone has tried to set me up. I'd done business with a fellow Morris a couple of years earlier and I got a call using his name as a reference and asking me to meet some people at the London Hilton. He and I had made a bit of money and they said, 'We'd like to talk something over with you'.

I went up there and one of them was correctly dressed — it was in the days when people wore suits and ties — but the other who looked like a powerhouse was in jeans and an open neck shirt. Lots of gold. They were both Colombians. Joseph was the smart one and the other was Peter. I suppose it was really Pedro. They put it to me they wanted to operate in London and could supply as much cocaine as I wanted. I thought I was talking to proper people and I told them I could place it but it might take a couple of weeks. I came home and phoned some people in Manchester, Liverpool, Birmingham and so on and they said they'd take £100 or £150 K each so I came back to the Colombians and said, 'Yes, if the price is right'.

They were a funny pair really. They'd seen I smoked cigars and they gave me a box which was nice of them but they were constantly repeating, 'We're confident we can trust you' which seemed a bit odd. The next thing was how the exchange was going to work out. There had to be some tests and I didn't like the idea of three or four of my friends with attaché cases loaded with money sitting in the foyer of the Hilton or by the Peter Pan statue or somewhere. I thought about it and said, 'You keep saying you trust me so give me the gear and leave the rest to me. Let me run it my way, this is London. Give me five kilos'. But they wanted to do twenty at a time. I told them again that I could shift it all in one afternoon. 'Give me five. I'll be back with the money, then give me ten' and so on. I was the one running around. But so far as they were concerned it had to be done wholesale. I said I didn't feel that way. If it went wrong these people from the north would be nicked and it would be down to me. So we were at a stalemate.

It's funny how when you've got one bit of business going you've suddenly got two or three. If you're reliable your name gets passed around like a parcel and in the early 1960s John Berkery introduced me to an Iranian princess or something like that. Would I go and have tea with her in the flat she'd taken on the Embankment. I went along, suited and booted, and gave my name to the reception. Go on up to the 12th floor, top of the building. I must have pressed the wrong button because I got off at the 11th and when a woman answered the bell she told me she was the maid. They had the top two floors. I went on up and here was the Princess. Would I like a drink? I said I'd have tea. What sort of tea? Green Tea, Camomile? I'd never drunk Green Tea and I'd never even heard of Camomile. I said just ordinary thank you. It came in a glass with a metal holder. What could I do for her? She said she wanted a passport. Now, there's two sorts of passports. I could get her a forged one or I could get her a genuine one. I said, 'It'll cost £5000 for the forged or £7000 for the genuine', and she said she'd have the genuine. Off she goes to get the money and I'm looking at the tea spoon. I could see the marks. It's solid gold. Then I look at the glass holder and that's gold as well. So's hers. If I'd known that before I set a price it would have been double.

That bit of business went all right and I became her man in London. Would I get her this, could I do that? Then one day when the Colombians were around she rang me from Paris, would I come and do a job there.

She wanted another fellow from the Middle East done. The price was right. £100,000. It was nothing to me; I didn't know the fellow. But there were problems. I couldn't take a gun to Paris and I didn't know where to get one there. I didn't speak French and I couldn't start going into bars in Montmartre showing a piece of paper saying, 'Voulez-vous sell me a pistol?' to the barman, could I? It's not the sensible way of doing things. This was in the days when the Zemmour brothers were running things there. Jewish boys they were. And I'm working for an Arab.

I told Peter and Joseph I was going to be away a day or so and I had to go to Paris. Lo and behold, they've got an office in Paris so they'll see me there. I thought, 'That's all right then, they'll help me out'. I meet the two up in Montmartre near the music hall and I put what I needed to them and Peter turns and says, 'Is it political?' And that was when the second strike came up so to speak. Why had they insisted on dealing in everything in one go? And now that's not a remark from someone who's involved in crime. If they were who they said it would have been nothing to them to get me a gun. Next day I saw them again and they never mentioned a gun. No 'Here's what we've got for you', and I didn't mention it either. The only reason people have done business with me is because I'm a sensible fellow and I began to smell something. Now, there might be an explanation for that but why ask, 'Is it political?' That sent another alarm bell ringing. All through the day it kept on bouncing off me.

So, I thought, I'll do it another way. I had a knife with me and with it being summer the chances were the man wouldn't be wearing a coat; it would be just one quick thrust and out. He lived out near the racecourse in the park there and I'd had my card marked he was going to be alone. But when I got there a woman in an apron opens the door. That was it as far as I was concerned. I'd been clocked. I was out of things. I wasn't there to harm innocent bystanders. I just said, 'Pardon, wrong house' and walked to the nearest Metro.

I hadn't blanked the Colombians off but as far as I was concerned it was something to put on the back burner. Things come in threes. I don't know why but all of a sudden I get a call from Tony Ferrante, Would I come over as soon as possible? I was to go there and then after a bit to go down to Miami and see 'Little' Nicky Scarfo who was then working under Bruno and he'd been exiled. Now generally you dealt with the captains, the rally top men were kept isolated. I may have met them in the Colony but that didn't mean they was going to invite me to their homes. So, Mr Scarfo himself I thought I'd hit the jackpot. There was the Colombians, then there's been a bit of disappointment with the Paris business no that I hadn't had something of a fee, and now I was going to see a really high ranking Mafia man. I told Joseph I had to go to the States to New Jersey and he said well, we could continue talking over there.

I bought my own ticket to the States but it was refunded when I got there and I was comped all the way after that. When I was having dinner with Tony before I flew down to Miami I told him about Peter and Joseph and he told me not to mention them to Scarfo who was very much against drugs. I said, 'But that's where the money is surely, Blacks and Cubans and Colombians are in it, earning more than you people'. I knew him well enough by now to say things like that without causing offence. He just smiled and said, 'We don't touch it but they can't do business without our say so. We run the city. They may have to give us something every week but we're not involved'. Things have changed now, of course.

I got down to Miami and the hotel said Mr Scarfo was out on his boat talking to the writer Mario Puzo. He called me at my hotel when he got back. What he wanted was for me to arrange to place his machines in clubs and bars. What I didn't realize at the time was they weren't just one armed bandits they was electronic, early versions of these machines you see everywhere now. Anyway could I place 500? I said that was a lot. He said, 'Yes, but can you do it?' and I said I could try but they wouldn't all be in London. I could place a hundred there but I could certainly put some in clubs in Leeds and Manchester as well. He said he'd send someone over with the cash to get a warehouse together for the machines. Then he asked where I was going next and when I told him where he arranged for me to be put up at at the best hotel in town and told me to go to the VIP desk to check in . A suite is what he'd arranged for me. All comped. Then when Harrah's Trump Casino opened in Atlantic City in the '80s on one of the last trips I did I found he'd put me in Frank Sinatra's suite. The whole of one floor. The carpets and curtains were burnt-orange and blood-red and there was brass trimmings all over. It was spectacular but it wasn't very restful. I'm told it's all gone now.

People said he was dangerous. Cold hearted and psychotic are a couple of the words people used but I have to say I never had any trouble with him. There again I never crossed him nor did I ever have any intention of doing. Nor with any of them.

And then the Colombians got in touch again — Mary had told them where I was — and Tony Ferrante arranged for me to meet a man, another Italian he knew in New York. Tony vouched for him and when we met up he said he didn't want cocaine and he produced a little jar about the size of a cigarette packet full of dark liquid. It was difficult stuff to get hold of but if the Colombians could then he'd be in business. Within a couple of days Joseph found some and gave it to me. Now I was in business again as the go-between and I set up a meeting in New York. It's only an hour, an hour and a half, drive and Joseph and Peter collected me in a black stretch limo only this time it's driven by a giant of a man, a white fellow. 'Hello Bert; I'm Sam'. I sat in the front with him and he starts asking me questions. He's much more than just the driver. He's trying to lead me on to talk about things I didn't want to talk about and he mentions me wanting a gun in Paris. Now why would he do that? I asked myself. What had it to do with him? Then he goes on about how big my end will be when the deal goes through.

It could have been a bit like what happened with Charlie Kray years later but it didn't seem right to me. We were to meet the other man in the foyer of one of the hotels up by Central Park. I could see him at a table waiting and I said to the three of them I'd go and get him and bring him up. They sit at another table where they can see me and I go over to my man. He knows he can trust me. I've come through Tony Ferrante.

'OK Bert?'

'No. See that big fellow. I don't fancy him.'

'You feel uneasy?'

'I don't feel happy'

'Drop it out then. Don't worry'.

I went back to the others and said, 'He's just checked me off. He'd said, 'I expected you to come with one man not three'. Sam said he'll go and talk to the man. I said, ' Don't make it worse. As big as you are — meaning in the underworld not his size — they do business their way. Don't worry, Sam I'll get the deal back on'. But he wants to know, 'Why can't we do it now?'

I said, 'You can't dictate with these people'. Now they're getting anxious. 'When can we meet again?' It's when, when, when. Now I realise I've got to get myself out of this. It's a week before Christmas and they're all over me. 'Come and stay with us over Christmas'. I said no, I wanted to go home to the family. I kept going between them and my man and finally said it was on again and I'd be back the first of January. They saw they weren't getting anywhere and eventually they left it at that. That's how I got out of it. That was a collar. They had to have been the Drug Enforcement Agency or the FBI, one of the two, but they just pushed that bit too hard. They were just too eager and the more they pressed the more leery I became of the whole thing. I'm a sensible sort of fellow. That's why people do business with me. Poor old Charlie was just too greedy.

It was also while I was with John Berkery that I first met Frank Sindone and Tony Caponigro. At the time Angelo Bruno was doing thirty months for contempt when he refused to give evidence at a Crime Commission and Sindone was looking after things. At the time I'd never met Sindone and when John introduced me, 'This is a friend of ours from London', he was very reserved, friendly but wary of me. Next night John picks me up again from where I was staying in Cherry Hill and we go to the same place. This time there's Sindone in the car park waiting for us.

'Hello John, hello Bert', then he turns to me and says, 'There's a friend of yours inside Bert'. 'Of mine?' And who's there but Tony Ferrante? He's with a young girl he introduced as his niece. He gets hold of my hand and holds it and says to John, 'Hey John, me and Bert go back a long way. I should have been told he was here'. He's more or less telling John off so I jump in and say, 'Tony, John didn't know I was coming or even that I knew you'. All Tony says is, 'Next time I wants to know he's coming.'

It was while I was in Cherry Hill that a man Felix, who was with Tony, contacts me. 'Someone's coming to see you. He's a very important man and he wants to talk to you. You've got to be ready. 6.45.' I said of course I'd be there. He didn't give me the name and he makes it sound like Al Capone at least. Dead on the dot Felix rings, 'He's arrived, come down, he's here.' I go the bar which has the lights dimmed. There's three men at the bar, two of them minders. Felix says, 'This is Bert' and the third man, about ten years older than me, losing his hair, says 'I've heard about you. I've got a problem and want to ask you a couple of questions. It's really important.' All this is just having a look at me. Would I have dinner with him in New York the next evening. Felix would drive me. It was around eighty miles but that didn't mean anything to them.

That man was Tony Caponigro, known as 'Tony Bananas', not because he was mad but because his father had an import business. We went to a place in Little Italy and there he tells me that the Crime Commission is looking for him to give evidence. 'You know there's been a few killings and I don't want to answer questions'. He could talk to me. Angelo knew I could be trusted. What he wanted was to skip and come to England. Could I help? I told him he shouldn't stay in any of the big hotels where ex-Scotland Yard detectives were likely to be security. I said I could find him a house outside London, somewhere like Virginia Water or Egham. He could play a bit of golf and if he wanted a girl I could arrange that as well. I'd come out every day and drive him around. There was plenty of money on offer. Would I come and meet his lawyer tomorrow evening?

These men fascinate me. They've come from poor families and they control a city. I shouldn't have done it but just as he was about to dip his spoon in his soup, I asked him, 'Looking back on your life are there things you regret?' He thought for a second, put his spoon down and said, 'Naaw, Bert, naaw'.

Nothing came of it. Next evening I met the lawyer and he'd advised Tony that if he skipped and got a tumble, as a result he'd be looking at years while he reckoned he could get him just a few months. 'Makes sense,' said Tony.

It wasn't all that long afterwards that Angelo Bruno was shot behind the right ear in his car in March 1980. His driver John Stanfa was shot with him but he survived. Angelo was sitting outside his home. He'd had dinner in the Cous' Little Italy restaurant where I'd been taken once.

It was only a matter of a few months after that both Tony Caponigro and Frank Sindone are shot dead as well. Tony went first in the April. His body was found in the boot of a car in the South Bronx. He had really been done over. He'd been stripped naked and there were 14 bullet and knife wounds in him. His mouth and backside were stuffed with money, a sure sign he'd been killed because he was too greedy. A fellow Joe 'Mad Dog' Sullivan admitted on television he'd done it. Alfred Salerno, Tony's brother-in-law, was found around the same time. He'd been shot behind the ear and he'd also been beaten up before he died.

Frank didn't last much longer. At the end of October he was found shot in the head in a back alley in South Philadelphia. His body had been stuffed into two trash bags. From what I gathered he'd been pleading for his life before he went because his trouser knees were covered in muck. But it may have just been he was told to kneel before he was topped. All summer he must have known it was on top. It was probably because they'd defied the Mafia Commission and gone ahead with the killing of Angelo without permission. It didn't matter to me. I was already friendly with Nicky Scarfo and he continued to use me over here.

It wasn't all heavy lifting of course. Once Meyer Lansky got in touch with me through Dino about buying greyhounds for a track in Florida called Flagler Dog Track. Right before the Biddy Gold murder it was and a

**Right:**

Bert (Top Center) with "Big" Tony Boffa smoking a cigar with the rest of his Clerkenwell friends in the late 40's

© BERT RO... ...JSE... PRIO... ...RITTEN ...PERMISSION

**Left:**

Another of Bert (Top Center) with Clerkenwell friends in the late 40's

**Right:**

A signed photo of Jack Dempsey to Bert for taking care of him on both visits to London for the Ali v Cooper fights.

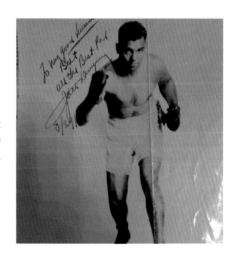

**Left:**

Bert (center) with friends Tony Schider (left) and Tony Ferrante of the Gambino Family. (right)

**Right:**

Bert (center) with life-long friend, Dennie Mancini, known as one of the best boxing corner men of his time. (right)

**Left:**

Bert (right) with dear family friend, Terry Haley

**Above:**

Bert's Nephew Jimmy, Enjoying
Christmas 2011, months before
suffering a near death car accident
in March 2012. Jimmy has recently
made a full recovery with the help and
support of Great Uncle Bert, Mother
Kathy and all his Family.

**Above:**

Bert and Family want everyone to
know Jimmy is back on track both
mentally and physically. Pictured above
with Uncle Bert March 2017 after an
interview at the Hilton Hotel with The
Sunday People

**Above:**

Garry Delaney, former commonwealth
light heavyweight champion amongst
other titles and one of Berts favourite
boxers of the 90's. Also a best mate of
Jimmy for over 30 years.

**Above:**

Terry Adams and his family have been
Clerkenwell neighbours and genuine
friends with Bert for many years.
Business man and art lover.

**Left:**

Bert enjoying a McDonalds lunch.
Even at 94 years old.

**Right:**

A signed, framed portrait Ronnie Kray
gave to Bert in 1991 called
"Down but not out"

**Left:**

Home from home, Bert still enjoys a
bet on the racing.

**Above:**

All dressed up and ready to hit London on his 93rd Birthday.

**Above:**

Bert enjoying a cold drink outside the York pub in Islington.

**Above:**

Bert at the Hilton Hotel in Islington after the interview with Tom Pettifor, Chief Crime Editor for the Mirror newspaper

**Above:**

Bert with his portait and acclaimed artist Charles De Felde

Bert

Michael Mansfield

Boris Johnson

**Left:**

Berts home where he rubs shoulders with the likes of Foreign Secretary Boris Johnson and top QC Michael Mansfield

**Left:**

Berts neighbour Michael Mansfield QC (left) at his own book signing with his friend Mohammed Al Fayed.

**Right:**

Boris Johnson, Foreign Secretary and next-door neighbour to Bert.

**Left:**

Donald Trump and wife Ivana with Don king at the Trump Castle Casino and Hotel for the boxing in 1985

**Above:**

Bert, Nice and warm at his home in London

**Above:**

Relaxing and having lunch in London

**Above:**

Bert with BOMP documentary maker Simon.

**Above:**

Bert proudly displaying his book.

couple of years before poor Dino died. And it was another thing which stood me in good stead. For some reason the owner of the track had been having trouble getting dogs and he needed thirty or forty. They run eight in a race and of course it's much more dangerous for the dogs which keep getting knocked over and so they're always wanting fresh meat so to speak. Now I didn't know one end of a greyhound from the other. I knew, of course, how to stop them but I didn't know which ones would be good chasers. And forty dogs is a lot in one haul. I had £100,000 deposited in an Irish bank from Santo Trafficante over in Florida. Santo was one of the old-school Mafia bosses who operated in Florida and Cuba. It showed me how much Trafficante trusted me to put that kind of money in the bank, so off I went to see a trainer at Wimbledon. Ireland is the place to buy puppies so the next week he and I go to Dublin for greyhound sales and we stay at the Gresham. Now at greyhound sales you see them trial in pairs, see they really will follow the hare and won't fight each other on the bend and then they're put up for sale. Through the trainer and his agent I buy half a dozen or more dogs but when I go back to the hotel the trainer opens his room door and says, 'We've got trouble, Bert'.

He and the agent have had a visit from the IRA who've somehow found out I've been buying for these people in Florida and it turns out they've had a quarrel with them. It's got to stop. I can keep the dogs I've bought but he can't buy any more for me. I try to say that with the people behind me there won't be any problems but the agent is in a panic. He points out we're not in Florida now. 'You don't know Bert, they can burn my farm down, just like that'. So now I'm on my own.

Next day I went to the track again and watched the dogs. There was a fellow there I'd seen the previous day and he said he thought I'd bought a few good animals. He seemed a nice fellow and I could see he wasn't Irish. We chatted a bit more and it turned out he came from Manchester and he bought a few dogs, got them up to racing standard and then either sold them on or raced them himself. Would he like to do a bit of buying for me? I made a few phone calls and the end was that I gave him cash there and then and dropped out of the picture. But he bought the dogs and arranged for them to be shipped over to Florida. The funny thing is I kept the bank note wrappers at home in my wardrobe and the coppers found them when they was looking at me for the Biddy Gold murder. That was part of their case. And they brought the Manchester man down to give evidence against me. Didn't do them any good.

# 14 : BOXING

I've got this lovely picture. Angelo Bruno give it to me. They're all Italian world champions and they've all signed it. One of the things I did for the Mafia was look after their boxers and ex-boxers when they came over here either to box or to do promotions. I must have had over a dozen world champions through my hands. I'd collect them from the airport, drive them around, go and watch their training sessions. That's how I knew whether they was up for it or just there for the pay day and how to bet. There wasn't mean to be betting on the boxing at the arenas– a big notice up at the Albert Hall and Harringay, 'No betting' but there was and of course there was plenty in the shops and on the corners.

Tony Mella got very excited when he hears Rocky Marciano is over and I know him. 'Do you think he'd come and have Sunday lunch with my parents, Bert?' he asks me. I put it to the Rock and he says that would be fine but then he gets in touch and says Lord Forte's asked him to lunch. What should he do? I said he's have to go with Forte 'He's got hotels over the world, you'll get comped every time'. I tell Tony and he doesn't take it well and in a way I can't blame Tony for being upset. 'But he promised'. He thinks its something to do with Rocky's PR man than when he decided to go up and have a straightener. 'I'll go down', he says. If he sorts out the PR man then he's bound to have to face up to the Rock and he thinks he can take him. Where? In the foyer of the Hilton or in Trader Vics? So it takes me to smooth things out. What I do arrange is for him to have his photo taken with Rocky and he's really pleased about that. Tony was a mangler of words. One day were having lunch in Peter Marios and discussing boxing and he says of one fighter he's 'dismatched'. I think he meant he was completely gone.

I'd take the boxers to Tolaini's Latin Quarter in Wardour Street and very often they'd see a hostess they fancied. Now some of the girls just did their shift there and went home to their husbands but others were on the game and you'd make inquiries. If the girl was a brass then she'd be over the moon to be seen out with a top class fighter. Anyway Rocky fancies this girl and I go and see the manager. 'Does she play?' And he said she did.

Next morning Rocky's not at the Hilton and I go round to Hampstead and they're still in bed. While he was getting dressed I had a word with her. 'He wants me for the week,' she says.' I said Well, I'm not paying. I give her £25 for the night. My treat and that was all I was forking out.

What luck for the girl to be seen with Rocky. Chance of a lifetime. Might not have been good for his training. In the days when he was in the ring Sex wasn't meant to be good just before a fight. The boxing manager and trainer Denny Mancini told me that in the old days trainers put rubber bands round their fighters' cocks at night so that if they got an erection and were going to have a wet dream the bands would tighten as their cocks grew and the pain would wake them up.

That was the stay when I was driving Rocky back to the flat in Hampstead of the brass.. It's late at night, the roads are clear and he pushing me to get on with it. I stopped at a red light down near Kings Cross and I must have sat there six minutes or more. I think they're broken and there's no traffic so I go across. All of a sudden the coppers are on me out of nowhere come the coppers. I went through the usual spiel about how sorry I was but then one of the coppers looks in and sees its Rocky in the passenger seat. 'Is that Mr Marciano?" Autographs all round and the red light's forgotten.

1966 it was when Floyd Patterson come over to fight with Henry Cooper. I remember walking down Shaftesbury Avenue with Henry, Bert Marsh and Jim Wicks and Bert was talking to Wicks more or less telling him what to say. Anyway Wicks leaves us and we all stand around on the pavement. Then he comes out and shakes his head and says 'No, they don't want to know. That's it' Cooper just shrugged his shoulders and said 'If that's it, that's it'. I know Henry always tried to win but some fighters have no control. If they don' t do what their managers say then there's no fight next time. I know Henry got knocked out in four that fight. At the Wembley Empire Pool it was.

Then there was Jack Dempsey, he came over to London a few times. I remember 2 occasions when he came across with Muhammad Ali and Angelo Dundee to fight Henry Cooper. You will see a lovely personalised signed photo of him on this page, that he signed to me as a thank you for looking after him while he was over here.

From time to time Albert's name surfaced over the years. Through no fault of Terry Downes his fight with Paul Pender left a sour taste in a number of mouths. July 1961it was. Now Pender was a tough Brookline firefighter who'd defeated Sugar Ray when he was on the way down; and beat him again in a rematch Six months earlier Downes had been stopped in seven but this time Pender stayed on his tool at the beginning of the 10th round. The contest had not been a hard one. There were slight cuts to both men and Pender had taken the 9th round. Pender's trainer Al Lacey said his eye was too bad to continue. Ike Powell the referee did not look at the eye but called Downes to the centre of the ring as the winner. Later Lacey said that Pender had had a series of injections for flu and was not fit to continue.

Albert lost a good bit of money backing Pender. The Boston promoter Sam Silverman was beaten up on 12 July as he left a night club off Piccadilly. He had been with his friend, Elliot Price, a big time gambler, after Downes beat Pender. The next morning at the Carlton Towers Hotel, Silverman's face was said to be more bruised than Pender's and the promoter had bruises on his ankles. The boxing writer Frank Butler said Silverman recognised Albert but wouldn't name him. Very sensible if he's right.

I could mix with straight people and they could mix with me. One of the men I was closest to was Denny Mancini, one of the straightest I ever met. His real name was Antonio but he was always known as Dennie. His uncle Alf Mancini who had a twenty round draw with Len Harvey, fought punishing fights in the 1920s. Look up his record on line. He had 148 fights in all and won most of them. Fifteen rounds on Monday and another 15 on Wednesday. Have a rest for a week and it was another fifteen followed by a twenty. No wonder so many old pros had brain damage.

Dennie damaged his hands as an amateur and never went in the ring as a pro but he was a wonderful cuts man trainer and manager. People said having him in their corner was worth a round start to them.

I remember he had a man boxing for a European title in Monte Carlo and said did I want to come along. He books us into a hotel and the first person I see is Nipper Read, who'd done the Krays. He's out there as representative of the British Boxing Board of Control. I can see he thinks he knows me but he's not sure who I am. At the time I've got two passports and I'm under the name Deforza. I told Dennie that was what he had to call me. Anyway the next morning at breakfast there's a photographer taking pictures of everyone and he takes one of me sitting chatting to Nipper. I told Dennie he must get a copy for me.

What I'd wanted it for was to put on my mantelpiece at home. I was getting regular spins and I thought if I had it on show a copper would come in and see me with Nipper and even though he'd retired it might make them think twice and that I had an in. But Dennie was smart. He never did get me the photo. He wasn't going to set Nipper up even accidentally.

It was the same another time. A fellow in Paris owed me £17000 and suddenly Dennie rang me saying he was there negotiating a fight. I couldn't believe my luck. It would save me a trip and the fares. I asked him to go and pick up the envelope for me but he wouldn't. He wouldn't get involved. But it didn't spoil our friendship.

You like some people better than you like others and it was the same with the boxers who come over. One man I did like was 'Jersey' Joe Walcott.

We used to have dinner together and one day told me the story of how he became world champion. He'd been a pretty decent boxer but he was never getting near another title fight. He'd been knocked out by Joe Louis 'I had a family to keep and I'd had enough of getting fit and then being told I wasn't on the bill' so I started work on the docks' is what he told me. He was always on the undercard even though at one time he'd had 12 straight wins. It was while he was doing a shift that a group of mafia guys saw him without his shirt on and called him over and one of them said 'Aren't you Jersey Joe Walcott? What are you doing here?' That's when he told them why he was fed up with boxing. The mafia man was actually Colombo Crime Family mobster Crazy Joe Gallo, and he said,, 'Finish here and get back in proper training and I'll get you the fights.' And sure enough he loses on points to Ezzard Charles and then knocks him out in seven for the title. He eventually got knocked out twice by Rocky Marciano but so did everyone.

He became a referee after that but in 1965, he was given the world heavyweight championship rematch between Muhammad Ali and Sonny Liston, who was in the Mob's pocket. Ali knocked Liston down and then Walcott lost the count as he tried to get him back to a neutral corner. When Walcott looked outside the ring to try and get the count back on track, Liston got up and him and Ali went at each other before Walcott had told them to restart. Then Joe suddenly stopped the fight in Ali's favour,stopped the fight. Walcott was never again appointed as a referee and he took up wrestling for a bit and then went into politics. He was the referee in the first fight Joe Louis had as a wrestler when with Jersey's Joe's help he knocked out Cowboy Rocky Lee. There's a bit of it on You Tube and you can see who's doing the work. After that Joe went into local politics.

He told me that every Friday he and his sisters who were nurses went round to his father's for dinner. His old man was a Pastor and said grace before dinner. Think of that. What a family, saying prayers before they fucking ate.

I never met Jake LaMotta over here but I did when I was in New York. I was in the same loft with him in an empty building the Mafia used for meetings and nothing else. Jake always spoke out against the Mafia but I reckon that was because he was always in debt to them through his gambling.

I looked after the great boxer Willie Pep a few when he came to

London. Even though Willie was in a plane crash that near killed him he ended up making a full recovery and went on to defend his featherweight title yet again. He also loved to have a bet so we would always go to my favourite casino, the Victoria on the Edgeware Road. Willie was a lovely guy but what an unlucky gambler. One day he asked if I would take him horse racing which I did.

We went to Epsom Downs and I was so happy because he won roughly £1400 which was a lot of money in the early 1970's.

Anyway Willie was on a high now after that scoop on the horses, and I don't know why but I could feel it coming when he turned around and said to me "Bert do you think we could go to the dogs tonight?" but it would have been too much of a rush so I said we could go the following evening, which we did.

We went to the Wembley dogs night, and I"ll tell you what my heart sank for him when everything that he won at Epsom he lost at Wembley.

So at the end of the night and on the way back to the Hilton where he was staying, I asked if he was disheartened at the loss, and he just said "Bert thats gambling fro you, and its just like boxing - you win some and you lose some".

I thought to myself what a good way to analyse it. Imagine if Willie won at the horses and at the casino as much as he did in his boxing career, he would have certainly ended up a very wealthy man. His boxing record was one of the best of all time as well, with 229 wins, only 11 losses and just the 1 draw. Willie Pep was one of the best boxers of all time, no doubt about it in my eyes.

Willie used to go to the track with Jake LaMotta as well, and one-time when Willie was going to be late he gave Jake money to put on a horse. When he arrived he saw the horse had won and when he met up with Jake he asked for his money. 'I'm sorry,' said Jake, 'I forgot to put it on'. Willie said he'd never spoken to him again. He reckoned Jake had just kept the winnings and given him his stake money back.

The mafia weren't too keen when Jake La Motta's daughter

Stephanie fell in love with John Conteh. He was married at the time — you know how strict those old Mafiosi can act if they want to be — and I was asked to have a quiet word with him. Poor girl , she was a model and she got multiple sclerosis at a very early age but she's still fighting it.

When Ali came over with his manager Angelo Dundee I made sure everything was sorted for them and they were all well looked after during their time in London. I did it more for Angelo and his brother than I did for Ali if I'm honest with you. It's almost sacrilege to say so but I thought Ali was flash and I'm not convinced he won that fight against Ken Norton.

Tony Graziano once asked me why I didn't set up as an agent, open an office and they could go through me. I turned it down. I didn't want to sit in an office the whole time.

A fellow I tried to help was Vinnie di Carlo. He'd been half way decent fighter but now he was a punch drunk from Philly without a couple of bob. His manager made him stop fighting. 'Bert', he said, 'I just had to pull him out'. What had happened was I got a call from Naples —Italy not Florida. All that year there'd been a load of kidnappings and the people over there were sitting on three or four million in ransom money but it's one thing to have dirty money and another getting it cleaned. Did I want to buy any or know who would? Probably it would cost a bit under half the face value. So I had Vinnie go over as a minder while I thought about things and shopped around to see who would. He's in Italy about three weeks and I get another call. He's had a heart attack and dropped down dead. His wife Mary rang me and of course she wanted to get him back home. Now I was extended at the time in the casinos and although it broke my heart I had to tell her I was borassic. A few weeks later I had a touch and sent her five grand but I wish I could have done it at the time.

# 15. MURDERS

As I said at the start, that reporter from a television company once said he thought I'd killed as many as eleven people both here and in the States. Bastard. Be that as it may, of course I've known a lot of people who've either been killed or been done for killing them but I've only ever been charged with one murder. The law's been round more than once or twice though.

I did work for Scarfo, Gambino and Bruno in the States and here and it wasn't filling skips with sandbags but I'm not going to say exactly what it was or where. Do you think I'm fucking mad? When they wanted something, I'd get a phone call, 'Can you come over tomorrow?' I'd get my ticket, let them know when I was arriving and I'd be picked up at the airport and there'd be a hotel room booked. Maybe they'd take me out to dinner that night but of course seven p.m. would be midnight to me so depending on things I might just have something light in the hotel. Next morning someone would pick me up and drive me wherever and then point out the subject. It might be the day after that I'd get a call. 'Nice bit of work'. I'd be picked up, given an envelope and driven to the airport. 'Maybe see you again soon', and I'd be home for breakfast. I'd travel in the back. There was too few in Business in those days. Your face would be remembered. That's the last thing you want.

It's no use thinking, 'Oh it's all so long ago no one's interested. Wrong'. What is it they say, 'There's no statute of limitations on murder'. Just after the war there was a brass was shot in Carnaby Street. It was pretty seedy then well before it become the street of Swinging London. 1946 and

I think it was November, a girl called Margaret Cook, well that was one of her names, a dark-haired girl who called herself an Exotic Dancer in a club called the Blue Lagoon which meant she took her clothes off.

She was shot by either a punter or a boyfriend who just disappeared into the crowds round Oxford Circus. Murders cause trouble for us. The coppers swarm around the place, pushing into clubs and pulling people, in questioning them and they expect answers. They know they won't get answers of say a breaking but they expect them in a murder. It disrupts things. Anyway they got nowhere. Apart from saying they thought the killer come from Scotland it all died down until last year when a fellow who's 91 walks into a police station in Canada and says he's done it. He's got cancer and killing the brass is on his conscience. The last I hear the DPP was trying to extradite him here. Shows you can't be too careful.

A killing that shocked the Hill was the one the papers called the Holy Lady murder. The Holy Lady was Anne O'Connell who lived near St Peter's and kept a shop at Victoria Buildings in the Clerkenwell Road selling religious stuff like rosaries and scapulars, that sort of thing.

She was battered to death in the early evening one day in October 1962 and it wasn't a successful robbery because she always wore a money belt stitched in her skirt and it had over £600 in it when she was found. Whoever did it cleared only a few quid from the till. She'd probably been killed about 7. 30 that evening because the prosecution thought the tolling of the church bell for Mass had drowned any noise there was.

What was even worse was the boy they done for it was Robert Reed, the son of my old mate who I was convicted with back in the war years. And it was a topping offence. Whoever killed her wasn't going to get any sympathy from the Home Secretary. There was a fingerprint of his on a newspaper and another bit of paper in the shop. Robert had just got married and he said he'd been there earlier to buy a St Christopher medal for his baby. He was picked out on an ID by a fellow who'd been at school with him as having been near the shop but he said it was nothing to do with him and he'd plenty of money so there was no need for him to rob anyone let alone her. He had that brilliant brief Victor Durand defend him and after two juries disagreed the prosecution offered no evidence the third time around. A funny thing was that while he was in Brixton he was with Harvey Holford who was charged with shooting his wife in Brighton. Harvey's defence was that he was involved with Albert and Billy Hill over gaming machines and he had a gun because it had all gone wrong and he was afraid of them. While they were on remand Robert had given Holford a religious medal for luck and it must have done the trick because he got a not guilty as well.

Funnily the police never came near me over the death of Ernie Isaacs, a man who I'd had a row with a few days earlier. That was on a Friday night and within the week he goes home one night and is found the next morning shot dead in his basement. He was a flash bastard from around the Angel, a cunt like Jack Buggy. Isaacs was another unpleasant man — putter up, receiver, wife beater you name it. He did a bit of street trading and he called himself a Prisoners' Welfare Officer which meant he touched people for money for those in the nick but how much got to them or their families I don't know. He was the sort of man who would hold a grudge for ever. He always had a mouth on him and a lot to say for himself. I was having a drink and talking with Bobby Warren in a pub when Isaacs comes over and starts making funny remarks, so it's 'Bosh'. I put him on the floor where he belonged. I put him in his place .

The night he died he had been dropped off at his home by another friend of mine the old time Alfie Allpress, father of Danny, the driver in Bertie Smalls' team of robbers in the 1960s. The killer fired five times, hitting Isaacs with four of them. The fifth shot hit the skirting board. He was probably killed with one of his own guns, a Webley or Enfield service rifle, which the killer knew would be in the flat. I know a .38 revolver of the type which fired the bullets was missing and a .9mm Luger was found wrapped in a piece of cloth in the piano. His body was found by his live-in girlfriend when she woke at around 5 a.m. She told the police she had heard nothing unusual during the night.

There was no question of robbery. Isaacs had £215 in cash and £200 in bonds on him when he was topped. There was, however, a lot of names in the frame. Isaacs was a violent man and a lot of people loathed him.

Isaacs had been a friend of George Cornell and when George was shot he made no secret of the fact he believed the Krays had done it. But there was plenty of people who would have been happy to help him go. He'd pulled off a robbery at an Arab bank in Moorgate a few weeks earlier and there were stories he hadn't accounted properly. The law decided that they had no proper evidence against the people they really fancied and in any event Isaacs was so hated generally any number of people could have killed him. The word in the underworld was that Reggie Kray had pulled the trigger but there was no against him at all and I can't believe he'd have done it personally. I'd have been at the bottom end of the queue for that one.

Years later a fellow called Anthony Patrick Austin confessed, saying the Krays had paid him £500 and he had thrown the Luger pistol he said he had used in the nearby canal. But it turned out he had been in prison at the time of the killing. He'd also been sent to Rampton secure hospital. And that was the end of that.

One of the ones the police here have been to see me about was the death of Solomon Lever, the ex-mayor of Hackney. If there was ever jewellery or a safe involved I was one of the first people to be seen. His wasn't really a murder. He had a heart attack when someone snatched him on his own doorstep.

That was a funny case altogether. He was the secretary of some Friendly Society. Apparently it was one of those things like a Christmas Club. You paid in money each week and when it came to it you could borrow. He was home one Saturday night in July 1959 when around 1 a.m. he got a call to say there was a fire in an office next to one he looked after in Sylvester Path just behind the Hackney Empire. He's got to go down.

Next thing is a man who says he's a copper turns up at the door — Lever's wife said he was tall and dark so it can't have been me. The Levers didn't ask for any ID and whoever it was took him to the offices, had him open the safe and nicked over £7000. A couple of hours later his body was found in Epping Forest. A passer-by thought he's been the victim of a hit and run. At some time he'd been gagged and his wrists had been bound and so that was quickly ruled out. He'd had a bad heart and I suppose the strain of it all was too much. I don't suppose whoever it was intended to kill him, he just passed out on them. Anyway the jury at the Coroner's Court said it was a case of manslaughter, but no one was ever charged. If he hadn't died you'd say it was a clever snatch.

The way the Train Robbers spent money was one of the reasons they were caught and was also one of the reasons that Scotch Jack Buggy got killed. He was a Scotsman but his family went to Nebraska when he was a kid before they came back to Motherwell and he came south. He was a minder and a robber as well. A horrible man who thought he could do what he liked. I'll give you an example. He was a good snooker player but when he was playing he'd put the stake money in one of the pockets and if he didn't like the way the game was going he's pick it up and walk out. No one dared stop him. Buggy thought he could just come to London and be someone. Instead he was carried out in a carpet.

He was a thieves' ponce as well. Just like the Twins . He fancied he could get to The Ulsterman who was said to have set up the Train Robbery and Brian Field who did some bird of it who was the only way he could get in touch. It seems that Field was ambushed upon his release from prison by Buggy , who gave him a good kicking with an eye on getting some of the loot from the robbery. Field subsequently went to ground.

Buggy did nine years for shooting a fellow outside a club in Piccadilly. What had happened was he had a friend who was having a party and Buggy, who'd been on the river, thought Shirley Bassey who was singing at the club might like to come along and sing at it. He tried to get in her dressing room and when he was barred he hung around the club until an electrician tried to clear him out. Buggy wasn't having none of it and a couple of waiters tried to throw him out. There was an all-in wrestler there worked under the name of Al Reeder and when he was egging the waiters , Buggy hit him with a plate and Reeder said, 'Outside'. Buggy said 'It's going to be with tools you know'. Reeder told him he wouldn't need tools but what he didn't realise was that Buggy had a gun with him. Of course, the moment they're outside Reeder knocks him down so Buggy shows him the meaning of the word tool and shoots him. Fortunately the bullet just went straight through him. Buggy was picked up three weeks later in a caff down the East End. He went to the Court of Appeal but they threw it out.

He doesn't learn his lesson. Six months after he came out of prison he turned up in the sea off Newhaven shot in the head and bound up with wire. What he'd done this time was try to lean on Franny Daniels who'd been on the Airport Robbery which went so badly wrong and who was running the Mayfair Bridge club just off Grosvenor Square. Guess who owned the club? It was Sammy Lederman and Eddie Fletcher who'd been at the Palm Beach when Babe Mancini stabbed Hubby Distleman. The Mount Street was also known as Lederman's and bridge was about the only game they didn't play there. Mostly it was kalooki.

There were big games at the Mount Street Club and I used to play in them. They could run into thousands on the table. It was well worth leaning on. Eddie was a soft touch when he had the club. A man who used to come round late in the evening was Lucian Freud trying to raise a few quid selling him his pictures. It might be as late as half past one in the morning he'd appear and Eddie would give him £25 or £30 for them. I remember Eddie telling him once, 'But you were here Tuesday' just like you'd say to these people who come round with a bag of dusters and boot polish and expect you to buy them. I think he felt sorry for the man. I had a look at them and I though they were rubbish, which shows how much I know. I don't know what Eddie did with them.

Anyway Eddie and Sam invited Franny Daniels to join them. Franny's nephew Waggy Whitnell also worked in the club along with Abe Lewis who was more or less the gopher.

Roy James, who was on the Train, bought himself a new Jaguar E type. He used to come to the Hatton Garden club I was running and after he was nicked I wanted to see if I could give him any help. Waggy comes over one day driving this Jaguar. I said to him, 'Whose is it?' I knew he couldn't afford one in those days. At first he says 'mine' and then when I give him a look he says, 'Actually it was Roy James. He give it to me'. That was when Buggy started to think there was some money about and began to go to the Mount Street Club to start to lean on Franny.

Shortly after Buggy floated into view one Derby Day, I got a pull. It was routine really. Round up the usual suspects. They were quite polite this time. After they'd searched the house Mary made them a cup of tea. Why were they coming to see me I wanted to know. 'Your name's in his phone book'. 'Whoever did him, done London a favour. He deserves a pat on the back', I told the police. 'What surprises me is that you're worrying who done it. Do you believe even if I did know I'd tell you'.

Years later an Australian conman Donald Wardle told the police it had been Franny and Abe Lewis and they went on trial at the Old Bailey but the case never really got off the ground. The Aussie was doing nine years and wanted out of it. I'm pleased to say Franny and Abe both got Not Guilties. I know some coppers went to Vienna to see Waggy Whitnell, and at one time they was looking to bring him back from France, but they never did.

Then I got questioned over the death of the bookmaker Harry Barham who'd been buying jewellery in Hatton Garden just before he was kidnapped in Holborn and shot. February 1972 it was. That TV reporter said I'd done it but he was wrong. Harry was due up at the Bailey over a VAT or a tax fraud and it was reckoned if he could pay off the money he owed he might stay out. He was buying small stuff and turning it round as quick as possible. It was said he'd managed to put £40,000 together in 24 hours. In the afternoon he went to a greasy spoon called Lesley's café in Red Lion Street near where he had his office and had his tea there. And he was seen in Russell Square about 5.15. He'd cut someone up in the traffic who'd taken his car number and that was that. He was found shot in the head in Windmill Lane, Stratford in his car about an hour later. There wasn't any jewellery and there wasn't any money.

178

But Harry was foolish. He should never have let people know he was carrying that sort of money and, if he had to, then he should have had someone like me as a minder for the afternoon. There's plenty of us who'd have minded him for a couple of hundred quid until he got the money into a bank or to his brief. There was another story floating about and that was he'd got wind of a big blag and either he was blackmailing the people involved to get a few quid or people thought he might blow the whistle for a reward. And of course he'd have got brownie points at the Bailey if he had. But I didn't know if it was true. If you asked me I think he was killed over the jewellery and he knew his killer which was why he had to go. But since I wasn't there I can't be sure. The file at the National Archives about Harry's death is closed for 75 years so we'll never know what the law thought. Not in my lifetime anyway.

Another name in the frame for Harry's death, so to speak, was the old Spot man Teddy Machin and I have to admit that Teddy wasn't everyone's cup of tea, even if I did get on well with him. Some people thought he was a tapper. You only had to meet him and he'd be on to you for a non-repayable loan. But I never found him like that. Someone had had a go at him when they shot him at his home a year or so before Harry went. Then Teddy was taken out in the street. May 1975 and the police was round sharpish to see me. I told them I hadn't ay quarrel with Teddy and in fact they found he'd been shot by a fellow whose aunt Machin had been tapping. He wasn't very kind to women and a fellow, whose aunt was tapping, shot him. He ran accident and the first time the jury couldn't agree. Next time round he pleaded to manslaughter and got three years. But since he'd been in custody waiting trial he was let out more or less at once.

Then again people have put Alfie Gerard's name up for it. With nothing to support it. Now Alfie was a seriously hard man. He was one of the ones Alf Donaghue named as shooting Frank Mitchell on behalf of the Twins. He was built like a brick wall but funnily enough he was a very good cook. He had a café over the water in Lambeth called The Blue Plaice.

One case I could have helped the law with if I'd wanted but they never asked was the shooting of Freddie Mills in an alley just outside his club, Freddie Mills' Nitespot, which he ran with a Chinese fellow Andy Ho up the top end of the Charing Cross Road. It was near where the Astoria cinema used to be and where they're turning it into a railway station and more or less opposite the Artists and Recreation Club, the drinker which Mickey Regan and Ronnie Knight ran. July 1965 it was when he died .

He'd been shot in the eye with a fairground rifle when he was seated in the back of his car. Now that was a bigger case than all the others put together and it was one no one will agree on even nowadays. Was it suicide or murder and whichever it was why? Why would Freddie, one of the most popular figures of his day in sport, want to kill himself? Why would anyone want to kill him?

He'd been world light heavyweight champion when he beat the American Gus Lesnevitch at the old Harringay Arena. It's been pulled down long ago. He was brave as a lion, he never knew when he was beaten. He was good looking; he'd saved some money from his days in the ring and he'd bought a few houses in South London; he had a lovely wife and two daughters and you couldn't turn on the radio or television without him being on it. He had starred in an ice show and appeared in pantomime. He was a regular on Six Five Special.

On his earnings from the ring he also opened up a Chinese restaurant and very popular it was. Chinese restaurants weren't two a penny in those days but everything has its time and when the Chinese themselves opened up in Gerrard Street his began to fade a bit. It was then he turned it into a nightclub. The Twins were regular visitors to the Nitespot and one story is that on one occasion Mills had a row with them and told them to go. The Twins were regular visitors to the Nitespot and another story is that on one occasion Mills had a row with them and told them to go. They went and it was after that lighted matches were stuffed down the padding of a banquette in the club, which had also been slashed.

They went and it was after that he was killed. There's a photograph of Reggie with his wife Frances, Mickey Fawcett from West Ham and other friends in the club and there's Freddie, a cigarette in his hand, with his arms around two of the men. In truth the club, and before that the restaurant, had always been a home for the likes of us.

Most nights of the week Mills would drive to the club from his home in South London and would often go for a sleep in his car parked in the yard. That night he told law student Robert Deacon, the club's part time doorman, to wake him at 11 p.m. When he did Mills told him he wanted to sleep on and Deacon went back to the car at a quarter to midnight. It was then he realised something was seriously wrong and raised the alarm.

It seems Mills had borrowed an air rifle from a May Ronaldson, who had a shooting gallery at Battersea funfair, to kill himself. The police who investigated his death along with the pathologist Keith Simpson, and the coroner, were all convinced it was suicide. The only real question raised then was why he had done it

So why would Mills, in his time almost as popular as Henry Cooper, Frank Bruno and David Beckham rolled into one, want to kill himself? Well, things had started to go sour for him. All the time he'd often been boxing heavier men than himself and had taken some bad beatings. Now he was suffering from headaches and his speech began to slur a bit and so he was no use to television and radio.

Then money-wise things weren't what they had been. When Freddie died his estate amounted to a bit under £4000 and, when all debts had been paid, less than £400. Where had it all gone? There is no doubt that Mills had been bleeding money. His south London houses had been sold and he had also taken out a mortgage on his home. He was gambling and was said to be 'borrowing' £10 or £20 a week from the club.

Then there was the club itself. It was not top of the market and was having a hard time competing with much bigger and smarter ones such as Churchills and the Embassy. I know that summer clubs generally were not doing well and July is a notoriously quiet time in the trade. An effort to boost the takings by having the singer Mandy Rice-Davies, fresh from her involvement in the Stephen Ward case, hadn't been helped by a mistake in the advertisement in the Evening News which billed her as 'Mangy Rice-Davies'.

There'd been a bit in the papers that it was full of brasses who were expected to get the punters to buy a couple of bottles of champagne. Then they would meet them at a local hotel but some of the girls were also running the corner game, arranging to meet punters away from the club, taking their money and then not turning up. Just before his death Freddie and Ho were fined £50 each for licensing offences at Marlborough Street court.

According to Deacon, who knew the Ho family well, another reason the club was doing badly was that Andy Ho was stashing away money taken from the club in cardboard boxes.

There was also sex stories. One story is that Mills had had an affair with a young girl which had caused trouble in his marriage. There was however a greater problem, particularly in those days for a man like Freddie. It was said that Mills fancied men and the suicide of his close friend the singer Michael Holliday had taken a serious toll on him. He may even have had a relationship with Don McCorkindale, his wife's first husband. Mills' supporters claim there was no way he could have been homosexual but there were persistent rumours that he had had a relationship with Ronnie Kray. My friend Bill Ackerman said that he saw them together in the Society, which was a club in Jermyn Street, and later in other venues. 'They'd always sit side by side and they were just like a man and a woman together', he told me. It was something Ron denied, saying that he would never have sex with a man as opposed to a boy and I always thought Ronnie liked youths not fully mature men.

Michael Howard, writing about his father my old friend Billy Howard, has a story that the singer Michael Holliday had indeed had a homosexual affair with Mills and, both being bi-sexual, had picked up girls for what were described as 'mild sado-masochistic acts on them for titillation before Mills and Holliday had sex with each other'. The story goes that around 1959 on one occasion things had got out of hand and a girl had died. Mills had disposed of the body and then persuaded Holliday not to go to the police. For a time Holliday and Mills had drifted apart but then the same thing happened again. Billy Howard had warned Mills that it was likely he would be arrested.

Blackmail? Well if those stories are right there's every reason to think he was being blackmailed. What about having to pay protection? Well, even if he was it wouldn't have been more than he could afford.

There've been books written that Freddie was Jack the Stripper, a man who killed prostitutes in the Hammersmith area between 1964 and 1965 and that Freddie was about to be arrested. In fact at one time Reggie Kray was questioned over the murders. in some versions of the story Freddie is said to have left a detailed confession of the killing of the girls but I don't know.

There is also a story which has never gone away that on the night of his death Freddie was caught in a West End urinal nodding and smiling at an undercover policeman. That boxer Nosher Powell, who was the stunt double for Gert Frobe as the German officer in Those Magnificent Men, thought 'You could accuse Freddie of murder or robbery and he'd hold his head up high but to be charged with being a poofter was more than he could take'.

Chrissie Mills and Mills' stepson Donnie McCorkindale and the boxing world generally were all convinced that he had been killed as an example by gangsters who were extorting a fortune in the mid-1960s from club owners. I don't think there's anything in the protection bit. Even if he was paying protection it wouldn't have been anything more than he could afford. And you don't kill golden geese.

Yet another theory is that Mills was killed by mafia hitmen on the orders of Meyer Lansky because he was trying to blackmail boxing promoter and Mafia associate Benny Huntsman for the £2500, he needed to keep the Nitespot open, by threatening to expose the Mafia takeover of gambling in London. He'd had a big public row with him. According to Roger Huntsman, Benny's son, in the book Shadowland he was sent to tell Freddie that he was going to be given the money after all. And Roger was being set up in a typical Mafia trick to lure Freddie into a sense of false security. Meanwhile the Mafia men had arrived in London. Maybe that's right but would they shoot him with a ropey gun like the one that was definitely used? From what I knew of them it would be in — bosh — and out. And from I knew people like Meyer Lansky there was never a hint of any suggestion of it.

Then there was the story he'd been killed by Triads who wanted the club to use for drug dealing. Now don't forget the Chinese were starting to make bits of Soho their own and for every decent man who ran a restaurant there'd be a couple of Triads wanting a bit of business. It was like Mary's little lamb, wherever the Chinese community went the Triads were sure to follow. The great benefit was that the back of Mills' club was in shadows and you could get to it from both Oxford Street and the Charing Cross Road. Drug dealers would have been able to come and go with relative safety. Mills had, according to one of the stories, turned down several offers and he was killed because he wouldn't cooperate.

I don't know. The argument that someone wanted a ready made place from which to deal drugs is just about all right but it may have all been much more simple; no Triads, simply one man and that was Andy Ho forcing Mills' hand. Maybe he just wanted the club for hisself.

And if I'd been asked by the law what I knew, what would I have said? A week or so before Freddie died Ronnie told me that Andy Ho wanted Mills out of the club and that there was money in it for them if they got him out. I told Ronnie that I didn't think it was a good idea. Freddie wasn't going to take any nonsense from them and he'd have hit them. Commonsense should have told them that. Then they'd have had to up the ante so to speak and maybe it would have got out of hand.

But I did agree to go and see Freddie and told him that Ho had gone to people in the East End and I said, 'Your back's to the wall. Give a little or there'll be trouble.' I left him in what you might think was an uncertain state of mind'.

After that I saw Ronnie and told him to leave things alone for four or five days. Then if Mills said he was prepared to go, he could tell the Chinese it was down to him and he would get the credit. I remembered saying to him , 'If need be do what you have to do'. But I didn't want any part of it. Five, six, seven days later all of a sudden Freddie's dead in the car. I was horrified. I went straight to Ronnie and asked what he'd done. Ronnie said it was nothing to do with them and I said, 'Are you sure?' And I believed him when he said he hadn't. I could usually tell when he was lying. He wasn't good at it.

People have often asked why, given how they claimed to be devoted to boxing in general and Freddie Mills, would the Twins even entertain going against him at all? Simple it was business. There was money in it. That and they never thought things through.

And then there was the Biddy Gold murder the law come to see me about. And that was much closer to home.

# 16: GAMBLING

When I say that although he was like a brother to me Albert had no brains, I mean it. Charlie Mitchell from Fulham, who was later with the Twins, gives him some dope and a syringe like an enema tube so he can do a few dogs. 'We're going to make some money,' Albert tells us. It wasn't a question of getting into the kennels and sticking the tube up their backsides. There wasn't the security at the actual tracks like there is today. When the dogs was paraded before a race it was possible to get up close ,give them a spray on their coats and they'd start to itch in a few minutes. They'd still be scratching when the traps opened and that would be the end of their race. We'd had a try at Harringay; a fellow Nicky and me that is. I'd been wearing a dun coloured coat as a sort of camouflage and when the dog passed I gave it a spray. We lay the dog to lose but it got out of the traps all right and that was that. Albert would always give me argument. 'You can't have done it right'. 'Of course I did, I could see the shine on its coat'. But he'd never have it.

So next the three of us go down to Brighton where Albert knew a bookmaker's clerk and we could do a few bets with him. Albert goes away to talk to the bookmaker. This time Nicky's got the syringe under his coat and we're on the rails. I can see a man standing a bit away from him. He's looking at us and I can smell copper. He's still there a few minutes later and I tell Nicky to go off and get rid of the syringe under someone's car. By the time he's back and Albert's joined us the coppers have swooped. They took us into an office and started questioning us. ' What are you doing here?' 'Come here to back a few dogs, same as everyone else'. But there was nothing they could do and they just turfed us out. Later I found out the stuff never even worked. I think Charlie Mitchell give it to Albert as a joke.

It was in the '70s when I fell foul of the slum landlord Peter Rachman when he opened a casino in Knightsbridge. One day when I was in Soho to see Bert Marsh I met a fellow Lennie Western who ran the Chicago Club there and he asked how was I doing. 'I've lost, lost, lost', I told him. 'I'm bang out of form.' He told me he was opening this club for Rachman. 'Why don't you come up? I'll give you £200 credit.' So up I went, played chemin de fer — you play against the banker and you're dealt two cards and you can draw a third. The court cards count zero and the idea is to get your count nearest to a nine —and lost the lot in half an hour. There were some prominent people around and I was just about to give up my seat when Lennie comes up and gives me another £200. And I lost that lot just as quick. This went on all through the night, him giving me the money and me losing it straight back, and by the end I'm in so much trouble I've done £2000.

There was no way I could pay and Rachman can see this great big hole in the accounts. He must have had Lennie in and asked him who'd lost the money and he'd said, 'Bert Rossi'. So he sent for me. He had that all-in wrestler Mad Fred Rondel with him. People said he was a Russian monk but was German originally. He's had a hard life. His family who were Jewish abandoned him in Berlin when he was about six and they went to Palestine. He came over here on Kindertransport and trained to be a rabbi but got into trouble and spent some time in a mental hospital and then he wrestled as Vladimir Waldberg, the Polish Eagle. He told me he'd given it up because after the war there were still a lot of Polish refugees who came to see him and started talking to him in Polish but he couldn't understand a word. Fred wasn't a bad fellow. He was short like me but twice as round. Didn't know what pain was. Mad as a hatter. He once thought he'd killed a man in Tottenham Court Road. 'He wouldn't stop looking at me', he told me, 'I told him to stop but he wouldn't and so I hit him and his head rolled across the pavement.' What he'd done was hit a tailor's dummy standing outside a shop. Rachman'd also got that other wrestler Peter Rann with him. Blonde, good looking but a nasty piece of work. He used to practice his break falls on the concrete in Hyde Park. They both worked for Rachman evicting tenants in Notting Hill. Fred used to say he did nothing but sit and smoke a cigar but that would be quite enough for most people.

Anyway Rachman says, 'Where's my money?' There's Fred sitting smoking a cigar and Rann picking his nails and looking nasty. He could have played the part of a Nazi officer in one of those war films. I tried to row Lennie out of things, saying I was the one who pushed him into letting me have the chips instead of the other way around. If they want they can give me a really hard time. 'Where's my money?' he says again. I just brazened it out. I said, 'You're not getting any fucking money out of me. If I have any trouble I can have you shot'. And I could and would have done. He just swallowed it and I walked away.

I never saw him or Rann again and the next time I saw Fred was in Brixton when I was on the Gold murder charge and he was accused of organising the Spaghetti House robbery which turned into a siege with all the waiters being held hostage. He wouldn't talk to anyone except me or maybe they wouldn't talk to him because by now he was a health fanatic and spent his time chain-chewing cloves of garlic. He stank from a yard away. One day we both had solicitors visits at the same time and I could see into the next room where his solicitor had a handkerchief out. Afterwards Fred says to me 'I can't understand what he says. He's got his hand over his mouth'. I said, 'That's because you stink him out'. He just laughed.

It was just before that that I had a really good touch. It could have been a lot better but, when it come to it, it stood me in good stead over the Gold case. It came to me through a class Italian conman Mario Fortini, a very sensible clever man. Over the years I've done a lot of business with him and in 1976 he comes over from Switzerland where he was living, books into the Hilton in Park Lane and sends word he wants to meet me, said we were going to get quite a bit of money. At the time in casinos there were two sorts of roulette wheels, French with one zero and American with two. He's brought them with him and what he wants from me is to get into a particular casino he has in mind and switch the wheels. 'It's not going to be an easy coup,' I tell him. There's a very limited time when they're not open; something like 4 a.m. to 1 p.m. and you're not going to want to do this in daylight. You've got to get a locksmith to get into a casino and they're going to be all belled up anyway. You a tame croupier and then you've got to have someone at the table who's not going to be suspicious. If I went in and started splashing money about and winning there'd be a stewards' inquiry. So we have to find a Greek or an Arab, someone with plenty of money and who'd probably be known there as a big punter. That's the second problem.

The first I solved after a chat with a friend. Go in at the same time as the cleaning ladies go in. They were always women in those days. The casino didn't leave any of its staff here to supervise them. That meant getting into one of the girls to leave a door open. As for the punter I went into Soho to the Bar Italia in Frith Street where the croupiers used to go before they started work and spoke to an Italian boy I knew. Did he know of anyone he could trust? 'Yes', he said, 'There's a Greek fellow. His father's in oil and the boy's a playboy. He's flash, got a girl on each arm. That sort of thing. He comes in two or three times a week and play two or three thousand. He's lost thousands. He'd be interested in winning. I could have a word with him'. 'He plays for us and he gets money, you get money. Can you lay on a meet?' 'He'll love it,' said my contact.

The next day or so he fetches the fellow along — he is Greek, a bit under thirty I'd think, and we have a coffee. 'Don't be flash,' I tell him. 'Don't go mad. I'll show you how to win. Don't go for a really big hit. Something under £20,000 and stop. Then you can go back again. If you take £60,000 or so someone will start to be suspicious. Then you go back a few days later and so on. When we get to £80,000 we'll turn it up, drop £7,000 or so back to them.'

Mario reckoned the wheel switch would take ten minutes and we got hold of one of the women and arranged she'd get the other girls away from the door and then let us in. We'd be wearing white coats so we looked official and they wouldn't sus a thing. It was a French wheel being played and at 4. 30 she let us in. Mario had our wheel in a green beige bag, took the club's one out, put ours in and we're off. She shuts the door and we're away. Now we can milk them over weeks. That day I show the Greek boy what to do and that night Mario and I are waiting in the Hilton on the first floor where we can overlook the street. We know our croupier has a white Mercedes. We're just waiting for it to come and suddenly he's there. 'It's beautiful,' he says, 'the Greek won £28,000'. I can see Mario's face drop. 'He was told not to win more than £18,000'. Still we had to accept it. The croupier was told to bring him along that afternoon. He gives us the £28,000 and we give him a stern talking to. He'd wanted to impress the bird he was with. 'You can do that with £18,000 as well as with £28,000,' I tell him. 'You've got to do as you're told'.

The next night we're waiting for him but only the croupier turns up. 'You don't know what happened,' he says. 'When we went to work the manager put a new croupier on the wheel. He was a novice, a German fellow. There's no punters of course in the early afternoon and he starts spinning the wheel on his own'. What did he do? It was all too obvious. He'd seen a sequence — say every nine plays 27 come up — and called over the manager who naturally tumbles and thinks of the Greek boy. He takes the wheel out and, of course, it isn't the casino's wheel. That night in walks the Greek boy with a girl on his arm. The manager calls him into the office and says he's got the wheel. He wants his money back or he'll call the law. Now Mario's worried. If we don't give the money back we'll be nicked. In fact it turns out right. The boy goes to his father who pays up and we kept the money less our exes. It could have been so much better but it did me a good turn when I was asked in the Gold murder how I came to have so much money handy. The coppers thought I'd had it as my share of the contract.

# 17 : THE GOLD MURDER

As I said at the start, the law could never make up their minds whether I was the middle man, the look-out or the actual gunman while Erroll Heibner, who was also known as John, acted as lookout, or just to have been the go-between who gave the gun to Heibner when he shot Biddy Gold. This is what one of the coppers, DCI Reginald Dixon, said to me when I was being questioned in November 1975. Straight off at the start of the interview:

In my estimation, Mr Rossi, you are the vile and treacherous person who planned this murder for your own ends or for someone else.

That wasn't the sort of thing he should have come out with if he wanted my help. But I didn't answer back. I was perfectly polite. There was no point in asking for a clip, which is what you could have got in those days, for getting him more riled up than he already was. So I just said, 'You're entitled to your opinion Mr Dixon and you'll have to do your job won't you?'

It all came about that year after what you might call the woman about town Beatrice 'Biddy' Gold was shot in her office in Clerkenwell when her husband Eric and the company secretary, Sheila Brown, had gone to buy a bottle of wine and some fish food a day or so before Gold and his wife were going to the States to celebrate their silver wedding. It all turned on a package I gave to Heibner who I'd been buying jewellery from. The police said it was a gun. I said it was just a packet of jewellery given to me by George Meisl and Matty Constantinou to give back to Heibner.

Of course if a wife gets done the first person the law looks at is the husband and he was down there at the station making a long statement with a solicitor in no time at all. He told them he and Sheila Brown had been out of the office for the half hour around 5 o'clock when she was shot. Apparently she'd known the Golds for years and out of the office was a friend of them both.

What was more peculiar was that when the police got to the Gold's safety deposit box it was stuffed with gold, jewellery and Krugerrands but they never took it away or sealed it. When some other coppers went back the next time it was gone.

There was certainly some thought that the contract had been on offer for months, maybe as long as a year. In fact so far as I could make out from what the coppers who interviewed me thought she was meant to have been done at her home a few days earlier. It was all over some land she'd thought she'd bought in Florida but which didn't exist — the land not Florida. She'd been going out to have a look and that's when the contract come about; then she decided not to and it was off and then when she finally decided to go it was on again.

Whoever wanted the contract done was said to have gone through a lawyer and a couple of other people, then to me and then to the killer. It may have gone through the first few phases but it didn't go through me, and Heibner's been saying he was innocent for the last thirty years. And there's more than a few people agree with him.

Now looking at things from the law's point of view, before they can look at me they have to get to Heibner. What was the evidence against him? Really it was mostly what you would call accomplices. Not accomplices to the murder but to other things.

The one who really put him away was a fellow Charles Fagan who was in the nick when he talked to the police. He said that Heibner had tried to recruit him to hurt someone. He'd promised him a grand and he'd more or less gone along with it but when he found it was a bit more than just hurting he'd backed out. He'd seen John a couple of day into September and they went to a pub when Heibner told him that it wasn't just a beating and the woman had to be done on 8 September at a clothing factory in Clerkenwell. That's when he backed out. He agreed he'd never have said anything about it until Heibner shopped him on some robberies they'd been on together but he claimed what he said was true.

What John did was lose his nerve. There were threats his family would be done for receiving and, after a couple of days in the nick, he confessed that he was the lookout and he went and signed a statement that he was and that I'd given him the gun. The law wasn't sure that it was right. They rather fancied him as the shooter. That is, when they didn't fancy me for it.

There was also some evidence he'd been skint before the murder and that he'd burned some of his clothes after it. He'd got £600 on him when he was nicked.

Now where do I come in? Well, they'd seen me and Heibner several times before the murder and they saw us on the day near the Strand Palace Hotel. They'd been keeping a look-out on John and they'd seen me give him a box and later drop him off near the Angel tube. The other thing against John was that a constable said he saw him near the Angel around 5 o'clock as he was coming off duty.

Heibner knew my boy Peter from when he worked in the print. When I had the club Heibner had a load of Coronet wines and I bought them off him for £300. He should have collected the money the following day but I'd lost it gambling. I'd give him a £20 here, a £50 there until it was down to £150 and then we settled for £100. But after that he was always on to me to find him work.

The law had also seen me with him at Harringay dog track and also in Exmouth Market. It shows how I'd kept out of sight because none of them knew me until I left an empty bottle of milk on a wall and a copper took it and got my fingerprints off of it.

Now, I knew John Heibner was stealing jewellery because he was fencing it through Georgie Meisl. It all came about because Georgie didn't like Heibner coming into the offices. Now the law knew perfectly well what

George and Matty were up to but it didn't need to be obvious and they were taking money off them every Friday, so as I've said they had a bit of a licence. The last time I went to give them some of the stolen tom I took John with me. I put stuff on the table, George priced it and then said, 'We don't want you coming on the meet any more, John. It's bad for business. We'll price it and Bert'll tell you.' Once Georgie said Heibner wasn't welcome, I said next time he had something to sell I'd pick it up and bring it in. And that's what we did.

A bit before, me and Mary had had to move from the top floor in Hatton Garden because the owner wanted to let it on a long let so we moved to Finsbury Park where Reggie Price had a flat. We'd been given £1000 to move out but I still kept the club on the floor below.

Reggie wasn't a villain. He was a ducker and diver. The sort of game he'd run was to go to Harringay dog track and he'd select six mug punters and give each of them a dog in a race. One of them had to win and he hoped to get a couple of quid off of the winner. Races would be close and so he could probably tap the fellow he'd given the runner up saying, 'Bit of bad luck, sir. But I've got this dog in the seventh'. When they nicked me the law thought I was going under his name.

The law came round about three in the afternoon the day I was arrested. 24 October it was four days after John. They didn't say what they wanted but they searched the place, found nothing, put a sack over my head, bundled me into a police car and took me down to Kings Cross police station. They took Mary in a separate car. It was only when I was at the station that they said it was about the Mrs Gold murder. There was no need to take Mary; she was a sort of hostage. They questioned me for a couple of days; for a long time I didn't get a shower or a wash and I was anxious about what was happening to Mary. She's a straight girl.

Our little dogs were locked up in police kennels. They weren't Rottweilers or anything like that; Susie was a bit of a mutt and Blackie was a Manchester Terrier. Immediately he heard, Dino Cellini had Mary go up to the Hilton where she was given £3000 to help her out. I was on remand for thirteen months and Alfie Anish from Stamford Hill ran the club with her while I was gone.

Eventually they said I was going to be charged and that was when I said I'd make a statement if it was done at Brixton. I got a screw to sit on the interview I had with D I O'Brien who now seems to be in charge. so they couldn't fit me up but in any event the law had been taping it. And what I told them was that one day Frankie Albert came to me and said he wanted my help. He said there was a guy in Soho, Tony Zomparelli, who had some papers off of him. Some people said Tony was Albert's right hand man but that was all newspaper talk after he died. 'I need them back and he won't give them to me,' says Frankie. 'I know he'll take notice of you but I can't make headway'. I think the truth is that Frankie's scared of Tony. Now, I know Frankie's in with the law and it can't hurt me to do him a favour so I went to see Tony, told him the papers don't belong to him and he's got to hand them over. 'You don't realise Frankie is connected to the Yard. Pay attention. They'll get rid of you'.

Eventually he agrees and I was satisfied he would hand them over and wasn't just saying so. How he got them in the first place, I don't know and it was nothing to do with me anyway. I want to do right with both of them and I ring up Frankie and he says we'll meet up, at 2 p.m. the next day on the corner of Old Compton and Frith streets, just where Albert and Spot had had their set-to. We meet and we haven't been there two minutes when a car pulls up and out jumps three law and one of them is Ken Drury who was a commander in the Flying Squad. He was a nasty piece of work. He used to control who opened porn shops in Soho and he had a rake off from them. As I say Frankie was his bagman. I was annoyed; Frankie's set this up. I said, 'I'm off' and I walked away leaving Tony and Frankie with them. Now I'll always believe that had something to do with Biddy Gold.

The evening the copper has been to see me a PO, that's a Principal Officer, top screw, comes in my cell. 'You've had a meet with DI O'Brien. You might have further information you want to give him. Don't put down to see the Governor, just let me know and I'll arrange it'. Now I know that every time you ask to see the Governor, even if it's only to buy a tube of toothpaste, it goes in the book. This way it's not going to and so I know the PO's working with the law. Same as that PO did with Nipper Read when Alf Donaghue turned against the Twins. But it's not for me.

When you're on a murder charge you go onto the hospital wing while they assess if you're fit to stand trial. After a week or so the Chief Warder who's the real boss of a prison comes to me to say I'm being moved that afternoon. Now my brain starts going tick-tock. I don't want to be moved. It's too easy for the coppers to have a slag put in with you and before you know where you are he's in the witness box telling the judge how you confessed to him out of the blue. And the reason he's telling the court this is not because he's expecting his charges dropped or favours in sentencing it's because he can't stand murder. Bollocks. When that actor John Bindon, who was in films like Cathy Come Home, was on trial for killing Ronnie Dark up popped a cell mate to say John had confessed. And the reason he says he's come forward is that he doesn't like murders but murder's exactly what he's on trial for himself. The good thing is John got a not guilty and the grass got a guilty. So I tell the screw I'm happy where I am but he's says I've got to move and there's no use arguing any further. But when I walk into my new wing there's Taters Chatham and the ex-boxer Billy Williams, good fighter he was, light-heavyweight, who's waiting trial for running over a fellow twice, and half a dozen others I know and it's, 'Bert, hello Bert' all round. It was as if I was the Queen coming in. But, nice thought it is, that sort of thing doesn't do you any good. You want to fade into the background as much as you can.

During the thirteen months, I was kept away from Heibner the whole time except when we went to court for hearings. At one time a High Court judge signed an order that I wasn't to have any visitors until further notice. No one asked me what I had to say about that before he made the order.

There were some high class men in Brixton that year. Bobby Maynard and Reggie Dudley, who were wrongly convicted of a couple of murders and it took the better part of thirty years for their convictions to be quashed; men from the Bank of America job like Lennie Wilde who they called the King of the Keys, Mickey Gervaise who became a supergrass, Billy Gear and Peter Colson who knew my son. Their trial finished a couple of days before mine and they drew some heavy bird. Twenty three years I think it was for Lenny. There was also one of the Reilly brothers; Tommy Hole who was later killed down the East End; he's had a not guilty over killing Nicky Gerard who had a not guilty himself over Tony Zomparelli. Then there some of the Arifs, a big family from South London; IRA men and Mad Fred Rondel who was accused of organising the Spaghetti House robbery which turned into a siege. He wouldn't talk to anyone except me or maybe they wouldn't talk to him because he was a health fanatic and spent his time chain-chewing cloves of garlic. He stank from a yard away. He got a not guilty at the end of it all.

We used to have a kick about with a football in the yard but the IRA men just walked round on their own. I asked them to come on over and join us but next morning one of our fellows comes over to me and says, 'We don't want them to play with us'. 'Why not?' I wanted to know, 'You're all nicked for personal gain, they stuck their lives on the line for a belief. They done it for a cause. They're fucking better people than any of us'. They were dangerous but compared with us they were churchgoers. After that they joined in the games.

As I say another old mate who was in at the time was Billy Williams, drove over someone a couple of times so the law said. He'd been a good boxer in his time; light heavyweight, won ten fights in a row in America. I'd got him out there through Dino and he was with Angelo Dundee. But then for some reason the Mafia wanted him to drop the eleventh to one of their men. He couldn't bring hisself to do it and he sort of compromised by kneeing the other fellow in the bollocks. That was the end of him over there. Angelo give him a plane ticket back here and said that was the best he could do for him. He used to spar in Canning Town. He told me you didn't get paid much over there when you was on the undercard. In those days it may have been around $200 but there was security work and you were put up in swank hotels and fed well.

In fact there's about 40 well known faces in the wing over those 13 months. Right at the start there's also a fellow I don't know came in on his own for a bank. After we're unlocked in a morning we'd often go into someone's cell for a chat while we have tea and this fellow comes in and sits at the back. As far as I know since he's in for a bank he's a good 'un. The talk's pretty free among us and it seems like Peter Colson and one or two of the others is going to try and make a break for it. Do I want to come along? No, is the answer, I don't.

Why didn't I take up the offer to try and break out with Peter? I've never known any one on the run who's stayed out. Peter and the Boche, they had £800 000 on the outside waiting for them and they may have had a chance but they'd have been bled white by people. They couldn't stay in England. I hadn't that sort of money and anyway I had Mary. Couldn't ask her to come on the run and she meant more than anything to me.

Getting back to my cell I look out and I can see another young fellow mopping up. 'Where are you from? 'Soho'. 'How long you here for?' 'Two months'. That's why he's allowed out to do cleaning. I give him a couple of packs of cigarettes because we were allowed to have them on remand in those days. At one time we could also get half a bottle of wine or a pint of beer a day if someone brought them in. 'Look', I says', 'I want you to pay attention. The PO comes round when people are locked away and I want to know whose cell he goes to'. Next day the boy says, 'It's Cell 17' and that's the cell of the newcomer no one knows who's in on a bank raid. The fellow's a wrong 'un. So, soon as I can, I tell Peter, 'If you've told him anything, scrub it out'.

It was being in Brixton which I reckoned caused me to lose my whack over a £2 million touch. When I had the club, there was a little fellow used to come in sometimes and sell me bits and pieces. I don't think I ever gave him more than £80 for anything. Well spoken, well turned out and one day I say, 'Stay and have a coffee'. We got talking and he told me his name was Simon, he'd been born in Ireland, been to a good school and he's been more or less disowned. He'd taken his mother's necklace and sold it for more or less nothing. It was obvious he was gay. Queer, he'd have been called then. He came in the club one day with a black eye. Someone had given him a whack and I asked if he wanted me to have a talk with the fellow. I'd become a bit protective of him. 'One of those things,' he says.

Anyway, I don't see him for a bit and while I'm in Brixton there's a report in the papers of a big currency raid at Heathrow. Couple of days later I'm being escorted from A wing and I hear a voice, 'Bert, it's Simon. I've been looking for you'. What's happened is that he's been part of the raid. I never learned if he was actually on it or was just changing the money down but a fine fist he made of that. He'd come looking for me and when he found I wasn't at the club he and a mate had taken it to Ireland but there was a strike on at the banks. So they decide to go to Paris and start to spend some of it. They'd gone to a man's shop and started buying shirts. They were lucky they'd anything to spend. While Simon was looking for me they left the money in the boot of a car overnight. Anyway the manager thinks its forged money and he called the local law. What a waste. I could have changed it down for him through Abe Kosky or a couple of people in France or even knocked it out in Las Vegas.

I heard later that while I was in the nick a firm of solicitors wrote to the law saying Roy Edgler had information which might help me, but whether it ever got passed on I don't know. My brief never mentioned it to me. Roy Edgler was a fellow who'd been done for the murder of Barbara Gaul, the ex-wife of the property dealer. She'd been shot in a contract killing which some people said had been set up by Charlie Kray .

Mary came to see me every single day except for the ones when I wasn't allowed visitors. We were allowed our own food in those days and she fetched me cigarettes and pie and mash for my dinner.

The trial began in October 1976 and came to a grinding halt pretty soon. A woman juror said she thought she was being followed. Nothing to do with me but they started again. One of the top men at the Bailey Michael

Corkery was prosecuting and I had Jeremy Hutchinson. He was the best barrister I ever saw and I was prepared to wait for him to become available. What a nice man; no side to him at all. John had some bad luck when his brief pulled out overnight and he was left with what they call the junior and another fellow standing in.

The police said the money I had on me had been my share of the contract but I was able to show it came from the roulette wheel swindle and money I'd been given to buy greyhounds for the Mafia and their dog track in Florida. They called the fellow who'd bought the dogs in Ireland for me and Mary saw him on the way to the Bailey to make sure he called me Rossi or Mr Rossi and not by my first name.

They ladled it on calling Fred Lambert who was head of security at The Sportsman, the casino at the beginning of Tottenham Court Road where I used to play. In the box he goes and pulls out a sheaf of papers. How would you assess Rossi as a gambler? He studies the papers as if he didn't know the answer and then says, 'A high roller'. And then he goes on to say that around the time of Biddy Gold's death I had lost £13,000 which was quite right.

When I was in the box my brief Jeremy Hutchinson says to me words like, 'You've heard Mr Lambert say how you lost all that money in a few days. Do you mind telling us where you got the money?' The judge is listening; the jury's listening. I said, 'I didn't win it I stole it.' Hutchinson's on his feet saying, 'Hold up, Don't implicate yourself'. But I saw there was nothing for me but to tell them the truth. 'I stole it from a casino. I didn't rob it. I did it by means of a trick. If you send one or two officers down to the casino they'll find that what I'm telling you is the truth'. £28,000 I'd got which was serious money in 1976.

I told the court that when I met Heibner on the day of the murder I had been going to the Strand to a weigh-in and that I had met him to give him some jewellery back. Remember George wouldn't have Heibner in the office and I was the go-between. Heibner had wanted £5000 and Meisl would only give him three and a half so the jewellery had to go back.

I was polite and said how I respected Mr Corkery the man who was prosecuting. I said I knew he was only doing his job but what he was suggesting that I had passed the gun over didn't make sense. If I had wanted to give Heibner a gun I would have met him at a block of flats and passed it over in the lift out of sight of everyone. I wouldn't do it in broad daylight. I suppose technically I was receiving stolen jewellery but that's a very different thing from supplying a gun in a murder. And anyway I didn't know that that particular bit of jewellery was stolen.

I also told them that Bernie Silver who was a big man in Soho – he ran clubs and porn — had told me Biddy Gold was deep into pornography. I also told them Tony Zomparelli had been killed and that Frankie Albert had flown off of a roof. Then I went on to say that the word around town was that anybody who'd got involved with Mrs Gold's affairs was playing with dynamite.

It was then I discover Heibner's been in the law's pocket. Feeding them things so he could stay out and do a bit of work. He'd been in on bank robberies, smash and grab. I should have known. How did he ever get bail on these robberies unless they wanted him to work with them? I told him he shouldn't give evidence and I was right. The judge just sort of led him on asking what weapons, guns and coshes he'd used , how bad people had been hurt. And he couldn't give an answer which didn't hurt him. Any decent pros can do that to you. There's always been a saying that the best moment for the defence is when the prosecution finishes its case and that was what happened with him. That sort of thing. I thought he was going to bring me down with him.

The jury was out just over three hours and when the foreman said they agreed on a verdict and it was 'Not Guilty, my Lord' the judge didn't look as though he could believe it. You don't get a lot of not guilties in big murder trials at the Bailey or anywhere else for that matter.

What can't have hurt was that the week the jury went out in my case a few coppers from the Vice squad went down in another court at the Bailey. Our jury must have through that coppers didn't always get things right.

Once the judge said I was discharged I didn't stay to see what happened to John. There were a couple of friends in court with Mary and after I'd gone down to the cells and picked up my things it was out of the back door into a cab and home for a bath and a decent bit of Mary's cooking

Johnwas found guilty on a majority verdict. 10-2. I've always thought Bernie Silver was right and the murder was to do with porn in Soho and the death of Frankie Albert. But the Florida land story may be just as right.

# 18: WINDING DOWN

Over the years I'd do business with most people but what I wouldn't do is deal in heroin. Cocaine, well if people want to stick that up their noses or marijuana, good luck to them but I've seen what heroin does to people and I've never had any part of it. I remember once being in a club playing cards in South London near the Elephant, when a girl, she can't have been more than fifteen, sixteen, all twisted up comes over trying to sell herself to buy drugs. How could anyone do that to someone's daughter?

When I had the club in Hatton Garden a fellow, Henry Cohen, come to me through Billy Hill. Henry wanted machines put in some clubs and I went to see him one Monday morning in Stamford Hill. I ring the bell. He opened the door and behind him there was a long corridor with doors off on the left. Almost simultaneously the doors were opened, heads popped out and popped back in again just as quick. I didn't recognise any of the faces and I said to Henry, 'What are they doing here?' He said, 'They're the law. I've had a tip off. One day I'm going to be robbed when I open the door. One of them's going to be dressed as a copper'. Henry had got the tip that a firm from Hoxton was going to do a tie-up for money. He'd even got a name, Johnny. So that was what the law was doing. They were staying camped out at Henry's house.

Anyway I talked to him about the machines and when I was driving home I thought what I should be doing. I'm not involved in any shape or form but can I let these Hoxton fellows walk into a trap which is going to cost them seven plus?

One of the fellows I knew in the Garden was Reggie Price and I asked him if he knew a Johnny from Hoxton who was into crime. 'Tell him I want a word with him'. I wasn't going to involve Reggie telling him what it was about. Johnny never rings and then suddenly on the blower is Billy Gentry another fellow I know from Hoxton and I ask him why Johnny hasn't been in touch. It seems he thought he was in trouble with me and I was going to hurt him. 'No, I say. 'I just want to give him some advice. Tell him to come up to the club'. But he's still leery and so I say I'll meet him at 1 p.m. outside the Italian church. When I get there, they're in a car, Billy's in front and Johnny in the back and it's Billy doing the talking. I told them not to go on with the job because it's a trap but instead of saying, 'Thanks Bert' they are querying it. I wonder just what nut cases I'm dealing with. 'Look,' I said, 'One of you is going to be dressed as a copper'. They look at each other and now they know. 'You didn't believe me,' I said and now they were a bit sheepish.

Another with me over machines for a time was the American 'Duke' Case when he had them in London. He'd put some in clubs and he was having trouble with people who wanted a pension from him. That's when he asked me for help. He got deported back to the States in the early sixties and about time too. He was an animal, a horrid person. The language he used was unbelievable. He was the sort who pinched waitresses' arses when they bent over to serve him. One day I told him, 'What the fucking hell's wrong with you? You don't come over here and do that'. He lived with two women and a child when he was here before he got thrown out. When he did he left me to look after his interests.

It was the early 1990s when a friend of mine was approached to help George Walker. Who was George? Well, he started life as a minder for Billy Hill. He was part of the team which took a boat into the Med and smuggled cigarettes for a few months. It all ended in tears and the boat went up in flames. After that Walker was caught stealing over £1700 worth of nylon stockings in London's Victoria Docks. According to legend, it took a van-load of coppers to subdue him. George's counsel told the judge he'd only been paid £3 and the judge called him a 'gullible fool' as he gave him two and a half years.

Seems to me the judge was the gullible one if he believed that fanny.

Whatever George was he wasn't a gullible fool. Then his brother Billy turned professional boxer. George had been in the ring himself as the Stepney Steamroller. In fact he fought for the British light-heavyweight title and he was winning against the Welshman Dinny Powell. He knocked him down seven times when Dinny hit him with what must have been about his last effort and damaged his eye so badly he couldn't continue. That was the end of him in the ring.

When he finished with Billy Hill, George became his brother Billy's manager. Billy was never quite top class but he was close to it. Very good looking boy with blond curly hair. The women loved him and he had a knockout punch but he wasn't that good if you had him on the back foot. Still he made a lot of money and George and him opened a fast food chain, Billy's Baked Potato. I'm talking about the 1960s now. George also had a disco, Dolly's in Jermyn Street which was popular for a while. And he then went on from strength to strength. The next thing is he's bought up a run down greyhound track at Brent Cross near Hendon in north-west London and develops it into a shopping complex. And he set up Brent Walker which became a public company.

Then in 1993 it all went pear shaped. He'd over extended himself and he was charged with fraud. That's when, through the boxing manager Burt McCarthy, he went to my friend for help. Could he square a couple of jurors?

Nowadays getting to a juror is more difficult than it used to be but you have more time to do it. Of course that also means they've more time to go bent on you. In the old days the names and addresses of jurors were printed out but you didn't have long to work. Back in the 1960s even a murder trial or a big fraud could be over in days. Now you've got time but you don't have the names and addresses as a starting point.

So the first thing you do is have a look at the jurors; see what they look like. There's no point at all going after a man who's got bugger's grips, a rose in his button hole and the Daily Telegraph under his arm. You can forget him. You select a likely one or two and have them followed when they go home at the end of the day. The coppers are going to have jurors minded in very big trials but they can't watch every single juror in every single trial and fraud's not the one which gets the most attention. So now you know where they come from. If they're seen going to church on a Sunday you leave them well alone. Next thing is have someone in the area get in touch. Follow them into a sweet shop or something like that, strike up a conversation, football, golf, cricket. Then its on to talking about the law and your man lets slip he knows the defendant; knew him years ago. He wasn't a bad fellow then. 'What's he done now?' and when he's told it's' I can't believe it'. Plant a seed of doubt in the juror's mind. And then it's, 'How would you like a few grand?'

Anyway my friend manages to square a couple and he goes back to George. But George isn't convinced. He's shrewd with his money, doesn't want to pass it over for nothing and my friend comes to me and wants to know how he can convince him. What I tell him is to get George to give him two of his ties, ones he can recognise easily. Next day the jurors are wearing them. How's that for a clincher?

It all turned out all right for George. Not Guilty, my Lord. My friend's saved him a minimum of four inside. But it didn't turn out so well for my friend. George give him £17,000 but he was expecting double. Of course he should have fixed a fee in advance; the rich are bastards when it comes to money. They don't like parting with it at all. My friend did make him pay the workers however.

The amount of advice I've given over the years and never taken a penny for it should get me some sort of gong as a one man Citizens Advice Bureau. And a lot of people haven't been that grateful either.

What I also did was I acted as a referee. I dealt with anything that arose. Like I said at the start I've done some advising, bought and sold a few things and done a good bit of mediation work when people have fallen out and they need things to be sorted before they get really out of hand. If a row broke out one of the parties would come to me and I'd quieten things down. If you've got people shooting each other then you've got the coppers interfering and that just interrupts business.

Say someone's been shot but not killed then there's likely to be retaliation. That's what mediators are for. Both parties come to someone they can trust, say what they want and agree to abide by the decision. Pay this, don't go there, hand over that share, take a beating. The world could learn a lot from us really.

Take that time with Ray Rosa. A fellow from the Angel came in the club a few times and then one day who walks in but Ray. I hadn't seen him for a while. We all have a chat and then a couple of weeks later this fellow comes in on crutches. What's happened is Ray has shot him. They'd both been doing a bit of minding in Paris and there's been some quarrel. I told him he had to drop it out. When he had to go back to give evidence he had to say it wasn't Ray who shot him. And he did, otherwise no one knows what trouble he'd have been starting.

Over the years and in all countries there have been people who have done that. Somebody who's trusted by everyone is asked to sort out a dispute. The last thing we want is the law involved and if things can be patched up one way or another it's that much better. There was that fellow in Paris a bit after the war, Pierre Cuccari, who had a bar up near Montmartre. He used to sort out the disagreements between pimps and their girls. He claimed half the award for himself which was something I never did. But there again I didn't get shot dead over a brass like he did.

Every few years there'd be a get together of the top men in the cities when something needed sorting out and I remember one the year Ronnie died. It was in the Moat House in Liverpool and people came from Scotland, Manchester, Belfast, Leeds; all over the place. I remember one fellow there started throwing his weight about going on about how he was now the 'Boss of the Underworld'; stupid remarks like that and I had to calm things down. If he hadn't been careful and I hadn't been there someone would have laid one on him and who knows where it might have ended. It was the same the whole world over. There was a big meeting once in Melbourne when people met in a restaurant. One of them a fellow Tony Mokbel started mouthing off about and he got a good hiding which led to people taking sides and a gang war which lasted for years. That's what I was there for – to stop things like that; the voice of reason you might say.

Funnily I've never had a really, really big touch, although quite often I saw more in one touch than many people would see in a year. I think the most in one hit came to £300,000 for a lorry of spirits but that had to be split.

There's some things will go on forever and one of them's contracts. That's life. It doesn't have to be the full thing. Someone with money will have a problem which they can't sort out for themselves. There's probably one being set up as you read this.

Going back nearly a couple of hundred years now there was a fellow in New York who carried a sort of tariff around with him. If you wanted someone just punched that was $2 but if you wanted an arm or leg broke it went up to $19 and $25 for a stabbing. What he called, 'Doing the big job' was $100 and up. And that was good money then.

I'll give you an example of how things worked. No names in this case but a top racing man came to me at the races one day and asked to have a word. We went off for a cup of tea and he says, 'Someone's fucking about with my wife.' 'What do you want?' I ask. It's always better for them to come out with things rather than you suggest them. 'I want him put in hospital'. Now there's putting in hospital and putting in hospital. It will all depend on what harm the contractor wants done and what he or she'll pay. He tells me just how bad he wants the man hurt and then it's up to me to see if I think the money he's offering is worth it. I'm not into cutting off his pecker or anything like that which you could get in the States. Sometimes you'll even get a fellow who wants to be shot; help him get out of a court case for a bit. That safebreaker Jackie O'Connell was one. He wanted a few pellets in his leg so he could send in a medical certificate but the man got too close and Jackie lost his leg. It's funny but apparently if you lose a leg or a hand or something you can still get pain where it used to be. It got worse for

Jackie over the years and eventually he topped himself.

I wouldn't take money in advance of a contract. People weren't going to turn me over. If they'd seen what I'd done on their behalf then they weren't going to leg me over. I'd say give the money to a stakeholder, someone we both trusted. I've held money for people and then paid it out. I didn't take a cut, just did it as a friend.

You can't say a contract is worth £10,000 or £200 or even £50. It's what is agreeable between both sides. The Gold contract was said to have been worth £40,000. The biggest I've ever been offered was £100,000 in the last two years and I turned it down. Far too much aggravation. I've known men who've gone on working in that line well into their sixties. You don't have to be a weightlifter to pull a trigger.

Charlie Kray was said to be an arranger after he came out from doing his ten and before he got his twelve. He was said to have brokered the killing of Barbara Gaul, the property man's wife, and that of Donald Urquhart, a fellow shot as he come out of a pub in Marylebone, as well. Could be right.

I'd still get calls from the States from time to time. For example, one day I got a call from Tony Ferrante. Did I know a Johnny? I said I did. 'How well? 'I wouldn't say he's a friend. I know him to have a drink with and meeting him in spielers but we're not close'. This fellow came from a large family of brothers in North London and they were friends with the Krays. I knew how they were getting a living but it was nothing to do with me. Good luck to them. They weren't stepping on my toes, you understand.

Ferrante said, 'We've got a man over with you and Johnny is trying to interfere'. He must have wanted a piece of the action. I said, 'Do you want me to have a word with him?' Ferrante told me, 'Don't say no more on the phone. No, let it go'. I got the message, 'You're in touch; you know where to find him if we have to send someone over'. Even so I went to see Johnny and told him he didn't know what he was taking on. He should drop it out and that's what he did. It never came to it but that's how close he came to being killed. It's that sort of world. Be careful whose toes you tread on.

And over the years they've helped me out. It was Santo Trafficante from Florida, who was another suspected of being involved with a plo to kill Castro, who helped get a boy out of England after he was wanted for a tie-up job. We had to go to Amsterdam together and then he was sent to Canada to friends of the Volpes. The man I took him to in Holland had the biggest piano I've ever seen. All silver and the length of a wall. I just left him there and he was passed on until he got to Toronto. Unfortunately the fellow didn't stick it over there. He came back and did something like seven years and later I heard he'd been shot in a post office raid.

Trafficante also had a valid interest in a casino like all the mob used to. When I used to go Vegas to watch the fights, he used to put me up in his casino and always gave me £10,000 in free chips to go and have some fun in the casino. one time I turned up with some friends, and had a 10k tab. I won about 40k and went to the counter to cash up. The cashier lady only paid me 30k back, and I thought hold up, where's the other 10k?. She said "Mr Rossi, it doesn't work like that, the house gets the 10k back if you win". So if I had lost all that 10k they would have just let it go. You see, this is where you really see how your Mafia friends were very powerful, very generous, but always very business minded people.

# 19 : WHERE HAVE THEY ALL GONE?

A lot of us did what that girl who was involved in the Profumo scandal Mandy Rice-Davies, said about life and declined slowly into respectability. There again one way or another you lose touch with people even with your friends and most of mine have died. Darby Sabini became a rails bookmaker and died in Hove in 1950. We were all a bit surprised how little money he left but, shortly after, the man who had been his clerk was stopped leaving the country with £36,000 which was big money in those days. I lost touch with Harryboy.

It all ended for me with Abe Kosky when one day he tells me he's going on holiday to the south of France and the next I heard he'd dropped dead on a beach there.

Bert Marsh had a heart attack in 1961 when he was driving to see his daughter who'd become a model and who lived in Hampstead. Albert Dimes had cancer and died in 1972. The story is that when he was dying he said the police should be told who killed Jack Buggy but I don't believe it. Albert would never say anything like that. The Krays sent a wreath but Albert's family wouldn't have it at the funeral. I went of course. Big, big turnout.

The Twins of course never came out from their sentences in the McVitie and Cornell murders. Well, I suppose technically Reggie did but it was only for a few days while he died in 2000. Charlie died in the nick while he was there for that drugs sentence. Same year as Reggie; Ronnie had gone in 1995. There was a terrible scandal because the law had taken Ronnie's brain for examination. The funerals were amazing with miles and people lining the streets and running along side the cars but I didn't go.

The nobs used Billy Hill when they needed him. Take that Lady Docker. Billy invited her and her husband Sir Bernard to the launch party of his book. I forget where Docker'd made his money but they was a flashy pair. Daimler Dockers they was called. The party was in Gennaros restaurant in Soho which is now the Groucho Club. There's a picture of me there standing next to Frankie Fraser and Billy . It was a warren of a place with rooms everywhere. She disappears with Billy and when Albert went to look for her he finds Billy giving her one on a pile of fur coats. So Albert gives her Ladyship a slap. Albert was a bit straitlaced in those things. He thought it disrespectful to her husband. I was downstairs where a fellow dressed in a policeman's helmet was playing the piano for us. When Albert told me I just laughed.

I don't know if Sir Bernard ever found out but if he did it didn't stop their Graces going to Billy when their jewellery was nicked. I think he just had a quiet word with Taters Chatham. Same with the jockey Gordon Richards when someone nicked his trophies. Billy had them back for him. This time I think it was Billy.

Benstead who'd had them away. And it was just the same with Darby Sabini all those years ago. Someone had the Duke of Norfolk's bins away at Ascot but Darby had them back before the last race.

After is book was launched Billy more or less called it a day in 1957 and it was then Albert and I inherited so to speak. Billy died in 1984 leaving, it was said, over £1 million in Switzerland. He had a son Justin by a dancer at Raymond's Revue Bar who was brought up by Gypsy and she kept him shielded from the press and public. She died of cancer in 2004. In turn the boy wrote his memoir saying although they were never poor there was no money stashed away abroad.

In early January 1995 Terry Hogan, another who'd been on the Eastcastle Street job, was killed in a fall from a window in Brentford. He'd only ever served one short sentence. He was only 65 and he'd been suffering from depression.

Jack Spot aka Colmore, Comer, Comar, Comor, Comacho and probably half a dozen other names, take your pick, died in March 1995 at Nazareth House, Isleworth. He was more or less broke. He'd split up with Rita some time earlier and ironically he worked in a bacon factory. Towards the end of his life he picked up a conviction for stealing a small amount of the bacon and got the sack. I heard some of his ashes were later scattered in Israel. Rita had died a few years before when she was sixty in September 1988 at the Charing Cross Hospital. She'd been suffering from cancer for some time.

Billy Howard was another who slid down the rankings. He died in 1984. He'd started drinking and that's fatal.

Tony Zomparelli was gunned down in an amusement arcade in Old Compton Street by a fellow Maxie Piggott and Nicky Gerard, Alfie's son. He was playing on a machine called Wild Side or something like that. They just walked in and, so Piggott said, Nicky shot him. Nicky was acquitted and so was Ronnie Knight, who was once married to Barbara Windsor., He was said to have paid for the contract after Zomparelli killed his brother David at the Lautrec Club above Toliani's in Wardour Street. It seems Zomparelli was a bit unlucky. He just happened to be there when a fight broke out rather than him starting it. Ronnie eventually said that he did in fact pay Gerard and Piggott. In turn Nicky got shot and beaten to death a few years later when he was leaving his daughter's birthday party. I don't know what happened to Piggott after he'd finished his life sentence. Tommy Hole , Nicky's cousin was put on trial for Nickey's murder and got a not guilty but he was killed, shot dead in the Beckton Arms down the East End, a few years later along with a fellow they called Joey The Crow.

Tommy Smithson got topped by the Maltese he was mean to be protecting but who he was leaving on. His last words after he was shot in Paddington were said to be 'Good morning, I'm dying'. There were all sorts of stories about Fay Sadler, his girlfriend. One was that she married Tommy's friend the club owner Dave Barrie who was with him when Spot and Billy Hill cut him up but I don't know if that was true. Another was that she went to Australia. She could have done both.

I think Harry Bryan died in prison. I kept in touch with Jock Wyatt after he come out but later on he developed dementia. At least Jock had some money put aside.

The last time I saw Billy Benstead was when I had the club in Hatton Garden. He just put his head round the door one day and I told him to come in. He was in a dreadful state. He could hardly speak — whether it was throat cancer, emphysema or something else I don't know — and he'd come to tap me. Now I don't mind that, I'd always let him have a few quid, but he was Billy Hill's man. Why wasn't he tapping him?

It was always likely Taters Chatham would die penniless and he did; living in a small ground floor flat in Fulham. He kept at it until he was 76 when he stole a load of furs. The paper said that he'd stolen over £100 million of stuff during his lifetime. He was 85. What he said he had was a lot of sad memories and thirty years in prison. Peter Scott, 'The Gentleman Thief', was another who died bankrupt owing nearly half a million. In 1998 he was sent down for three and a half years for receiving a Picasso which had been stolen from a Mayfair gallery. The police said he was helping John McVicar's son, Russell, try and get ransom money from the insurance company. He wrote a book about his life and died when he was 82. His rival Ray Jones had emphysema and died a few years ago. He'd been in sheltered accommodation. The fence, little Stan Davis, only died last year or the year before. He'd married a black girl, Ugandan I think she was and she looked after him. He lived out Sutton way. He'd have been in his nineties.

After his acquittal George Walker went into business with his wife selling cigarette machines in Russia. He also opened betting shops in Moscow and had British horse and dog racing transmitted by satellite. I don't know where he got the energy. He'd already had a couple of heart attacks and had stomach cancer. He died in March 2011 when he was 81. One of his daughters married into the aristocracy.

Lou Canastri, 'Lou the Bandit', died on his own sitting in an armchair in a room off the Caledonian Road.

Bobby Ramsey, who we slashed over Spot, and later was with Ronnie and Reggie worked as a doorman in a South Woodford nightclub until he was 75. He was another game fellow. He died a few years ago in an old folks home. I think he'd had cancer as well.

The law eventually got Joey Pyle from south London in a drugs sting. Joey went down for fourteen but it got knocked down to nine. When he came out his health started to fail and he died ten years ago this year.

The Rosa brothers are both dead. Jack was killed in a car crash and Ray fell out of a window. Jack, who didn't have a licence, was said to have told the law that found him dying at the roadside, 'I wasn't driving'. Game to the end.

Poor Billy Gentry went down for seventeen years with John McVicar and a few others in an attempted raid over in Deptford in 1966 which went seriously wrong. What had happened was a kid saw one of them with a shotgun and got his father to call the police. There was a long chase and shots were fired at the police and that can just about double a sentence. Billy told the coppers that he thought the driver who chased them had been brilliant and if he'd drive for them next time he could have five grand. Billy came out of that all right but then in 1982 he went down again when his girlfriend shopped him over stealing mailbags from trains. He got a nine for that.

I did a bit of work with Charlie Richardson. Eddie was involved more with machines but Charlie had a few Long Firms going with Kenny Bloom —now there was a brilliant LF man—and I had a share in some of them. I'd always have a word and a drink with them when I saw them but they were south of the river and I was north so we were never what you would call close. I respected them though. Charlie's dead now but Eddie's written a few books and he's a good painter. Charlie told me a funny story once. Funny peculiar that is. There'd always been stories about pictures of Johnny Bindon taken with Princess Margaret but there was another set of pictures he told me about, this time taken not far from where I lived and this time it was with a black fellow, Michael X. Now the actor Richard Harris was another like Stanley Baker, always liked to mix with the rough stuff, and he went to Charlie to see about getting them back. I don't know who had them but they weren't going to do anyone any good if they got out in the open. Charlie got them back and met Richard Harris is a pub down in Surrey to hand them over. Harris just chucked them on the fire; never looked at them Charlie wouldn't take any money for the job. I heard the black fellow went back to Jamaica where a bit later he got hung. But that may just be talk.

As for the coppers. Tommy Butler, the one who chased me and Billy Blythe to Ireland, was involved in the Great Train Robbery. Now there was a secretive man. Lived with his mother in Hammersmith and he didn't really mix with other coppers. He became obsessed with catching Bruce Reynolds who he reckoned was the mastermind of the robbery and he took to spending his holidays on the beaches in the south of France with a pair of binoculars trying to spot him. At least that's what he said. He was actually allowed to stay on past retirement age to try and get him and he eventually did but it was in Torquay rather than Nice. After that he did retire and he died in 1970.

Ken Drury went down at the Bailey in 1977 on something like five counts of corruption. He got eight years and as far as I was concerned it wasn't a day too long.

As for the Gold case, John Heibner was released after serving something like 25 years. He's always maintained he was innocent and in 2014 the Court of Appeal heard what was something like his third appeal. They wouldn't listen. Everything his brief argued they said didn't count and they turned it down. He's still fighting on but I doubt he'll get anywhere now.

O'Brien, the copper in the Gold case, got suspended because he failed to report a meeting with that bent copper Alec Eist in July 1977. There was also some sort of suggestion he'd tried to cover up another bit of corruption. He went and retired on medical grounds. Funnily enough a few years ago Mary was in the street and she heard a voice calling her. Who was it but O'Brien. She invited him in for tea but he said she should ask me first.

I didn't mind, it was all so long ago and he was doing what he thought was right. I think he became an insurance assessor.

As for the Americans, towards the end of his life Meyer Lansky lived in the Imperial House, a high-rise waterfront condominium in Miami Beach. He died of cancer at Miami's Mount Sinai Hospital. He was 81 years old. He'd tried to get into Israel but he'd been blanked by the authorities.

In 1976, Dino turned up in Hamburg, Germany with Freddy Ayoub and Joseph Nesline, working with Wilfrid 'Frieda' Schulz who was the top man in Hamburg's red-light district. Dino certainly became involved in Resorts International in Atlantic City, New Jersey, which was the first legal casino in the U.S. outside of Nevada. There was also a story he was involved with swindler Robert Vesco in the embezzlement of over $240 million from the mutual fund Investors Overseas Service but I don't know if it's true. Dino was another who got cancer and he died at the beginning of November 1978.

George Raft died in 1980 in Los Angeles. He'd had leukemia. Some people said he was 85 but he told me he'd been born in Hell's Kitchen, which is around 8th Avenue from 34th up to 59th street in New York, in 1902 so he'd only have been in his late seventies. He'd been a childhood friend of Bugsy Siegel and he said before he became a dancer he'd done a bit of driving for the Mob.

Henry Shapiro, who was with me in the junkets, got called before the New York Federal Grand Jury over the skim from the off-shore gambling casinos. I read he was stopped when he stepped off of a plane at Kennedy Airport with a load of returning gambling junketeers. Old Henry had $30,000 in cash and $90,000 in cheques in his pockets. I haven't heard what happened to him.

I was sorry to see Nicky Scarfo died. Well, not sorry in a way. He was never going to come out unless Donald Trump pardoned him when he ended his being President and that wasn't likely. It can't have been any sort of life at Nicky's age. People say he had a vicious temper but I can only speak as I found him and I never had a moment's trouble with him.

Maybe it was his own fault that he was a bit too high profile and there's no doubt a lot of people hated him. It was in 1980 I think that he was first done for the murder of Vincent Falcone. The murder was all about respect. Falcone started running down Nicky Scarfo and his nephew Phil Leonetti behind their backs saying the concrete factory Nicky had set up was no good. In fact it was a very good piece of business. Nicky was supplying the concrete for the building which was going on turning Atlantic City from a run down dump into the gambling city its become. And who do you think was one of the people buying his concrete for his hotel? Donald Trump.

As for Don King he ended up serving time for manslaughter but then went on to become the world's biggest boxing promoter, after he co-promoted alongside Jon Daley "the rumble in the jungle" fight between Muhammad Ali and George Foreman. He then went on to co-promote several other boxing fights in Atlantic City, with none-other than the current US President, Donald Trump.

I was first introduced to Trump at a Boxing show that I attended with Big John Berkery, Scarfo and Frank Sindone were there, and it was Scarfo who made the introduction. Scarfo said to me "he might look a bit dodgy with the hair but finance wise he was a powerful man, contact wise a powerful man, business connections a powerful man...you get it?". Who would believe that 30 years on from that same conversation, that same Donald Trump becomes president of the US? But what's even more bonkers is that my next door neighbour Boris Johnson who started out in politics, becomes mayor of London, and then ends up becoming foreign secretary. You couldn't write it!

It was in 1979 Nicky had him shot by Phil Leonetti while Nicky was sitting drinking scotch. A bit like Jack Buggy at the Mayfair Club here, Nicky had him wrapped up in a carpet and taken away. One man who supplied the gun, a fellow called Joe Salerno, rolled over but Nicky and Phil and a third fellow got not guilties.

But the FBI wouldn't leave him alone. He did a couple of years for possessing a firearm and then at the end of the 1980s they threw the book at him, Phil Leonetti and fifteen others on racketeering charges and anything else you could think. Joe Salerno gave evidence again. They were all found guilty in May 1989. Nicky got fifty five years Phil 45 and the rest thirty and up. Next thing was they did him for the murder of Frankie Flowers D'Alfonso who got his name from running a flower shop. He was shot on a south Philly street in 1985 . People said Frankie had been shot back in 1985 for refusing to pay Nicky a street tax but I don't know if that's right Now there was a few more prepared to turn rat against Nicky Lawrence Merlino turned rat and so did Nicky's nephew Phil Leonetti. As I say just who is staunch when the chips are down? The deal he made was so good Phil got out after five years and, believe it or not, he married the girlfriend of Vincent Falcone. Then he just disappeared from view. There was said to be a half million dollar contract on him but it has never been carried out. Nicky's sons hard a hard time. One broke away from the family , the second hanged himself and so did the third.

Carlo Gambino died of a heart attack just after watching the Yankees win the pennant in 1976. It must have been too much excitement for him but what a way to go. The priest said he died in a state of grace but I wonder about that. I didn't go to his funeral. Firstly, they're not for me and I couldn't have gone if I'd wanted because I was waiting trial over Mrs Gold. I'm told there was over a hundred cars and a load of lawyers and judges as well as his crew and the police.

I'm pleased to say John Berkery's still alive and going strong. He's written two really good books about his life in Philly. I'm in regular contact with him.

Back in 2009 I was also approached by some Hollywood film people, asking if I could tell them about Dino Cellini as they new he was a big name in the Mafia with Meyer Lansky. They obviously wanted to make a film about his life story and knew that I had been with Cellini all the time at the Colony Club with George Raft as well. We had 3 meetings over the next 6 months to help them put the missing pieces of the jigsaw together. Then one day in 2010 I got a nice letter to say thanks for all your time but the

Cellini film was being put on hold for undisclosed reasons. I have to admit that I was sorry to hear this but the pain was soon eased when attached to the letter was a cheque for £15,000 for my time which I thought was nice gesture as I had never asked for a penny. But there you go, its funny how things went around in my life really.

As for the boxers I knew, most of them are gone. Joe Louis gave up wrestling after Cowboy Rocky Lee accidentally stood on his chest. He became a greeter at a Las Vegas hotel and the Twins had him over here showing him off in clubs up North. He went downhill just like Ali but without the fanfare and he died at the beginning of the 1980s.

It's over ten years since my friend Dennie Mancini died after a series of heart attacks. He was just about the best cuts man in the world. Boxers used to say that having him in your corner was worth a round's start. I know when Willie Pep fell on hard times Dennie sent him a cheque every Christmas.

Vince Hawkins, the British champion who became a screw at Winchester and could so easily have turned me in, worked there for thirty years. Can you believe it? He'd lost his title to Dick Tiger, Randolph's brother, in the first bout in which a black man was allowed to fight for a British Empire title. He died in 2008 aged 85.

Paul Pender always had bad hands an hed never fought again after he beat Terry Downes in their third bout. He did a lot for boxer's rights saying that the worst thing that happened to managers was when boxers learned to read and right. He died in 2003. Like so many fights he had Alzheimer's. I'm glad to say though that Terry Downes is still going strong. After he left the ring he was in a few films. In his younger days he did a lot of work for charities. And not just appearing to have his hand shook. People could ask him to help shift stuff for them and he'd always turn up in a van and move things for them. He's in his 80s now.

By the early 2000s Albanian gangsters were said to control more than 70 per cent of brothels in Soho, with the women forced to service between 20 and 30 clients a day, charging as little as £30 and so undercutting the local talent. Police say that there were around 70 brothels in Soho but others say there may have been up to 1200 rooms from which girls worked.

Some things are still the same though. The Bar Italia in Frith Street is still top class. It doesn't seem to have changed over the years at all. Full of Italian football papers and Italian waiters off their shifts.

I was back down Saffron Hill the other day and that hasn't changed that much either. Of course like everywhere there's been gentrification, posh restaurants and offices, and The Griffin where Darby sorted out Monkey Bennyworth nearly 100 years ago, has become a pub with striptease in it. Darby would turn in his grave. Merlin Street Baths is long gone, turned into a block of flats in 1988. The Yorkshire Grey on the corner of Gray's Inn Road is still there; that hasn't changed much but the Globe cinema where we used to spent our Saturday mornings changed its name to the Rio and then disappeared in the middle fifties. It was pulled down and became part of a housing estate.

I haven't been in America for years but I read at that the end of the 1990s Roy DeMeo's Gemini Lounge was sold and turned into a church, The Flatlands Church of God. I heard Roy's landfill which was across the Belt Parkway, was shut down in 1985. I'm told it's all parkland now. In 2010 Angelo Bruno's South Philly house was sold for $300,000.

As for me, being 94 years old doesn't mean i'm stuck at home all day everyday passing the time. I've got no issues with people who want to do that but I like to get out an about when I can, and the only thing that can stop me is the rain.

Since my Jimmy bought me an electric scooter for my birthday last year it makes it so much more easier to get up the market to buy myself some fruit, or to head to the betting shop and see how my luck is, or to just see old friends and family.

I have even kept my American connections and frequently talk to Big John Berkery, as well as the sons and daughters, and even grandchildren of the Gambino families and other families, that I had the chance to befriend back in the 50's.

Everyone wants money but if you've got to stretch out for it then you've got to think, 'Do I need it?' I have people come and visit me today but there's no one today I want to work with. I've had the choice of working with young people but they're all tattoos, jewellery and drugs in and up their noses. I don't trust them.

I've always put people together and as a result they've given me a tickle. What is it the Italians say ? 'Bagnare il tuo becco -- Wet your beak'?. I've never demanded it like the Twins but over the years almost every job which went off from Soho to Islington a bit came my way. It was more a question of respect.

I've had plenty of opportunities to be a millionaire but it's never bothered me. I've been comfortable and happy. I've kept my money, live in a nice part of London Who'd have thought an Italian boy from the Saffron Hill slums would end up living next door to Boris Johnson?

I don't condemn myself. I'm not a grass. I don't do deals with the police. You'll never find any villain or any police office who can say I took a liberty with them. I was never a bully. I've never hurt anyone who didn't need hurting. Darby was the same sort of fellow. I've been a villain but I have respect for people and I've never been a hooligan. With all the ups and downs I don't think I'd have liked to change my life. Of course, there's some secrets I've got to take to the grave. People whose close families are still alive; I'm not going to say anything which will upset them.

It's a question of being strong if you come from the slums. If you're born poor it's the only way to survive. You can get a job and you're still doing the same thing thirty or forty years later. If you do what I did you have to accept the wheels can come off and you've got to do your bird. You take that on. It's a form of living. No one goes out thieving because they like it. If you've got no strength, you've got no chance.

I grew up in an era when if you didn't have money you were just rubbish. Take those people in the American Depression. Baby Face Nelson and people like him. They didn't want to be gangsters. They were strong. If you see your mother and father have nothing to eat you go out and get it. We should be called survivors not gangsters.

Regrets? Like the Sinatra song, I've had a few but only a few. There's some people I regret helping that I should have just let go. There were some things I fancied but I couldn't touch them. I got to know Cubby Broccoli who produced the Bond films through Dino at the Colony. Now his wife had a wonderful diamond necklace. It must have been worth a million. I fancied it something rotten but I couldn't touch I, could I? I couldn't do that to a friend. But I knew some who would have. One thing I do regret and that was not meeting Abe Koski years earlier. When we did meet he brought me to a different level. He opened my eyes to a new world. I really believe I've been a good fellow. If all the world was like me it would be a fucking better place.

My Jimmy's written a book about his life, its nearly complete and I've read a lot of chapters and without being biased its great read. He reminds me so much of a young me.

Do I believe in God? To me I'm an out and out agnostic. I don't believe in things like ghosts and flying angels. But millions of people do. How can people be so gullible? No, no-one's ever been able to prove it to me. Sometimes I think there's not much difference between people who claim to hear voices which have influenced them into chopping up prostitutes and those people in the nick who have seen the Light and heard Jesus talking to them so now they're saved. It's a funny old world. I may be wrong. I'll see soon enough.

I would like to thank not only my great nephew Jimmy Andrews, but my neice Kathy Andrews, the rest of my family, my old dear friends from here and across the pond and the always professional National Crime Syndicate, without whom this wouldnt have not be possible.